Logically Fallacious

The Ultimate Collection of Over 300 Logical Fallacies

Academic Edition

Written By

BO BENNETT, PHD

http://www.LogicallyFallacious.com

~~~~~~
For my kids, Annabelle and Trebor.
~~~~~~

Archieboy Holdings, LLC.
365 Boston Post Road, #311
Sudbury, MA 01776

Updated academic edition - May 6, 2021

publisher@ebookit.com
http://www.ebookit.com

ISBN: 978-1-4566-0737-1 (ebook)
ISBN: 978-1-4566-3184-0 (Amazon KDP paperback)
ISBN: 978-1-4566-0752-4 (generic paperback)
ISBN: 978-1-4566-2453-8 (hardcover)

Contents

There are some famous people who have mocked God and resulted in their untimely death. To give just one example, the designer of the Titanic said, "Not even God can sink this ship." Of course, we all know what happened to the Titanic. My question is,

Preface

There are those who say that we are living in a "post-truth world." This is the idea that the truth no longer matters. People back up their personal religious beliefs by stating "it's true to me, and that's all that matters." People support their political candidate despite lie after lie by finding a way to derive a kernel of truth from their candidate's lies. The media sells us their "version" of the truth based on the media empire's ideological position—and we buy it, hook, line, and sinker. But guess what, the concept of truth has not changed; what has changed is our willingness to sacrifice our intellectual integrity for information that supports our beliefs, personal values, and ideologies. We can also look at changes in our social environment that strongly contribute to our disturbing new relationship with the truth. For example, most of us get our "news" from social media and heavily-biased media sources that we choose based on what confirms what we already believe to be true. This creates an *echo chamber*, where such views are supported by the vast majority of those who comment on and share the views, only making us more confident that the information and perspective we receive is the "truth." This story does have a happy ending— or it can. Being able to identify errors in reasoning, known as *logical fallacies*, is a way that you can do your part to bring more truth back into our "post-truth world."

This is a book about **reason**, not formal logic. Fallacies have been discussed in philosophy since Aristotle first introduced them in his work, *On Sophistical Refutations*. Since then, prolific writers and thinkers have contributed to this area of study (directly and indirectly) including Francis Bacon (1620), Antoine Arnauld and Pierre Nicole (1662), John Locke (1690), Issac Watts (1724), Jeremy Bentham (1824), Richard Whately (1826), John Stuart Mill (1843), and Irving Copi (1961). For an excellent academic introduction to the philosophical side of logical fallacy theory, see the entry on logical fallacies in the *Stanford Encyclopedia of Philosophy*. The focus of this book is on the importance of good critical thinking through the awareness of and avoidance of common errors in reasoning when making and evaluating arguments.

In this latest edition,

- I have replaced the use of "opponent" with "interlocutor," meaning a person who takes part in a conversation or dialogue. The word "opponent" suggests competition and perhaps even hostility. Good, rational discourse should neither be a competition nor hostile; it should be seen as a partnership in order to get closer to the truth. "Opponent" does still work in some cases such as competitive debate or perhaps legal proceedings, but I do feel that "interlocutor" is a better word.

- I have added several more practice sessions and questions and answers in the back of the book, covering some of the highlights of the last two years.

- I have made sure that all the fallacies have at least two examples, often adding even more.

- I have reviewed the "pseudo-logical fallacies" and moved some of them to the "A-list" while removing others.

- I have added over a dozen new fallacies to this edition.

- I have added several dozen "also known as" names.

- I fixed several typos, added clarification, and made other corrections.

- I made sure each fallacy has either a tip or a "fun fact."

- I have updated many of the examples with more real-world examples where practical and added some more humor and light-heartedness to make the reading more enjoyable.

I did all this because I care about you, my favorite reader in the whole, wide, world.

Introduction

While this book is written for the layperson, I do need to introduce some concepts which may be new to you but play an important role in reasoning, as well as issue a few warnings, and explain how this book is organized. First, let me answer the question, "What's up with the title?"

The domain name was available. Moving on...

Reasoning

Humans have the capacity to establish and verify facts, to change and justify beliefs, and in general, to make sense of things. We do this by *reason*, and the process of doing so is called *reasoning*. While virtually all humans past the age of two or three are capable of reasoning, an alarmingly small percentage of us are really any good at it. We'll be exploring why this is the case throughout this book.

Arguments

When we hear the word "argument," we tend to think of an adversarial confrontation between two or more people, with bickering, defensiveness, and increased negative emotions. This is only one kind of argument—not the kind we will be focusing on in this book. Academically and logically, an *argument* is an attempt to persuade someone of something by offering reasons to accept a given conclusion. We make and hear arguments every day and often do not recognize them. We are constantly being bombarded with persuasion and led to conclusions, without being consciously aware. Sometimes the persuasion is very subtle, sometimes the reasons are implied, and sometimes the conclusion is assumed. For the purpose of this book, we just need to be able to recognize arguments when we hear them or make them.

An argument is made up of *premises* and a *conclusion*. The premises can also be referred to as *reasons*, *supporting evidence*, or *claims*.

Premise 1 (P1). Pizza is the best-selling food in America.

Premise 2 (P2). We can reasonably assume that "best-selling" means that people like it.

Conclusion (C). People in America like pizza.

If we just stated that "people in America like pizza," we wouldn't technically be making an argument; we would just be stating a proposition, assertion, claim, or even opinion. We cannot talk about logical fallacies unless they are in the context of an argument. Often, arguments are less formal as in

People in America like pizza. This is obvious because it is the best-selling food in America.

From this structure, we can still spot the premise and conclusion. Thus, we can talk about logical fallacies. Again, if we just asserted the conclusion, logical fallacies are unlikely to apply.

I use the terms "arguer" and "interlocutor" or "audience" to represent the one making the argument and the person or persons considering the argument, respectively. Keep in mind that the arguer could be a political candidate, Jehovah's Witness, a spouse, the 17-year-old kid at the returns desk in Walmart, or anyone capable of rational communication. The interlocutor/audience could be a police officer, your best friend, your spouse, or anyone else capable of rational communication.

Deduction is a form of reasoning and argument in which the conclusion follows **necessarily** from the premises. Sticking with the classic example:

Premise 1: All humans are mortal.

Premise 2: Socrates is a human.

Conclusion: Socrates is mortal.

If the premises are true, then the conclusion **must** be true. That is what makes an argument deductive. This is also referred to as a *formal argument*.

Arguments where the conclusion is merely based on probability, not necessity, are considered *inductive arguments*. These are usually constructed through *inductive reasoning*, which is the process of making general conclusions from specific instances. For example:

> Premise 1: The sun has risen every day so far.
>
> Conclusion: Therefore, the sun will likely rise tomorrow.

Because the sun could explode tonight, the conclusion is just very probable; therefore, this is an inductive or informal argument.

I will be using these terms throughout the book. If you don't understand them now, you will very soon.

Arguments are everywhere. You make them every day, and you hear them every day. Where you find arguments, you find fallacious arguments. Where you find fallacious arguments, you find fallacious reasoning.

Beliefs

A *belief* is defined as the psychological state in which an individual holds a proposition or premise to be true. Beliefs are formed in many different ways, which is outside the scope of this book, but it will suffice to say that many beliefs are not formed by reason and critical thinking. For our purposes, we are focusing on two aspects of beliefs: 1) the reasoning we use to form new beliefs, and 2) the reasoning we need to evaluate our existing beliefs.

Beliefs can often be stated explicitly as beliefs, stated as opinions, implied, or arrogantly stated as fact. Some examples:

> I believe that unicorns exist.
>
> In my opinion (or I think), we are actually simulations in a computer created by some advanced race of beings. And so are the beings who created us, and the beings who created them, ad infinitum.
>
> Hot dogs are delicious when ground up into powder and snorted.

If you are not baptized as an adult, you are going to Hell where you will experience an unimaginable level of suffering for all eternity. And Jesus loves you.

Beliefs can be wonderful, as in believing that humanity is overall good. Beliefs can be benign, as in believing the Red Sox are better than the Yankees. Beliefs can also be devastating, as in believing your god wants you to fly planes into buildings. But no matter how good a belief makes us feel or how good the potential outcome of a belief can be, **it does not affect the truth of the belief.** Although we are focusing on arguments, this book will help you find the truth of beliefs by examining any fallacious reasoning you may have used to form your beliefs.

What is a Logical Fallacy, Exactly?

The word "fallacy" comes from the Latin "fallacia" which means "deception, deceit, trick, artifice," however, a more specific meaning in logic (a logical fallacy) that dates back to the 1550s means "false syllogism, invalid argumentation."

An Error in Reasoning

One of the earliest academic discussions of logical fallacies comes from the book *Elementary Lessons in Logic: Deductive and Inductive*, published by MacMillian and Co. in 1872 where the modern definition of logical fallacies is used: "the modes in which, by neglecting the rules of logic, we often fall into erroneous reasoning." Today, this basic definition is still used, and often abbreviated to just "an error in reasoning." It is not a factual error.

Formal and Informal Fallacies

Two main categories of fallacies are *formal* and *informal*. Formal fallacies are classified by their structure (logical form), while informal fallacies are classified by their content.

Formal Fallacy Example

No X are Y.

Some Z are X.

Therefore, some Z are Y.

Informal Fallacy Example

Timmy is a poo-poo face; therefore, Timmy is wrong.

It seems simple enough. The problem is, however, real life is not a textbook with textbook examples. First, unless one is involved in formal debate, we rarely see one present a formal syllogism that is subject to a formal fallacy. What we find in real life is a bunch of words that need to be parsed into an argument. We often find when there is a flaw in the logical structure of the argument (i.e., a formal fallacy), there is also one or more problems with the content (i.e., informal fallacies). It is good to know these two general classifications, but don't expect to spot formal fallacies in everyday situations.

The Difference Between Logical Fallacies and Cognitive Biases

In the early 1970s, two behavioral researchers, Daniel Kahneman and Amos Tversky pioneered the field of *behavioral economics* through their work with *cognitive biases* and *heuristics,* which like logical fallacies, can affect the reasoning process. The main difference, however, is that logical fallacies require an argument whereas cognitive biases and heuristics (mental shortcuts) refer to a problematic pattern of thinking. Sometimes there is crossover. Logical fallacies can be the result of a cognitive bias, but having biases (which we all do) does not mean that we have to commit logical fallacies. Consider the *bandwagon effect*, a cognitive bias that demonstrates the tendency to believe things because many other people believe them. This cognitive bias can be found in the logical fallacy, *appeal to popularity.*

Everybody is doing X.

Therefore, X must be the right thing to do.

The cognitive bias is the main reason we commit this fallacy. However, if we just started working at a soup kitchen because all of our friends were working there, this wouldn't be a logical fallacy, although the bandwagon effect would be behind our behavior. The *appeal to popularity* is a fallacy because it applies to an argument. For example, "All my friends are working at the soup kitchen. Therefore, it must be the right thing to do."

I would say that more often than not, cognitive biases do not lead to logical fallacies. This is because cognitive biases are largely unconscious processes that bypass reason, and the mere exercise of consciously evaluating an argument often causes us to counteract the bias.

Factual Errors are Not Logical Fallacies

To illustrate this point, let's consider the *availability heuristic*, a cognitive bias that describes the tendency for one to overestimate the likelihood of more salient events, usually the result of how recent the memories are or how unusual or emotionally charged they may be. This bias can be demonstrated in believing that you are more likely to die in a plane crash than an automobile accident because of all the plane crashes you see in the news. As a result of this bias, one might argue:

> *Plane crashes kill more people than automobile accidents. Therefore, it is safer to drive in a car than fly in a plane.*

This is not fallacious; it's factually incorrect. If it were true that plane crashes kill more people than automobile accidents, the conclusion would be reasonable. The argument itself does not contain flawed reasoning; it contains incorrect information. Similarly, if I told you that the sun was about 30 miles from the earth and the size of a football stadium, I would not be committing a fallacy—but I would be a moron. Factual errors are not fallacies.

Logical Fallacies Can Be Committed by the Arguer or Audience

In this book, I will be using the term "fallacious" in the following ways, all of which support the primary purpose of this book—**to promote better reasoning**.

Fallacious Arguments. Arguments that are fallacious contain one or more non-factual errors in their form.

Just as a woman has the right to get a tattoo, she has the right to get an abortion. (Weak analogy)

Fallacious Reasoning. When an individual is using erroneous thinking (including bypassing reason) in evaluating or creating an argument, claim, proposition, or belief. This is where cognitive biases frequently play a role.

I was pro-abortion before, but now that this speaker made me cry by showing me a photo of an aborted fetus, I am against abortion. (Appeal to emotion)

Fallacious Tactics. Deliberately trying to get your interlocutor or audience to use fallacious reasoning in accepting the truth claims of your argument.

Look at this photo of an aborted fetus. How can you tell me that you still are pro-choice? (Appeal to emotion)

Note that fallacious tactics are not a deficiency in reasoning (morality, perhaps) on the part of the arguer, although people who fall victim to these tactics do demonstrate fallacious reasoning. While some of these tactics are labeled logical fallacies, the arguer would not be held responsible for committing a logical fallacy. When charities run ads, they don't bombard us with data and moral arguments; they show us a photo of a suffering child who needs our help. These charities know what they are doing. They are not lacking in reason; quite the opposite, in fact. They are using effective persuasion techniques.

If it were up to me, I would prefer to keep logical fallacies and fallacious tactics separate. For decades, people have been classifying select manipulation and persuasion techniques as fallacies. The problem is that there are many, many more of these techniques that aren't considered fallacies for no consistent reason, so what we have is a partial list of manipulation and persuasion techniques that we are arbitrarily calling logical fallacies. I include these for completeness, but let the record show that I object to this usage!

Logical Fallacies are Deceptive

Another characteristic of logical fallacies is that they are not always easy to spot, especially to the untrained mind. Yet they often elude our critical faculties, making them persuasive for all the wrong reasons—sort of like optical illusions for the mind. Some, however, are as clearly wrong as a pig roast at a bar mitzvah (yet still fool too many people). For example,

> *"Don't grow a mustache, because Hitler had a mustache. Therefore, you will be like Hitler!"*

After reading this book, you can probably match about a dozen fallacies with the above argument. The error in reasoning should be apparent—sharing a physical characteristic with a fascist dictator will not make you a fascist dictator.

Logical Fallacies are Common and Worthy of Identifying by Name

Over the years, I have received questions from perhaps hundreds of students of logical fallacies who have presented what met all the other criteria of logical fallacies but was unique, very specific, or already fit nicely under a more general category of logical fallacy. For example, the *appeal to emotion* fallacy is a general category of fallacies, and there are many in that category such as *appeal to anger*, *appeal to pity*, *appeal to fear*, and many more. These are all common enough to be worthy of their own fallacy. But what about "appeal to indignation?" This certainly could be fallacious, but so rare that it's just not worth naming since it fits under the *appeal to emotion* fallacy. If there is a general category under which the rare fallacy fits, it is less likely to be named.

Dr. Bo's Three Criteria for a Logical Fallacy

In this book, we are using what is referred to as the *argument conception of fallacies* (Hanson, 2015). That is, what we are identifying as a "logical fallacy" goes beyond the standard conception of "fallacy" where the error in reasoning must commonly apply to argumentation. More specifically,

1. **It must be an error in reasoning,** not a factual error.

2. **It must be commonly applied to an argument** either in the form of the argument or the interpretation of the argument.

3. **It must be deceptive** in that it often fools the average adult.

Therefore, we will define a logical fallacy as **a concept within argumentation that commonly leads to an error in reasoning due to the deceptive nature of its presentation**. Logical fallacies can comprise *fallacious arguments* that contain one or more non-factual errors in their form or deceptive arguments that often lead to fallacious reasoning in their evaluation.

Recall my objection to calling fallacious tactics "logical fallacies." This is because most fallacious tactics do not meet my second criterion of being commonly applied to an argument. I include the frequently-cited fallacious tactics under the main fallacy section and some of the others under the pseudo-logical fallacies section. Please keep in mind that there are many more similar techniques that are beyond the scope of this book and are not included.

On Reason and Rationality

If you are a parent, you know exactly what it is like to argue with someone who is unreasonable and irrational. Many attempts at logic and reason end with the parent coming down to the level of the child—basing arguments on emotion usually in the form of a tasty bribe or smacked bottom, depending on what the circumstances call for. Unfortunately, many people carry these success-repelling traits with them into adulthood. This makes communication, cooperation, and prosperity a real challenge.

As you might have guessed, those who are acting unreasonably and irrationally are either incapable or unwilling to accept that their arguments are fallacious, if in fact, their arguments are fallacious. In these cases, you can come down to their level, appeal to their emotions, and exploit their cognitive biases—but this takes some manipulative talent, and I would argue that it is not very ethical. You can simply give up and refuse to argue any further, which I have done at times. Or, if possible, you can show how their arguments and beliefs are inconsistent with other beliefs they hold. This is my preferred strategy because it is not patronizing, nor does it reflect my frustration.

Being a Smart-Ass

There are two general schools of thought on how to point out a fallacy to your interlocutor. On the one hand, you can tactfully explain why your interlocutor's reasoning is erroneous (1 smart-ass point), without mentioning the name of the fallacy. On the other hand, you can tell your interlocutor that his reasoning is fallacious (1 smart-ass point), tell him the name of the fallacy he committed (another smart-ass point), tell him why it is a fallacy (another smart-ass point), then extend his underwear over his head, and conclude with, "by the way, in Latin that fallacy is known as [insert Latin name here]." (10 smart-ass points)! Of course, you could take a path somewhere in between, but what you certainly should be prepared for, is your interlocutors pointing out your fallacies, and if you know about fallacies, you will be ready to defend yourself.

I caution you against correcting fallacies that your interlocutor might raise. As you will see in this book, fallacies go by many different names, and there are varying definitions for the fallacies. Except for a handful of fallacies that have been around since the time of Aristotle, most fallacies are under a continual redefining process that might change the name of the fallacy or the meaning of the fallacy. The bottom line is to focus on exactly what error in reasoning you are being accused of, and defend your reasoning—not a definition or name.

When All You Have is a Hammer, Everything Looks Like a Nail.

In my experience with dealing with claims of fallacies on a daily basis, I have noticed a strong tendency to force-fit fallacies where they don't belong. This seems to come from those who know just enough about fallacies to be dangerous. My guess is that the common perception is that fallacious arguments are false arguments (they're not necessarily false,) and if one can show a fallacy, they can refute the claim of their interlocutor.

Act in good faith. Apply the *principle of charity* (i.e., do your best to assume the most charitable interpretation of the argument) and resist the temptation to assume the worst from your interlocutor. This will move the conversation forward rather than create a branched argument about a potential fallacy that serves as an irrelevant distraction.

Methodology

As discussed in the preface, the core fallacies detailed in this book date back thousands of years to Aristotle. Academic resources were used when possible when compiling this list of fallacies. These resources include papers in peer-reviewed journals, peer-reviewed encyclopedias, and books published by academic presses. The majority of modern, informal fallacies have been defined and named by students of argumentation throughout the years and published in non-academic resources including web pages. On the one hand, this "wisdom of the crowds" approach has helped identify hundreds of errors in reasoning not previously identified due partly to advances in cognitive science, changing communication, and the sheer number of people contributing ideas. On the other hand, there are many so-called "logical fallacies" that are not worthy of that title by any reasonable definition. Through an exhaustive and ongoing search for the uses and mentions of logical fallacies, I catalog these and subject them to my previously mentioned criteria. Those that pass the test make it as a named logical fallacy in this book. Those that don't are either ignored, or if visible enough on the Internet, have a mention in the "Pseudo-Logical Fallacies" section at the end of this book.

Format and Style of this Book

If you haven't noticed by now, I like to have fun with both writing and learning. I understand that by using humor that I will inevitably offend someone, which is unfortunate, but a fact of life.

While this book can function as a reference book, I hope you will read this like a novel—from cover to cover. I define what I feel may be unfamiliar terms to the reader as I progress through the fallacies in alphabetical order. Therefore, if you do read the fallacies in order, unfamiliar terms and concepts will be revealed to you as needed—I do this to keep the book interesting.

While it may seem like a crazy number of fallacies to read through, I have done my best to make it enjoyable and educational. The fallacies that are seldom ever seen or not quite fallacies, and not worthy of a complete entry in this book, are just listed in the back section of this book with brief descriptions.

There have been many attempts to categorize fallacies, some of which may make fallacies easier to understand. The previously mentioned book *Elementary Lessons in Logic : Deductive and Inductive*, uses an Aristotelian classification system for the fallacies which might have worked in 1872 when there were a handful of fallacies. Beyond the distinction between *purely logical* and *semi-logical* (now commonly referred to as deductive and informal fallacies), it is no longer helpful, in my opinion. I have chosen to organize all fallacies, alphabetically by the names for which they are best known. I chose this method because:

- There is no official taxonomy used today, nor is there even a taxonomy accepted by the majority of those who classify fallacies.

- The ambiguous nature of most fallacies means that many of the fallacies can fit in a variety of categories.

- Focusing on faux-categorical structures distracts from the fallacies themselves.

Fallacy Name(s). Each fallacy begins with its most commonly used name, followed by the Latin name (if there is one). I then list all other known names for the fallacy. At times, there might be slight differences in the fallacies that go by other names, but unless I feel the differences are worthy of their own entries, I will just list it as another name for the fallacy. Keep in mind that fallacies are named and referred to mostly by common usage. The point of listing every known alias is not so you can memorize them; it's so that you might recognize them when referred to by these other names.

Description. My descriptions are all short and to the point, giving you the information you need to understand the fallacy, while sometimes adding in some extra commentary.

Logical Form. Most fallacies, especially formal ones, have what are called logical forms, which means that the general fallacy can be represented in symbolic language. I list the logical forms where they apply to help you better understand certain fallacies. With informal fallacies, I use a little artistic license to create a logical form to help you to understand the fallacy better. For informal fallacies, the form does not have be followed. Consider the *appeal to equity* where I list the logical form as

A equals B (when A does not equal B)

Y applies to A or B.

Therefore, Y applies to both A and B.

For an example, I have

If women get paid maternity leave, so should men.

There are many ways or "forms" to state or imply the same general argument. We can read the above as

Men are the same as women.

Women get paid maternity leave.

Therefore, men should also get paid maternity leave.

Example(s). I try to include realistic examples and, in fact, many examples are from actual debates of mine (real names protected). I feel that using realistic examples will help you to identify the fallacies when used in real situations—people aren't as stupid as they are portrayed in many examples. If the fallacy requires it, I will use an extreme example to make the fallacy clear, then include a second or even third example that is more realistic.

When examples are indented and italicized like this:

I am an idiot who says stupid and fallacious things.

This is not me speaking; it is the character. I get some comments from readers who tell me that I am committing an unrelated fallacy in my examples. I realize this, and good for you if you spot multiple fallacies in an example, but please remember that I do this purposely. My fictional characters are not very reasonable by design.

As mentioned, most of these examples are from actual arguments. Reality doesn't shy away from controversial topics, so neither do I. Remember that a bad argument does not mean that the conclusion is false; it only means we can't trust the conclusion based on the argument made. I do my best to be an equal-opportunity offender, no matter what your religion or political affiliation.

Exception(s). Fallacious arguments and fallacious reasoning are more often probability-based then based on an objective fact. Take the following informal or inductive argument, that virtually everyone would consider fallacious:

> *"Don't grow a mustache, because Hitler had a mustache; therefore, you will be like Hitler!"*

Perhaps some psychologist has some data supporting the idea that sporting a mustache, especially a Hitleresque one, can make that individual more susceptible to genocide (I would really like to see the details of that study!) Therefore, one can argue that this argument is not fallacious—the argument itself is strong and the reasoning that was used to construct this argument was sound. Showing this argument is fallacious can be an argument in itself, where it is all about providing stronger evidence and more sound reasoning to support your claim.

There are some arguments that use a formal or deductive structure and contain fallacies of form that are objective fallacies, that is, they are always fallacious in all situations. For example:

> *All humans are mortal.*
>
> *Phil is mortal.*
>
> *Therefore, Phil is a human.*

Actually, Phil is a groundhog. This is an example of a *syllogistic fallacy* (a class of fallacies), and it always will be, in all situations. Even if Phil were human, the form of the argument would still commit the fallacy. In formal logic, the truth of the premises guarantees the truth of the conclusion. The bottom line: never insist that an informal argument is definitely fallacious, and be prepared to defend your arguments against claims of fallacy.

Variation(s): If the fallacy has an alias but the alias is different enough to warrant an explanation, I will explain the difference in the "variation" section. I will also add a "[form of]" after the alias listed below the main fallacy name.

Tip / Fun Fact: In 2004, I wrote the book, *Year To Success*. In that book, I explain that success is like a game of chance where you control the odds by continually replacing behaviors that pull you away from success with behaviors that bring you closer to success. When appropriate, I include a tip that might be relevant to the fallacy, which will bring you closer to success in mastering fallacies—most of which are serious, but some... not so much (you will know the difference). Alternatively, I will include a fun fact—a little something about almost everything that has nothing to do with anything.

Let's get started!

The Fallacies

Accent Fallacy
accentus

(also known as: emphasis fallacy, fallacy of accent, fallacy of prosody, misleading accent)

Description: When the meaning of a word, sentence, or entire idea is interpreted differently by changing where the accent falls.

Logical Form:

> Claim is made with accent on word X giving claim meaning Y.
>
> Claim is interpreted with accent on word A giving claim meaning B.

Example #1: In the movie, *My Cousin Vinny*, Ralph Maccio's character, Bill, was interrogated for suspected murder. When the police officer asks him, "At what point did you shoot the clerk?" Bill replies in shock, "*I* shot the clerk? *I* shot the clerk?" Later in the film, the police officer reads Bill's statement as a confession in court, "...and he said, 'I shot the clerk. I shot the clerk.'"

Explanation: In the movie, it appeared that the police officer did understand Bill's question as a confession. So it did not appear to be a fallacious tactic of the police officer, rather a failure of critical thought perhaps due to a strong confirmation bias (the officer was very confident that Bill was guilty, thus failed to detect the nuance in the question).

Example #2: In the hilarious Broadway musical, *The Book of Mormon*, there is a musical number where one character is explaining how to bury "bad thoughts" by just "turning them off" (like a light switch). The character doing the explaining (in glorious song) is specifically explaining to the main character how to suppress gay thoughts when the main character's "bad thoughts" have nothing to do with being gay. After the instructions, the main character tries to make this clear by affirming, "*I'm* not having gay thoughts," to which the other characters respond "Hurray! It worked!"

Explanation: The stress on the "I'm" was ignored and confused for "Hey, I'm *not* having gay thoughts anymore!" Although this was comedy it portrayed an argument.

Tip: Our biases can cause us to miss the vocal nuance. Listen actively and critically, and try not to jump to conclusions. And you cannot turn off gay thoughts like a light switch.

References:

Damer, T. E. (2008). *Attacking faulty reasoning: A practical guide to fallacy-free arguments.* Cengage Learning.

Accident Fallacy
a dicto simpliciter ad dictum secundum quid

(also known as: destroying the exception, dicto secundum quid ad dictum simpliciter, dicto simpliciter, converse accident, reverse accident, fallacy of the general rule, sweeping generalization)

Description: When an attempt is made to apply a general rule to all situations when clearly there are exceptions to the rule. Simplistic rules or laws rarely take into consideration legitimate exceptions, and to ignore these exceptions is to bypass reason to preserve the illusion of a perfect law. People like simplicity and would often rather keep simplicity at the cost of rationality.

Logical Form:

X is a common and accepted rule.

Therefore, there are no exceptions to X.

Example #1:

I believe one should never deliberately hurt another person, that's why I can never be a surgeon.

Explanation: Classifying surgery under "hurting" someone, is to ignore the obvious benefits that go with surgery. These kinds of extreme views are rarely built on reason.

Example #2:

> *The Bible clearly says, "thou shall not bear false witness."*
> *Therefore, as a Christian, you better answer the door and tell*
> *our drunk neighbor with the shotgun, that his wife, whom he*
> *is looking to kill, is hiding in our basement. Otherwise, you*
> *are defying God himself!*

Explanation: To assume any law, even divine, applies to every person, in every time, in every situation, even though not explicitly stated, is an assumption not grounded in evidence, and fallacious reasoning.

Exception: Stating the general rule when a good argument can be made that the action in question is a violation of the rule, would not be considered fallacious.

> *The Bible says, "thou shall not murder," therefore, as a*
> *Christian, you better put that chainsaw down and untie that*
> *little kid.*

Tip: It is your right to question laws you don't understand or laws with which you don't agree.

References:

Bile, J. (1988). Propositional justification: another view. *Contemporary Argumentation & Debate, 9,* 54–62.

Ad Fidentia
argumentum ad fidentia

(also known as: against self-confidence)

Description: Attacking the person's self-confidence in place of the argument or the evidence.

Logical Form:

> *Person 1 claims that Y is true, but is person 1 really sure*
> *about that?*
>
> *Therefore, Y is false.*

Example #1:

> Rick: I had a dream last night that I won the lottery! I have $1000 saved up, so I am buying 1000 tickets!
>
> Vici: You know, dreams are not accurate ways to predict the future; they are simply the result of random neurons firing.
>
> Rick: The last time I checked, you are no neurologist or psychologist, so how sure are you that I am not seeing the future?
>
> Vici: It's possible you can be seeing the future, I guess.

Explanation: Although Vici is trying to reason with his friend, Rick attempts to weaken Vici's argument by making Vici more unsure of his position. This is a fallacious tactic by Rick, and if Vici falls for it, fallacious reasoning on his part.

Example #2:

> Chris: You claim that you don't believe in the spirit world that is all around us, with spirits coming in and out of us all the time. How can you be sure this is not the case? Are you 100% certain?
>
> Joe: Of course not, how can I be?
>
> Chris: Exactly! One point for me!
>
> Joe: What?

Explanation: This is a common fallacy among those who argue for the supernatural or anything else not falsifiable. If Joe was not that reasonable of a thinker, then he might start to question the validity of his position, not based on any new counter evidence presented, but a direct attack on his self-confidence. Fortunately for Joe, he holds no dogmatic beliefs and is perfectly aware of the difference between possibilities and probabilities (see also *appeal to possibility*).

Exception: When one claims certainty for something where certainty is unknowable, it is your duty to point it out.

Tip: Have confidence that you are probably or even very probably right, but avoid dogmatic certainty at all costs in areas where certainty is unknowable.

References:

This is a logical fallacy frequently used on the Internet. No academic sources could be found.

Ad Hoc Rescue
ad hoc

(also known as: making stuff up, MSU fallacy)

Description: Very often we desperately want to be right and hold on to certain beliefs, despite any evidence presented to the contrary. As a result, we begin to make up excuses as to why our belief could still be true, and is still true, despite the fact that we have no real evidence for what we are making up.

Logical Form:

> Claim X is true because of evidence Y.
>
> Evidence Y is demonstrated not to be acceptable evidence.
>
> Therefore, it must be guess Z then, even though there is no evidence for guess Z.

Example #1:

> Frieda: I just know that Raymond is just waiting to ask me out.
>
> Edna: He has been seeing Rose for three months now.
>
> Frieda: He is just seeing her to make me jealous.
>
> Edna: They're engaged.
>
> Frieda: Well, that's just his way of making sure I know about it.

Explanation: Besides being a bit deluded, poor Frieda refuses to accept the evidence that leads to a truth she is not ready to accept. As a result, she creates an *ad hoc* reason in an attempt to rescue her initial claim.

Example #2:

> *Mark: The president of the USA is the worst president ever because unemployment has never been so bad before!*
>
> *Sam: Actually, it was worse in 1982 and far worse in the 1930s. Besides, the president might only be partly responsible for the economy during his term.*
>
> *Mark: Well... the president kicks animals when nobody is looking.*

Explanation: Out of desperation, Mark makes a claim about the president's private treatment of animals after his original claim has been refuted.

Exception: Proposing possible solutions is perfectly acceptable when an argument is suggesting only a possible solution—especially in a hypothetical situation. For example, "If there is no God, then life is meaningless." If there is no God who dictates meaning to our lives, perhaps we are truly free to find our own meaning.

Tip: When you suspect people are just making stuff up, rather than providing evidence to support their claim, simply ask them, "What evidence do you have to support that?"

References:

Carey, S. S. (2011). *A Beginner's guide to scientific method.* Cengage Learning.

Ad Hominem (Abusive)
argumentum ad hominem

(also known as: personal abuse, personal attacks, abusive fallacy, appeal to the person, damning the source, name calling, refutation by caricature, against the person, against the man)

Description: Attacking the person making the argument, rather than the argument itself, when the attack on the person is completely irrelevant to the argument the person is making.

Logical Form:

> *Person 1 is claiming Y.*
>
> *Person 1 is a moron.*
>
> *Therefore, Y is not true.*

Example #1:

> *My opponent suggests that lowering taxes will be a good idea—this is coming from a woman who eats a pint of Ben and Jerry's each night!*

Explanation: The fact that the woman loves her ice cream, has nothing to do with the lowering of taxes, and therefore, is irrelevant to the argument. *Ad hominem* attacks are usually made out of desperation when one cannot find a decent counter argument.

Example #2:

> *Tony wants us to believe that the origin of life was an "accident." Tony is a godless SOB who has spent more time in jail than in church, so the only information we should consider from him is the best way to make license plates.*

Explanation: Tony may be a godless SOB. Perhaps he did spend more time in the joint than in church, but all this is irrelevant to his argument or truth of his claim as to the origin of life.

Exception: When the attack on the person is relevant to the argument, it is not a fallacy. In our first example, if the issue being debated was the elimination of taxes only on Ben and Jerry's ice cream, then pointing out her eating habits would be strong evidence of a conflict of interest.

Tip: When others verbally attack you, take it as a compliment to the quality of your argument. It is usually a sign of desperation on their part.

References:

Walton, D. (1998). *Ad hominem arguments*. University of Alabama Press.

Ad Hominem (Circumstantial)
argumentum ad hominem

(also known as: appeal to bias, appeal to motive, appeal to personal interest, argument from motives, conflict of interest, faulty motives, naïve cynicism, questioning motives, vested interest)

Description: Suggesting that the person who is making the argument is biased or predisposed to take a particular stance, and therefore, the argument is *necessarily* invalid.

Logical Form:

> Person 1 is claiming Y.
>
> Person 1 has a vested interest in Y being true.
>
> Therefore, Y is false.

Example #1:

> Salesman: This car gets better than average gas mileage and is one of the most reliable cars according to Consumer Reports.
>
> Will: I doubt it—you obviously just want to sell me that car.

Explanation: The fact that the salesman has a vested interest in selling Will the car does not mean that he is lying. He may be, but this is not something you can conclude solely on his interests. It is reasonable to assume that salespeople sell the products and services they do because they believe in them.

Example #2:

> Of course, your minister says he believes in God. He would be unemployed otherwise.

Explanation: The fact that atheist ministers are about as in demand as hookers who, "just want to be friends," does not mean that ministers believe in God just because they need a job.

Exception: As the bias or conflict of interest becomes more relevant to the argument, usually signified by a lack of other evidence, the argument is seen as less of a fallacy and more as a legitimate motive. For example, courtesy of Meat Loaf...

Girl: Will you love me forever?

Boy: Let me sleep on it!!!

Girl: Will you love me forever!!!

Boy: I couldn't take it any longer

Lord, I was crazed

And when the feeling came upon me

Like a tidal wave

I started swearing to my god and on my mother's grave

That I would love you to the end of time

I swore that I would love you to the end of time!

Tip: When you know you have something to gain from a position you hold (assuming, of course, you are not guilty of this fallacy for holding the position), be upfront about it and bring it up before someone else does.

Supporting this cause is the right thing to do. Yes, as the baseball coach, I will benefit from the new field, but my benefit is negligible compared to the benefit the kids of this town will receive. After all, they are the ones who really matter here.

References:

Walton, D. (1998). *Ad hominem arguments*. University of Alabama Press.

Ad Hominem (Guilt by Association)
argumentum ad hominem

(also known as: association fallacy, bad company fallacy, company that you keep fallacy, they're not like us fallacy, transfer fallacy)

Description: When the source is viewed negatively because of its association with another person or group who is already viewed negatively.

Logical Form:

Person 1 states that Y is true.

Person 2 also states that Y is true, and person 2 is a moron.

Therefore, person 1 must be a moron too.

Example #1:

Delores is a big supporter for equal pay for equal work. This is the same policy that all those extreme feminist groups support. Extremists like Delores should not be taken seriously —at least politically.

Explanation: Making the assumption that Delores is an extreme feminist simply because she supports a policy that virtually every man and woman also supports, is fallacious.

Example #2:

Pol Pot, the Cambodian Maoist revolutionary, was against religion, and he was a very bad man. Frankie is against religion; therefore, Frankie also must be a very bad man.

Explanation: The fact that Pol Pot and Frankie share one particular view does not mean they are identical in other ways unrelated, specifically, being a very bad man. Pol Pot was not a bad man *because* he was against religion, he was a bad man for his genocidal actions.

Example #3:

> *Callie: Did you know that Jake Tooten was a racist?*
>
> *Chris: I know Jake well. Why do you say he's a racist?*
>
> *Callie: He was on a podcast the other day...*
>
> *Chris: Did he say something racist?*
>
> *Callie: No, but the podcast host did an interview two years ago with a woman who said she supported an organization that had a history of racism back in the 1960s. Jake clearly supports racism!*

Explanation: In this case, Jake Tooten is the "source" who is viewed negatively (as a racist) because of his association with the organization referenced. Note that his "association" with this group says nothing about his beliefs, which makes this fallacious. It is even more fallacious due to 1) Jake being several steps removed from this organization and 2) the organization's history of racism rather than the organization's current position on racism.

Callie actually was right, but for the wrong reason. Jake runs a Nazi youth group.

Exception: If one can demonstrate that the connection between the two characteristics that were inherited by association is causally linked, or the probability of taking on a characteristic would be high, then it would be valid. In example #1, if Delores supported the "all men should be castrated" position, we can call her an "extremist." In example #2, if we used "murdered children" instead of "against religion," the claim of being a "very bad man" would be justified. In example #3, if Jake appeared on the podcast titled "I am racist, and you should be too," Callie's claim of Jake being a racist would be justified.

Tip: People change. Be forgiving of one's questionable past associations, especially if they realize and admit those associations were wrong.

References:

Walton, D. (1998). *Ad hominem arguments*. University of Alabama Press.

Ad Hominem (Tu quoque)
argumentum ad hominem tu quoque

(also known as: appeal to hypocrisy, "you too" fallacy, hypocrisy, personal inconsistency)

Description: Claiming the argument is flawed by pointing out that the one making the argument is not acting consistently with the claims of the argument.

Logical Form:

> *Person 1 is claiming that Y is true, but person 1 is acting as if Y is not true.*
>
> *Therefore, Y must not be true.*

Example #1:

> *Helga: You should not be eating that... it has been scientifically proven that eating fat burgers are no good for your health.*
>
> *Hugh: You eat fat burgers all the time so that can't be true.*

Explanation: It doesn't matter (to the truth claim of the argument at least) if Helga follows her own advice or not. While it might appear that the reason she does not follow her own advice is that she doesn't believe it's true, it could also be that those fat burgers are just too damn irresistible.

Example #2:

> *Jimmy Swaggart argued strongly against sexual immorality, yet while married, he has had several affairs with prostitutes; therefore, sexual immorality is acceptable.*

Explanation: The fact Jimmy Swaggart likes to play a round of bedroom golf with some local entrepreneurial ladies, is not evidence for sexual immorality *in general*, only that *he is* sexually immoral.

Exception: If Jimbo insisted that his actions were in line with sexual morality, then it would be a very germane part of the argument.

Tip: Again, admit when your lack of self-control or willpower has nothing to do with the truth claim of the proposition. The following is what I remember my dad telling me about smoking (he smoked about four packs a day since he was 14).

> *Bo, never be a stupid a—hole like me and start smoking. It is a disgusting habit that I know will eventually kill me. If you never start, you will never miss it.*

My dad died at age 69—of lung cancer. I never touched a cigarette in my life and never plan to touch one.

References:

Walton, D. (1998). *Ad hominem arguments*. University of Alabama Press.

Affirmative Conclusion from a Negative Premise

(also known as: illicit negative, drawing a negative conclusion from negative premises, fallacy of negative premises)

This is our first fallacy in *formal logic* out of about a dozen presented in this book. Formal fallacies can be confusing and complex and are not as common in everyday situations, so please don't feel lost when reading through the formal fallacies —do your best to understand them as I do my best to make them understandable.

New Terminology:

Syllogism: an argument typically consisting of three parts: a major premise, a minor premise, and a conclusion.

Categorical Term: usually expressed grammatically as a noun or noun phrase, each categorical term designates a class of things.

Categorical Proposition: joins exactly two categorical terms and asserts that some relationship holds between the classes they designate.

Categorical Syllogism: an argument consisting of exactly three categorical propositions: a major premise, a minor premise, and a conclusion, in which there appears a total of exactly three categorical terms, each of which is used exactly twice.

Description: The conclusion of a standard form categorical syllogism is affirmative, but at least one of the premises is negative. Any valid forms of categorical syllogisms that assert a negative premise must have a negative conclusion.

Logical Form:

Any form of categorical syllogism with an affirmative conclusion and at least one negative premise.

Example #1:

No people under the age of 66 are senior citizens.

No senior citizens are children.

Therefore, all people under the age of 66 are children.

Explanation: In this case, the conclusion is obviously counterfactual although both premises are true. Why? Because this is a categorical syllogism where we have one or more negative premises (i.e., "no people..." and "no senior citizens..."), and we are attempting to draw a positive (affirmative) conclusion (i.e., "all people...").

Example #2:

> *No donkeys are fish.*
>
> *Some asses are donkeys.*
>
> *Therefore, some asses are fish.*

Explanation: This is a categorical syllogism where we have a single negative premise (i.e., "no donkeys"), and we are attempting to draw a positive (affirmative) conclusion (i.e., "some asses").

On a somewhat related note, some lawyers are asses.

Tip: Syllogisms and identifying formal fallacies (at least by form) are common on intelligence tests. Know this and be more intelligent (at least on paper).

References:

Schuyler, A. (1859). *The principles of logic: for high schools and colleges.* Wilson, Hinkle & co.

Affirming a Disjunct

(also known as: the fallacy of the alternative disjunct, false exclusionary disjunct, affirming one disjunct, the fallacy of the alternative syllogism, asserting an alternative, improper disjunctive syllogism, fallacy of the disjunctive syllogism)

New Terminology:

> **Disjunction:** *A proposition of the "either/or" form, which is true if one or both of its propositional components is true; otherwise, it is false.*
>
> **Disjunct:** *One of the propositional components of a disjunction.*

Description: Making the false assumption that when presented with an either/or possibility, that if one of the options is true that the other one must be false. This is when the "or" is not explicitly defined as being *exclusive*.

This fallacy is similar to the *unwarranted contrast* fallacy.

Logical Forms:

> *P or Q.*
>
> *P.*
>
> *Therefore, not Q.*

> *P or Q.*
>
> *Q.*
>
> *Therefore, not P.*

Example #1:

> *I can't stop eating these chocolates. I really love chocolate, or I seriously lack willpower. I know I really love chocolate; therefore, I cannot lack willpower.*

Explanation: Ignoring the possible *false dilemma*, the fact that one really loves chocolate does not automatically exclude the other possibility of lacking willpower.

Example #2:

> *I am going to bed or watching TV. I am exhausted, so I will go to bed; therefore, I cannot watch TV.*

Explanation: It is logically and physically possible to go to bed and watch TV at the same time, I know that for a fact as I do it just about every night. The "or" does not logically exclude the option that is not chosen.

Exception: If the choices *are* mutually exclusive (either by necessity or indicated by the word "either"), then it can be deduced that the other choice must be false. Again, we are working under the assumption that one of the choices we are given represents the truth.

Today is either Monday or Sunday. It is Monday. Therefore, it is not Sunday.

In formal logic, the above is referred to as a *valid disjunctive syllogism*.

If you are thinking, "But it can be both Monday and Sunday if we are talking about two different time zones," then give your self three points for being clever, then subtract four points for missing the whole point of the fallacy.

References:

Kilgore, W. J. (1979). *An introductory logic.* Holt, Rinehart and Winston.

Affirming the Consequent

(also known as: converse error, fallacy of the consequent, asserting the consequent, affirmation of the consequent)

New Terminology:

Consequent: *the propositional component of a conditional proposition whose truth is conditional; or simply put, what comes after the "then" in an "if/then" statement.*

Antecedent: *the propositional component of a conditional proposition whose truth is the condition for the truth of the consequent; or simply put, what comes after the "if" in an "if/then" statement.*

Description: An error in formal logic where if the consequent is said to be true, the antecedent is said to be true, as a result.

Logical Form:

If P then Q.

Q.

Therefore, P.

Example #1:

If taxes are lowered, I will have more money to spend.

I have more money to spend.

Therefore, taxes must have been lowered.

Explanation: I could have had more money to spend simply because I gave up crack-cocaine, prostitute solicitation, and baby-seal-clubbing expeditions.

Example #2:

If it's brown, flush it down.

I flushed it down.

Therefore, it was brown.

Explanation: No! I did not have to follow the, "if it's yellow, let it mellow" rule—in fact, if I did follow that rule I would probably still be single. The stated rule is simply, "if it's brown" (the *antecedent*), then (implied), "flush it down" (the *consequent*). From this, we cannot imply that we can ONLY flush it down if it is brown. That is a mistake—a logical fallacy.

Tip: If it's yellow, flush it down too. Especially, if you are married and want to stay that way.

References:

Jevons, W. S. (1872). *Elementary lessons in logic: deductive and inductive: with copious questions and examples, and a vocabulary of logical terms.* Macmillan.

Alleged Certainty

(also known as: assuming the conclusion)

Description: Asserting a conclusion without evidence or premises, through a statement that makes the conclusion appear certain when, in fact, it is not.

Logical Form:

Everybody knows that X is true.

Therefore, X is true.

Example #1:

People everywhere recognize the need to help the starving children of the world.

Explanation: Actually, people everywhere don't recognize this. This may seem like common sense to those who make the claim, and to many who hear the claim, but there are many people on this earth who do not share that view and need to be convinced first.

Example #2:

Everyone knows that, without our culture's religion, we all would be like lost sheep.

Explanation: Everyone does not know that. Sometimes, without stepping outside your own social or cultural sphere, it might seem like what you might accept as universal truths are simply truths within your own social or cultural sphere. Don't assume universal truths.

Example #3:

There's no question that our president is a major idiot.

Explanation: As tempting as a claim such as this one might be for some to accept as true, it must be recognized as the fallacy it is. Simply saying "our president is a major idiot," then supporting that claim with evidence is very different than replacing the evidence with the statement of certainty (i.e., "there's no question that...").

Exception: Facts that would seem foolish not to assume, can be assumed—but one should be prepared to support the assumption, no matter how certain one may be.

We all know that, without water, we cannot survive.

Tip: Replace the word "certain" in your life with the phrase "very probable" or "very confident."

References:

Yoos, G. E. (2007). Deceptions, blunders, and confusions. In *Reframing Rhetoric* (pp. 245–255). Palgrave Macmillan US. https://doi.org/10.1057/9780230607514_25

Alphabet Soup

Description: The deliberate and excessive use of acronyms and abbreviations to appear more knowledgeable in the subject or confuse others.

Logical Form:

Person 1 uses acronyms and abbreviations.

Therefore, person 1 knows what he or she is talking about.

Example #1:

In programming CGI, a WYSIWYG interface doesn't handle PHP or CSS very well. If you sign up for my personal consulting, I will show you how to program effectively.

Explanation: Simply overusing acronyms is not the problem here; it's the deliberate overuse for the purpose of making people think the speaker is very knowledgeable in this area, or perhaps to use terms the audience is unaware of, making the audience think they need the consulting service more than they thought they did.

Example #2:

Am I good at public speaking? Let's see. I have a CC, AC-B, AC-S, AC-G, CL, AL-B, AL-S, and a DTM. What do you think?

Explanation: These are all designations from Toastmasters International. In fact, many of them have more to do with leadership than speaking, but the average audience member would never know that. Besides, getting all these awards just means the person did the work needed, not that they are necessarily good at public speaking—kind of like certificates given out in fifth-grade gym class to all the kids who do more than six sit-ups.

Exception: "Excessive" is subjective. Acronyms and abbreviations are perfectly acceptable in many situations.

Tip: Don't be so quick to assume nefarious intentions. Sometimes people simply are unaware that they are overusing this type of language.

References:

This is a logical fallacy frequently used on the Internet. No academic sources could be found.

Alternative Advance

(also known as: lose-lose situation)

Description: When one is presented with just two choices, both of which are essentially the same, just worded differently. This technique is often used in sales. Fallacious reasoning would be committed by the person accepting the options as the only options, which would most likely be on a subconscious level since virtually anyone—if they thought about it—would recognize other options exist.

Example #1:

> *Max: If you're not a witch, you have nothing to fear. If you're not a witch, you are not made of wood; therefore, you will sink and drown after we tie you up and throw you in the well. If you do float, then you are made of wood, you are a witch, and we will hang you.*

> *Glinda: Wait, how is it I have nothing to worry about if I am not a witch?*

Explanation: The argument is created so that any woman accused of being a witch will die, which is certainly a lose-lose situation.

Example #2:

Guy working a booth in the mall: Excuse me, but you look like you can use a vacation! Do you have a few minutes to chat about vacation destinations, or would you prefer I just send you some information by e-mail?

Explanation: Of course, other options include just ignoring the guy and keep walking; telling the guy, "no thank you," and keep walking; or respond, "I have some time to chat. My rate is $10 per minute. Do you prefer to pay me by cash or check?"

Exception: If you engage your critical thinking and realize other options exist and still choose one of the given options, you would not be guilty of fallacious reasoning.

Tip: Whenever you are presented with options, carefully consider the possibility of other options not mentioned, and propose them.

References:

This is a logical fallacy frequently used on the Internet. No academic sources could be found.

Amazing Familiarity

(also known as: argument from omniscience, "how the hell can you possibly know that?")

Description: The argument contains information that seems impossible to have obtained—like it came from an omniscient author. This kind of writing/storytelling is characteristic of fiction, so when it is used in an argument it should cast doubt.

Logical Form:

Claim X is made that nobody could possibly know.

Example #1:

The president is a good man and would have never cheated on his wife, and has never cheated in anything in the past.

Explanation: Clearly the arguer could not know this unless the arguer was with the president all the time. We might assume that the arguer has some special knowledge and find this argument credible when we should only accept it as an opinion from someone who can't possibly know what he or she claims to know.

Example #2:

God wants us to love each other, but he is okay with us killing each other if we are defending our land—we will still go to Heaven.

Explanation: Claims of knowing the mind of God are highly dubious. While we cannot rule out "divine revelation," we would need to weigh that possibility against the likelihood of a false belief.

Example #3:

Larry is pure evil.

Explanation: Larry may be an ass. He might have done many bad things. Heck, he might have even have ripped the "do not remove under penalty of law" tag off his mattress. However, to make claims of "pure" evil, one would have to be Larry. While making absolute claims about a person such as being "pure evil" might just be hyperbole, if we take the claim at face value, knowing the claim to be true would require the kind of omniscience reflected in this fallacy.

Exception: "Seems impossible" is not "impossible." It might be possible that someone actually has the detailed knowledge they claim. We need to keep that option open when thinking probabilistically.

Tip: By simply adding an "I believe" to non-factual arguments and claims, you can avoid many fallacies and be more honest while exercising more humility.

References:

This is a logical fallacy frequently used on the Internet. No academic sources could be found.

Ambiguity Fallacy

(also known as: ambiguous assertion, amphiboly, amphibology, semantical ambiguity, vagueness)

Description: When an unclear phrase with multiple definitions is used within the argument; therefore, does not support the conclusion. Some will say single words count for the ambiguity fallacy, which is really a specific form of a fallacy known as *equivocation*.

Logical Form:

Claim X is made.

Y is concluded based on an ambiguous understanding of X.

Example #1:

It is said that we have a good understanding of our universe. Therefore, we know exactly how it began and exactly when.

Explanation: The ambiguity here is what exactly "good understanding" means. The conclusion assumes a much better understanding than is suggested in the premise; therefore, we have the *ambiguity fallacy*.

Example #2:

All living beings come from other living beings. Therefore, the first forms of life must have come from a living being. That living being is God.

Explanation: This argument is guilty of two cases of ambiguity. First, the first use of the phrase, "come from," refers to *reproduction*, whereas the second use refers to *origin*. The fact that we know quite a bit about reproduction is irrelevant when considering origin. Second, the first use of, "living being," refers to an empirically verifiable, biological, living organism. The second use of, "living being," refers to a belief in an immaterial god. As you can see, when a term such as, "living being," describes a Dodo bird as well as the all-powerful master of the universe, it has very little meaning and certainly is not specific enough to draw logical or reasonable conclusions.

Example #3:

> Bernice: Do you support Black Lives Matter?
>
> Mildred: Of course, I do!
>
> Bernice: Then you should support me looting that store.
>
> Mildred: Wait... what?

Explanation: "Black Lives Matter" is a political ideology that has evolved from a simple declaration. Like all ideologies, it has many branches ranging from moderate to extreme. Bernice clearly has a different concept of Black Lives Matter than Mildred does. An argument can be had over who is perverting the ideology (we have seen this among different Christians for millennia), but the point remains that what is meant by "supporting Black Lives Matter" has become unclear.

Exception: Ambiguous phrases are extremely common in the English language and are a necessary part of informal logic and reasoning. As long as these ambiguous phrases mean the same thing in all uses of phrases in the argument, this fallacy is not committed.

Tip: Don't be afraid to ask for clarification, especially if the alternative is to assume your interlocutor is being unreasonable or deceptive.

References:

Jevons, W. S. (1872). *Elementary lessons in logic: deductive and inductive: with copious questions and examples, and a vocabulary of logical terms.* Macmillan.

Anonymous Authority

(also known as: appeal to anonymous authority)

Description: When an unspecified source is used as evidence for the claim. This is commonly indicated by phrases such as "They say that...," "It has been said...," "I heard that...," "Studies show...," or generalized groups such as, "scientists say..." When we fail to specify a source of the authority, we can't verify the source, thus the credibility of the argument. Appeals to anonymous sources are more often than not, a way to fabricate, exaggerate, or misrepresent facts in order to deceive others into accepting your claim. At times, this deception is done subconsciously—it might not always be deliberate.

Logical Form:

Person 1 once heard that X was true.

Therefore, X is true.

Example #1:

You know, they say that if you swallow gum it takes seven years to digest. So whatever you do, don't swallow the gum!

Explanation: "They" are wrong as "they" usually are. Gum passes through the system relatively unchanged but does not hang around for 7 years like a college student terrified to get a job. "They" is a common form of appeal to *anonymous authority*.

Example #2:

The 13.7 billion-year-old universe is a big conspiracy. I read this article once where these notable scientists found strong evidence that the universe was created 6000 years ago, but because of losing their jobs, they were forced to keep quiet!

Explanation: Without knowing who these scientists are, or the credibility of the source of the article, we cannot verify the evidence; therefore, we should not accept the evidence.

Exception: At times, an accepted fact uses the same indicating phrases like the ones used for the fallacy; therefore, if the anonymous authority is actually just a statement of an accepted fact, it should be accepted as evidence.

*Climate change is happening—and always has been.
Scientists say the earth is certainly in a warming phase, but
there is some debate on the exact causes and certainly more
debate on what should be done about it politically.*

Tip: Be very wary of "they."

References:

Greenwell, W. S., Knight, J. C., Holloway, C. M., & Pease, J. J. (2006).
A Taxonomy of fallacies in system safety arguments. Retrieved
from https://ntrs.nasa.gov/search.jsp?R=20060027794

Anthropomorphism

(also known as: personification)

Description: The attributing of human characteristics and
purposes to inanimate objects, animals, plants, or other natural
phenomena, or to gods. This becomes a logical fallacy when
used within the context of an argument.

Logical Form:

Non-human thing is described with human characteristics.

*Claim X is made that requires the human characteristics of
the thing.*

Therefore, claim X is true.

Example #1:

How dare you murder those carrots!

Explanation: Murder applies to humans, not carrots. By
definition, one cannot murder carrots. In this example, the
carrots are assumed to have the human characteristics that
make murder "murder" and not just "killing" or "eating."

Example #2:

Akoni: The Polynesian fire goddess, Pele, sacrificed her own daughter in the volcano to bring peace to the islands. This is how I know she loves us.

Ubon: Aren't the gods and goddesses immortal?

Akoni: Err, yes.

Ubon: Then what happened to Pele's daughter after she was thrown in the volcano?

Akoni: She was reunited with Pele in the heavens.

Ubon: So why was this a sacrifice?

Explanation: The goddess, Pele, and her daughter are given the human quality of the frailty of life in order for the concept of "sacrifice" to be meaningful.

Tip: If you want to make people laugh, give objects and small animals human qualities. Anthropomorphism is a comedy goldmine for stand-up comedians.

References:

anthropomorphism | religion. (n.d.). https://www.britannica.com/topic/anthropomorphism

Appeal to Accomplishment

(also known as: appeal to success)

Description: When the argument being made is sheltered from criticism based on the level of accomplishment of the one making the argument. A form of this fallacy also occurs when arguments are evaluated on the accomplishments, or success, of the person making the argument, rather than on the merits of the argument itself.

Logical Forms:

Person 1 claims that Y is true.

Person 1 is very accomplished.

Therefore, Y is true.

Person 1 presents evidence against claim Y.

Person 1 is told to shut up until person 1 becomes as accomplished as person 2.

Example #1:

I have been around the block many times, and I have had my share of success. So believe me when I tell you that there is no better hobby than cat-juggling.

Explanation: We can all admire accomplishment and success, but this is irrelevant to cat-juggling. There are many accomplished and successful people who are immoral, mean, insensitive, hateful, liars, miserable, and just plain wrong about a great many things.

Example #2:

I hold a doctorate in theology, have written 12 books, and personally met the Pope. Therefore, when I say that Jesus' favorite snack was raisins dipped in wine, you should believe me.

Explanation: While the credentials of the one making the statement are certainly impressive, in no way do these credentials lend credibility to the belief that Jesus' favorite snack was wine-dipped raisins.

Exception: When one's accomplishments are directly related to the argument, it is more meaningful.

I have been around the block many times, and I have had my share of success in real estate. So believe me when I tell you that, if you know what you are doing, real estate can be a great way to make a great living.

Tip: Many successful people attempt to use their success as a wildcard to be an authority on everything. Don't allow one's own success to cloud your judgment of the claims they are making. Evaluate the evidence above all else.

References:

This is a logical fallacy frequently used on the Internet. No academic sources could be found.

Appeal to Anger
argumentum ad iram

(also known as: appeal to hatred, loathing, appeal to outrage, etc.)

Description: When the emotions of anger, hatred, or rage are substituted for evidence in an argument.

Logical Forms:

Person 1 claims that X is true.

Person 1 is outraged.

Therefore, X is true.

Claim A is made.

You are outraged by claim A.

Therefore, claim A is true/false.

Example #1:

Are you tired of being ignored by your government? Is it right that the top 1% have so much when the rest of us have so little? I urge you to vote for me today!

Explanation: This is a common tactic to play on the emotions of others to get them to do what you want them to do. The fact is, no evidence was given or claim was made linking your vote with the problems going away. The politician will hope you will make the connection while she can claim innocence down the road when the people attempt to hold the politician to a promise she really never made.

Example #2:

> *How can you possibly think that humans evolved from monkeys! Does my nanna look like a flippin' monkey to you?*

Explanation: Ignoring the fact that we didn't evolve from monkeys (we share a common ancestor with modern African apes), the fact that the arguer is obviously offended is irrelevant to the facts.

Exception: Like all appeals to emotion, they work very well when used, in addition to a supported conclusion, not in place of one.

> *Are you tired of being ignored by your government? Is it right that the top 1% have so much when the rest of us have so little? I urge you to vote for me today, and I will spend my career making America a place where the wealth is more evenly distributed!*

Fun Fact: The great Yoda once said, "Fear leads to anger, anger leads to hate, hate leads to suffering." With all due respect to the cute, little, green guy, anger can be very powerful and effective, as well as lead to great things. Think of Martin Luther King, Jr.

By the way, Yoda's statement actually commits the *slippery slope fallacy*.

References:

Whately, R. (1854). *Rhetoric*. Griffin.

Appeal to Authority
argumentum ad verecundiam

(also known as: argument from authority, ipse dixit)

Description: Insisting that a claim is true simply because a valid authority or expert on the issue said it was true, without any other supporting evidence offered. Also see the *appeal to false authority*.

Logical Form:

According to person 1, who is an expert on the issue of Y, Y is true.

Therefore, Y is true.

Example #1:

Richard Dawkins, an evolutionary biologist and perhaps the foremost expert in the field, says that evolution is true.

Therefore, it's true.

Explanation: Richard Dawkins certainly knows about evolution, and he can confidently tell us that it is true, but that doesn't make it true. What makes it true is the preponderance of evidence for the theory.

Example #2:

How do I know the adult film industry is the third largest industry in the United States? Derek Shlongmiester, the adult film star of over 50 years, said it was. That's how I know.

Explanation: Shlongmiester may be an industry expert, as well as have a huge talent, but a claim such as the one made would require supporting evidence. For the record, the adult film industry may be large, but on a scale from 0 to 12 inches, it's only about a fraction of an inch.

Exception: Be very careful not to confuse "deferring to an authority on the issue" with the *appeal to authority fallacy*. Remember, a fallacy is an **error in reasoning**. Dismissing the council of legitimate experts and authorities turns good skepticism into denialism. The *appeal to authority* is a fallacy in argumentation, but deferring to an authority is a reliable heuristic that we all use virtually every day on issues of relatively little importance. There is always a chance that any authority can be wrong, that's why the critical thinker accepts facts *provisionally*. **It is not at all unreasonable (or an error in reasoning) to accept information as provisionally true by credible authorities.** Of course, the reasonableness is moderated by the claim being made (i.e., how extraordinary, how important) and the authority (how credible, how relevant to the claim).

The *appeal to authority* is more about claims that require evidence than about facts. For example, if your tour guide told you that Vatican City was founded February 11, 1929, and you accept that information as true, you are not committing a fallacy (because it is not in the context of argumentation) nor are you being unreasonable.

Tip: Question authority—or become the authority that people look to for answers.

References:

Hume, D. (2004). *An Enquiry Concerning Human Understanding*. Courier Corporation.

Appeal to Celebrity

Description: Accepting a claim of a celebrity based on his or her celebrity status, not on the strength of the argument.

Logical Form:

Celebrity 1 says to use product Y.

Therefore, we should use product Y.

Example #1:

Tom Cruise says on TV that Billy Boy Butter is the best tasting butter there is. Tom Cruise is awesome—especially in MI4 when he scaled that building with only one suction glove; therefore, Billy Boy Butter is the best tasting butter there is!

Explanation: Tom Cruise might be awesome, and perhaps he really does think Billy Boy Butter is the best tasting butter there is, but Tom is no more an authority on the taste of butter than anyone else; therefore, to accept the claim without any other evidence or reason is fallacious.

Example #2:

Mike Seaver from that 80's sitcom, "Growing Pains," is really cool. He is now a born-again Christian and apologist for the faith. Therefore, you should really believe what he has to say!

Explanation: Mike Seaver is awesome, but Kirk Cameron, the actor that plays that character? Even if Kirk were super duper (which he might be, I don't know him), his views on the truth of religion are equally valid as yours, or anyone else's who determines what he or she considers to be the truth through faith.

Exception: Some celebrity endorsements are authentic, where the celebrities are motivated by the love of the product itself, not the huge check they are getting for pretending to like the product. When these products are directly related to their celebrity status, then this could be seen as a valid (but not sufficient) reason for wanting the product.

Tip: If you are in business and looking for a celebrity to endorse your product, try not to pick one that is likely to be accused of killing his wife and his wife's lover, then taking off in a white Bronco.

References:

Kamins, M. A. (1989). Celebrity and noncelebrity advertising in a two-sided context. *Journal of Advertising Research, 29*(3), 34–42.

Appeal to Closure

(also known as: appeal to justice [form of])

Description: Accepting evidence on the basis of wanting closure—or to be done with the issue. While the desire for closure is a real psychological phenomenon that does have an effect on the well-being of individuals, using "closure" as a reason for accepting evidence that would otherwise not be accepted, is fallacious. This is similar to the *argument from ignorance* where one makes a claim based on the lack of information because not knowing is too psychologically uncomfortable. However, the *appeal to closure* focuses on accepting evidence and for the reason of closure.

Logical Form:

Evidence X is presented, and found to be insufficient (or evaluated with a heavy bias due to the desire for closure).

Closure is desired.

Therefore, evidence X is accepted.

Example #1: After the terrorist attack on the city, the citizens were outraged and wanted justice. So they arrested a Muslim man with no alibi who looked suspicious then charged him with the crime.

Explanation: Unfortunately, unsolved crimes are bad politically for those in charge and based on the number and percentage of false arrests, it is clear that appealing to closure has some serious consequences for many innocent people.

Example #2:

Art: Why didn't it work out between you and Marci?

Steve: It turns out that she was a lesbian.

Art: Did you know she and Jack just got married?

Steve: [experiences a hard hit to his ego]

Explanation: I heard from Suzi who told Tanya who told Jennifer that Marci simply thought Steve was a jerk but fed him the classic break up line, "it's not you, it's me." Steve, being the alpha male he is, couldn't deal with this psychological trauma of not having a firm answer to why Marci didn't want to be with him, so based on the fact that Marci once commented that a supermodel had "pretty eyes," Steve put the issue to rest by writing Marci off as a lesbian. Steve discovered that calling Marci a lesbian was actually just him projecting his own homosexual desires on Marci. Today, Steve is living happily with his partner, Raúl, and their white Persian cat, Mr. Muffins.

Exception: It has been stated elsewhere that "agree to disagree" falls under the *appeal to closure*. This is not the case because agreeing to disagree does not mean that either party is accepting the evidence of the other, in fact, it's the opposite. People can agree to "move on" or "table the issue," for many logical reasons. This is similar to negotiation and compromise. When people compromise, they usually do not agree to accept evidence they wouldn't otherwise accept. For example, if an atheist and theist are debating the existence of the Biblical God, they wouldn't say, "Okay, I'll agree that some kind of creator god exists if you agree that this god does not currently interfere in the universe."

Variation: The *appeal to justice* is also about closure, but "just" closure. The concept of justice is the focus where the facts and reasoning are secondary. "Do you want to live in a world where people can rob banks and get away with it? Then when it comes time for your verdict, vote Bad Boy Billy guilty!"

Tip: Remember that justice is a subjective term. When people cry "justice," they often have created a narrative with very clear heroes and villains, when the truth is far more often unclear.

References:

This is a logical fallacy frequently used on the Internet. No academic sources could be found.

Appeal to Coincidence

(also known as: appeal to luck, appeal to bad luck, appeal to good luck)

Description: Concluding that a result is due to chance when the evidence strongly suggests otherwise. The *appeal to luck* variation uses luck in place of coincidence or chance.

Logical Form:

> *Evidence suggests that X is the result of Y.*
>
> *Yet one insists that X is the result of chance.*

Example #1:

> *Bill: Steve, I am sorry to say, but you are a horrible driver!*
>
> *Steve: Why do you say that?*

Bill: This is your fourteenth accident this year.

Steve: It's just been an unlucky year for me.

Explanation: Based on statistical norms, it is very clear that anyone getting into fourteen accidents in a single year has a safety issue as a driver. Ignoring this obvious fact and writing it off as "bad luck," is seen as the *appeal to coincidence*.

Example #2:

Mom: This is the eighth time you have been sent to the principal's office this year. The principal tells me she has seen you more times in her office than any other student. Why is this?

Dwight: A teacher just happens to sneak up on me whenever I am doing something against the rules, which is no more often than any other student.

Explanation: Dwight is a trouble-maker—that is quite clear. Rather than face the facts, he is *appealing to coincidence* by suggesting he just gets caught more often due to bad timing.

Exception: Coincidences do happen. When the evidence points in the direction of coincidence, the coincidence might be the best option.

Tip: Remember that million-to-one thing happened to you? It was probably a coincidence. Given how many things happen to us every day, all of us should experience many million-to-one events throughout our lifetimes.

References:

Shermer, M. (2002). *Why People Believe Weird Things: Pseudoscience, Superstition, and Other Confusions of Our Time.* Henry Holt and Company.

Appeal to Common Belief
argumentum ad populum

(also known as: appeal to accepted belief, appeal to democracy, appeal to widespread belief, appeal to the masses, appeal to belief, appeal to general belief, appeal to the majority, argument by consensus, authority of the many, consensus fallacy, bandwagon fallacy, appeal to the number, argumentum ad numerum, argumentum consensus gentium, appeal to the mob, appeal to the gallery, consensus gentium, mob appeal, social conformance, value of community, vox populi)

Description: When the claim that most or many people in general or of a particular group accept a belief as true is presented as evidence for the claim. Accepting another person's belief, or many people's beliefs, without demanding evidence as to why that person accepts the belief, is lazy thinking and a dangerous way to accept information.

Logical Form:

> *A lot of people believe X.*
>
> *Therefore, X must be true.*

Example #1: Up until the late 16th century, most people believed that the earth was the center of the universe. This was seen as enough of a reason back then to accept this as true.

Explanation: The *geocentric model* was an observation (limited) and faith-based, but most who accepted the model did so based on the common and accepted belief of the time, not on their own observations, calculations, and/or reasoning. It was people like Copernicus, Galileo, and Kepler, who refused to *appeal to the common belief* and uncovered a truth not obvious to the rest of humanity.

Example #2:

> *Mark: Do you believe in virgin births?*
>
> *Sue: You mean that babies are born virgins?*
>
> *Mark: I mean birth without fertilization.*
>
> *Sue: No.*

Mark: How could you not believe in virgin births? Roughly two billion people believe in them, don't you think you should reconsider your position?

Explanation: Anyone who believes in virgin births does not have empirical evidence for his or her belief. This is a claim accepted on faith, which is an individual and subjective form of accepting information, that should not have any effect on your beliefs. Don't forget that there was a time that the common beliefs included a flat earth, earth-centered universe, and demon possession as the cause of most illness.

Exception: Sometimes there are good reasons to think that the common belief is held by people who do have good evidence for believing. For example, if virtually all of earth scientists accept that the universe is approximately 13.7 billion years old, it is wise to believe them because they will be able to present objective and empirical evidence as to why they believe.

Tip: History has shown that those who break away from the common beliefs are the ones who change the course of history. Be a leader, not a follower.

References:

Wagner, R. H. (1938). *Handbook of argumentation*. Nelson.

Appeal to Common Folk

(also known as: appeal to the common man)

Description: In place of evidence, attempting to establish a connection to the audience based on being a "regular person" just like each of them. Then suggesting that your proposition is something that all common folk believe or should accept.

Logical Forms:

X is just common folk wisdom.

Therefore, you should accept X.

Person 1 is a common man who proposes Y.

You are also a common man.

Therefore, you should accept Y.

Example #1:

My fellow Americans, I am just like you. Sure, I have a few private jets and homes in twelve countries, but I put on my pants one leg at a time, just like you common people. So believe me when I say, this increase in taxes for the common folk is just what we all need.

Explanation: There is no valid reason given for the increase in taxes.

Example #2:

You don't want a hot dog and beer? Eating hot dogs and drinking beer at a baseball game is the American thing to do.

Explanation: Here the person making the argument is appealing to the *tradition* of the common folk.

Exception: If the "common folk" appeal is made in addition to valid reasons, then it is not a fallacy, although I would argue it is cheap pandering that many people can easily detect.

Tip: If you are tempted to appeal to some folk, appeal to the folk that made the world a better place. Not only do people love inspirational stories, but these stories are also powerful motivators. Just be sure to use this technique in addition to reason, not in place of it.

References:

McWhorter, K. T. (2001). *Academic Reading*. Addison Wesley Longman.

Appeal to Common Sense

Description: Asserting that your conclusion or facts are just "common sense" when, in fact, they are not. We must argue as to *why* we believe something is common sense if there is any doubt that the belief is not common, rather than just asserting that it is. This is a more specific version of *alleged certainty*.

Logical Form:

It's common sense that X is true.

Therefore, X is true.

Example #1:

It's common sense that if you smack your children, they will stop the bad behavior. So don't tell me not to hit my kids.

Explanation: What is often accepted as "common sense" is factually incorrect or otherwise problematic. While hitting your kids may stop their current bad behavior, the long-term psychological and behavioral negative effects (including future bad behavior) can far outweigh the temporary benefits. Logically speaking, the example simply appeals to "common sense" rather than makes an attempt at a strong argument.

Example #2:

Don: If you drink alcohol, it will kill any virus you might have.

Tony: What evidence do you have to support that?

Don: I don't need evidence. It is common sense.

Explanation: Since we use alcohol to clean viruses from our skin, it might be "common sense" that it would clean our insides too. But this is not the case. First, the alcohol needs to be high concentration, like 60% or more to be effective. Second, it does nothing to kill a virus in your body. Third, Don does need evidence if he is trying to convince Tony he is right, and he should demand evidence for himself before engaging in a risky behavior because of what he believes is "common sense."

Example #3:

FlatSam: Common sense tells us that if the earth were a sphere, people on the bottom would fall off.

ReasonEric: I don't think you get to reference something you clearly don't have.

Explanation: FlatSam is attempting to justify his implied argument (the earth is flat) by appealing to "common sense." He appears to be offering a reason (i.e., people on the bottom would fall off), but that reason is itself a claim "supported" by the *appeal to common sense.*

Exception: What is "common sense" to one might not be to another. It is possible one might not accept something that is "common sense," so it could be argued that the error in reasoning falls on the person rejecting the assertion of common sense.

Tip: It's all about good communication. Keep your assumptions to a minimum when attempting to make a persuasive argument.

References:

Facione, P. A., & Facione, N. C. (2007). *Thinking and reasoning in human decision making: the method of argument and heuristic analysis.* California Academic Press.

Appeal to Complexity

Description: Concluding that because you don't understand something, it must not be true, it's improbable, or the argument must be flawed. This is a specific form of the *argument from ignorance.*

Logical Form:

I don't understand argument X.

Therefore, argument X cannot be true/is flawed/improbable.

Example #1:

Bill the Eye Guy: The development of the eye is monophyletic, meaning they have their origins in a proto-eye that evolved around 540 million years ago. Multiple eye types and subtypes developed in parallel. We know this partly because eyes in various animals show adaption to their requirements.

Toby: Uh, that sounds made up. I don't think the eye could have evolved.

Explanation: Yes, the evolution of the eye is confusing to non-biologists and those who are not familiar with evolutionary theory and natural selection. But the complexity of this argument is not a reason to reject it or find it less credible than a simpler claim (e.g. Zeus created eyes from clay).

Example #2: If a layperson criticizes a complex policy about which they know nothing or very little, they are probably *appealing to complexity.*

Explanation: Black and white thinking is found where one has a lack of knowledge about a topic. Policies such as national healthcare are incredibly complex where each change has benefits and drawbacks. Non-experts often will dismiss a 1000-page document and say something such as, "Look, it's simple. Do this, this, and this. Problem solved." No, it's not simple, and that wouldn't solve the problem.

Exception: When the one making the argument doesn't understand what they are actually saying, they are committing the *argument by gibberish.*

Tip: It is the job of the arguer to make the argument as clear as possible, and use language and terms that the audience can understand. This is a major problem in science communication. The *curse of knowledge* often leads to those trying to explain a complex topic in such a way where they assume the audience has as much knowledge in the fields as they do. If your audience fails to understand your argument, don't blame the audience; explain your argument differently.

References:

This is a logical fallacy frequently used on the Internet. No academic sources could be found.

Appeal to Consequences
argumentum ad consequentiam

(also known as: appeal to consequences of a belief, argument to the consequences, argument from [the] consequences, appeal to convenience [form of], appeal to utility)

Description: Concluding that an idea or proposition is true or false because the consequences of it being true or false are desirable or undesirable. The fallacy lies in the fact that the desirability is not related to the truth value of the idea or proposition. This comes in two forms: the positive and negative.

Logical Forms:

X is true because if people did not accept X as being true then there would be negative consequences.

X is false because if people did not accept X as being false, then there would be negative consequences.

X is true because accepting that X is true has positive consequences.

X is false because accepting that X is false has positive consequences.

Example #1 (positive):

If there is objective morality, then good moral behavior will be rewarded after death. I want to be rewarded; therefore, morality must be objective.

Example #2 (negative):

If there is no objective morality, then all the bad people will not be punished for their bad behavior after death. I don't like that; therefore, morality must be objective.

Explanation: The fact that one wants to be rewarded, or wants other people to suffer, says nothing to the truth claim of objective morality. These examples are also *begging the question* that there is life after death.

Example #3:

> *If there is no freewill, then we are not ultimately in control of our actions. If this is true, our entire system of justice would be seriously flawed. This would be very bad; therefore, freewill must exist.*

Explanation: The "freewill" argument has been around for thousands of years, and we may never know how free we really are to make decisions. Many philosophers recognize this problem as well as the consequences of not believing in freewill. For this reason, some suggest that we should just accept freewill as being true. While acting as if we have freewill might lead to a better outcome, actually believing freewill to be true because of the consequences is a compromise of one's rational integrity.

Exception: If the consequences refer to actions taken or not taken, it would be more of a warning than an argument, thus not fallacious.

> *If you continue to reflect the sun in my eyes using your watch, I will take your watch and shove it in a place the sun don't shine. Therefore, you should really stop doing that.*

Variation: The *appeal to convenience* is accepting an argument because its conclusion is convenient, not necessarily true. This is very similar to the *appeal to consequences* except that consequences are only positive and reasonably referred to as "convenient."

Tip: Realize that you can deal with reality, no matter what that reality turns out to be. You don't need to hide from it—face it and embrace it.

References:

Walton, D. (1999). Historical Origins of Argumentum ad Consequentiam. *Argumentation, 13*(3), 251–264. https://doi.org/10.1023/A:1007779527544

Appeal to Definition

(also known as: appeal to the dictionary, victory by definition)

Description: Using a dictionary's limited definition of a term as evidence that term cannot have another meaning, expanded meaning, or even conflicting meaning. This is a fallacy because dictionaries don't reason; they simply are a reflection of an abbreviated version of the current accepted usage of a term, as determined by argumentation and eventual acceptance. In short, dictionaries tell you what a word meant, according to the authors, at the time of its writing, not what it meant before that time, after, or what it should mean.

Dictionary meanings are usually concise, and lack the depth found in an encyclopedia; therefore, terms found in dictionaries are often incomplete when it comes to helping people to gain a full understanding of the term.

Logical Form:

The dictionary definition of X does not mention Y.

Therefore, Y must not be part of X.

Example #1:

Ken: Do you think gay marriage should be legalized?

Paul: Absolutely not! Marriage is defined as the union between a man and a woman—not between two men or two women!

Ken: Did you know that in 1828 the dictionary definition of marriage included, "for securing the maintenance and education of children"? Does that mean that all married couples who can't or choose not to have children aren't really married?

Paul: No, it just means they need to buy updated dictionaries.

Ken: As do you. The current Merriam-Webster Dictionary includes as a secondary definition, "the state of being united to a person of the same sex in a relationship like that of a traditional marriage."

Explanation: The dictionary does not settle controversial issues such as gay marriage—it simply reports the most current accepted definition of the term itself while usually attempting to remain neutral on such controversial issues.

Example #2:

Armondo: Mrs. Patterson was wrong to knock off 10 points off my oral presentation because I kept using the word, "erection" instead of building.

Felix: That was hilarious, but did you honestly think you would not get in trouble?

Armondo: No, my dictionary says that an erection is a building.

Explanation: Armondo may be right, but the dictionary is not the final authority on all issues, especially social behavior. More modern usage, especially in a high school setting, takes precedence in this case.

Exception: The dictionary works well when the term in question is a result of a misunderstanding or ignorance. For example:

Ken: Do you accept evolution?

Paul: No. Because life cannot come from non-life.

Ken: Look up "evolution" and you will see that it makes no claims to the origin of life.

Tip: Don't be afraid to argue with authority if you believe you are right—even when that authority is the dictionary.

References:

This is an original logical fallacy named by the author, but the victory by definition form has the following source:

Govier, T. (2009). *A Practical Study of Argument*. Cengage Learning.

Appeal to Desperation

Description: Arguing that your conclusion, solution, or proposition is right based on the fact that something must be done, and your solution is "something."

Logical Form:

Something must be done.

X is something.

Therefore, X must be done.

Example #1:

These are desperate times, and desperate times call for desperate measures. Therefore, I propose we exterminate all baby seals. It is obvious that something must be done, and this is something.

Explanation: No reason is given for why we should exterminate all baby seals. Perhaps the reason is that they all have a virus that will spread to the human race and kill us all, perhaps exterminating all baby seals will leave more fish for humans, or perhaps exterminating all baby seals will be a way to put an end to the clubbing of baby seals—but without these or any other reasons given, we have nothing to go on except the desperation that something must be done.

Example #2:

Chairman: We are out of money come Monday. Any suggestions?

Felix: I suggest we take what money we do have, and go to Disney World.

Chairman: Any other suggestions?

(silence)

Chairman: Since there are no other suggestions, Disney World it is.

Explanation: Desperate times don't necessarily call for any measure over no measure. Many times, no action is better than a bad action. Blowing what money is left on over-priced soft drinks and what appears to be rotisserie ostrich legs, may not be a wise choice—especially when investors are involved.

Exception: At times, especially in situations where time is limited, taking some action will be better than taking no action, and in the absence of better reasoning, the best available reason might have to do. However, a reason, no matter how poor, should still be given—not simply a conclusion.

Tip: Do your best to avoid situations of desperation where emotion very often takes the lead over reason. Although not all desperate situations can be avoided, many can, by proper planning and foresight.

References:

This is a logical fallacy frequently used on the Internet. No academic sources could be found.

Appeal to Emotion

(also known as: appeal to pathos, argument by vehemence, playing on emotions, emotional appeal, for the children)

Description: This is the general category of many fallacies that use emotion in place of reason in order to attempt to win the argument. It is a type of manipulation used in place of valid logic.

There are several specifically emotional fallacies that I list separately in this book, because of their widespread use. However, keep in mind that you can take any emotion, precede it with, "appeal to," and you have created a new fallacy, but by definition, the emotion must be used in place of a valid reason for supporting the conclusion.

Logical Form:

Claim X is made without evidence.

In place of evidence, emotion is used to convince the interlocutor that X is true.

Example #1:

Power lines cause cancer. I met a little boy with cancer who lived just 20 miles from a power line who looked into my eyes and said, in his weak voice, "Please do whatever you can so that other kids won't have to go through what I am going through." I urge you to vote for this bill to tear down all power lines and replace them with monkeys on treadmills.

Explanation: Notice the form of the example: assertion, emotional appeal, request for action (conclusion)—nowhere is there any evidence presented. We can all tear up over the image of a little boy with cancer who is expressing concern for others rather than taking pity on himself, but that has nothing to do with the assertion or the conclusion.

Example #2:

There must be objective rights and wrongs in the universe. If not, how can you possibly say that torturing babies for fun could ever be right?

Explanation: The thought of people torturing babies for fun immediately brings up unpleasant images (in sane people). The actual argument (implied) is that there are objective (universal) rights and wrongs (morality). The argument is worded in such a way to connect the argument's conclusions (that there is objective morality) with the idea that torturing babies for fun is wrong (this is also a *non sequitur fallacy*). No matter how we personally feel about a horrible act, our feelings are not a valid substitution for an objective reason behind *why* the act is horrible.

Exceptions: Appealing to emotions is a very powerful and necessary technique in persuasion. We are emotional creatures; therefore, we often make decisions and form beliefs erroneously based on emotions, when reason and logic tell us otherwise. However, using appeals to emotion as a backup to rational and logical arguments is not only valid, but a skill possessed by virtually every great communicator.

Tip: By appealing to both the brain and the heart, you will persuade the greatest number of people.

References:

Brinton, A. (1988). Pathos and the "Appeal to Emotion": An Aristotelian Analysis. *History of Philosophy Quarterly*, 5(3), 207–219.

Appeal to Equality

(also known as: appeal to egalitarianism, appeal to equity)

Description: An assertion is deemed true or false based on an assumed pretense of equality, where what exactly is "equal" is not made clear, and not supported by the argument.

Logical Form:

A equals B (when A does not equal B)

Y applies to A or B.

Therefore, Y applies to both A and B.

Example #1:

If women get paid maternity leave, so should men.

Explanation: There are some good reasons that men should get some form of paid **paternity** leave, but they are not present in this argument. There is an unstated assumption that what benefits women get, for whatever reason, men should get the same. This *begs the question*.

Example #2:

Gay marriage should be the law of the land because gays should have the same rights as heterosexuals.

Explanation: What do the "same rights" mean? Before gay marriage, men had the right to marry women, and women had the right to marry men. A man marrying a man is a different form of the "right of marriage" and needs to be argued as such. Again, there are many excellent arguments for gay marriage, but this isn't one of them.

Example #3:

> *Why should fetuses not have human rights, yet when they exit the womb as babies, they do have human rights? Clearly, fetuses deserve to have the same human rights as the rest of us.*

Explanation: This argument implies that fetuses and babies outside the womb are equal, and ignores the fact that one is dependent on the resources of the mother's body to survive. Like with gay marriage, there are many excellent arguments for extending human rights to fetuses, but due to the *appeal to equality*, this isn't one of them.

Exception: There is quite a bit of subjectivity in the analysis of this fallacy. Is what is made equal, "clear?" Is this equality supported by the argument? Consider the following:

> *People of all races are equal. Human rights apply to everyone, so members of the HootchyCootchie Tribe on the Island of PiddlyWiddly have the right to marriage and family.*

Unless we are talking about two or more of the same thing (i.e., A=A), then we really mean "equal in some way." Although not explicitly stated, "equality" is referring to having human rights, which seems pretty clear. The right to marriage and family is a universal human right, so this is supported by the argument.

Tip: Don't get outraged when one questions what you believe should be "equal." Very often, either you really mean "similar" or you and your interlocutor have different concepts of what exactly should be equal.

References:

This is a logical fallacy frequently used on the Internet. No academic sources could be found.

Appeal to Extremes

Description: Erroneously attempting to make a reasonable argument into an absurd one, by taking the argument to the extremes. Note that this is not a valid *reductio ad absurdum*.

Logical Form:

If X is true, then Y must also be true (where Y is the extreme of X).

Example #1:

There is no way those Girl Scouts could have sold all those cases of cookies in one hour. If they did, they would have to make $500 in one hour, which, based on an 8 hour day is over a million dollars a year. That is more than most lawyers, doctors, and successful business people make!

Explanation: The Girl Scouts worked just for one hour—not 40 per week for a year. Suggesting the extreme leads to an absurd conclusion; that Girl Scouts are among the highest paid people in the world. Not to mention, there is a whole troop of them doing the work, not just one girl.

Example #2:

Don't forget God's commandment, "thou shall not kill." By using mouthwash, you are killing 99.9% of the germs that cause bad breath. Prepare for Hell.

Explanation: It is unlikely that God had mouthwash on his mind when issuing that commandment, but if he did, we're all screwed (at least those of us with fresh breath).

Exception: This fallacy is a misuse of one of the greatest techniques in argumentation, *reductio ad absurdum*, or reducing the argument to the absurd. The difference is where the absurdity actually is in the argument or in the reasoning of the one trying to show the argument is absurd.

Here is an example of an argument that is proven false by reducing to the absurd, legitimately.

Big Tony: The more you exercise, the stronger you will get!

Nerdy Ned: Actually, if you just kept exercising and never stopped, you would drop dead. There is a limit to how much exercise you should get. At some point, the exercise becomes excessive and causes more harm than good.

Tip: People very often say stupid things. Sometimes it is easy to reduce their arguments to absurdity, but remember, in most cases, your goal should be diplomacy, not making the other person look foolish. Especially when dealing with your spouse— unless you really like sleeping on the couch.

References:

This is a logical fallacy frequently used on the Internet. No academic sources could be found.

Appeal to Faith

Description: This is an abandonment of reason in an argument and a call to faith, usually when reason clearly leads to disproving the conclusion of an argument. It is the assertion that one must have (the right kind of) faith in order to understand the argument.

Even arguments that heavily rely on reason that ultimately require faith, abandon reason.

Logical Form:

X is true.

If you have faith, you will see that.

Example #1:

Jimmie: Joseph Smith, the all American prophet, was the blond-haired, blue-eyed voice of God.

Hollie: What is your evidence for that?

Jimmie: I don't need evidence—I only need faith.

Explanation: There are some things, some believe, that are beyond reason and logic. Fair enough, but the moment we accept this, absent of any objective method of telling what is beyond reason and why *anything goes*, anything can be explained away without having to explain anything.

Example #2:

> Tom: Did you know that souls ("Thetans") reincarnate and have lived on other planets before living on Earth, and Xenu was the tyrant ruler of the Galactic Confederacy?
>
> Mike: No, I did not know that. How do you know that?
>
> Tom: I know this through my faith. Do you think everything can be known by science alone? Your faith is weak, my friend.

Explanation: It should be obvious that reason and logic are not being used, but rather "faith." While Tom might be right, there is still no valid reason offered. The problem also arises in the vagueness of the *appeal to faith*. Tom's answer can be used to answer virtually any question imaginable, yet the answer is really a deflection.

> St. Bingo: You need to massage my feet.
>
> Tina: Why?
>
> St. Bingo: My child, you will only see that answer clearly through the eyes of faith.

Exception: No exceptions—the *appeal to faith* is always a fallacy when used to justify a conclusion in the absence of reason.

Tip: Atheist and theist debate often reduces to the concept of faith, sometimes after many hours. It is often a good idea to start with the question, "Is faith a reliable method to know things?"

References:

This is a logical fallacy frequently used on the Internet. No academic sources could be found.

Appeal to False Authority

(also known as: appeal to doubtful authority, appeal to dubious authority, appeal to improper authority, appeal to inappropriate authority, appeal to irrelevant authority, appeal to misplaced authority, appeal to unqualified authority, argument from false authority)

Description: Using an alleged authority as evidence in your argument when the authority is not really an authority on the facts relevant to the argument. As the audience, allowing an irrelevant authority to add credibility to the claim being made. Also see the *appeal to authority*.

Logical Forms:

> *According to person 1 (who offers little or no expertise on Y being true), Y is true.*
>
> *Therefore, Y is true.*

> *According to person 1 (who offers little or no expertise on Y being true), Y is true.*
>
> *Therefore, Y is more likely to be true.*

> *Expert A gives her view on issue B.*
>
> *Expert A's area of expertise has little or nothing to do with issue B.*
>
> *Expert A's opinion influences how people feel about issue B.*

Example #1:

> *My 5th-grade teacher once told me that girls would go crazy for boys if they learn how to dance. Therefore, if you want to make the ladies go crazy for you, learn to dance.*

Explanation: Even if the 5th-grade teacher were an expert on relationships, her belief about what makes girls "go crazy" for boys is speculative, or perhaps circumstantial, at best. In other words, the teacher's expertise is in dance, not on the psychology of attraction.

Example #2:

> The Pope told me that priests could turn bread and wine into Jesus' body and blood. The Pope is not a liar. Therefore, priests really can do this.

Explanation: The Pope may believe what he says, and perhaps the Pope is not a liar, but the Pope is not an authority on the *fact* that the bread and wine are actually transformed into Jesus' body and blood. After all, how much flesh and blood does this guy Jesus actually have to give?

Example #3:

> Dr. Dean, TV's hottest new psychologist, says that coffee enemas are the "fountain of youth." Get me that coffee enema!

Explanation: Assuming Dr. Dean is actually a licensed psychologist, that does not qualify him to give advice about non-psychology related issues such as coffee enemas. Like the colon, Dr. Dean is most likely full of... obligate anaerobes. Extending his expertise from psychology to issues of the colon is fallacious.

Example #4:

> My accountant says that within the next 90 days, the president will be impeached! So we should take this claim seriously!

Explanation: Unless the accountant has some inside information to the presidency, her expertise in accounting has little to do with the current administration, political, and constitutional law.

Exception: Don't pigeonhole people into certain areas of expertise. A medical doctor can also be an expert in sewing. A fly-fisherman can also be an expert in law. And a patent clerk can also be an expert in quantum mechanics.

Tip: Beware of your *confirmation bias*. You may want a person to be an authority on the topic, and this desire will result in your seeking out confirming information and ignoring conflicting information.

References:

Hume, D. (2004). *An Enquiry Concerning Human Understanding.* Courier Corporation.

Appeal to Fear
argumentum in terrorem

(also known as: argumentum ad metum, argument from adverse consequences, scare tactics)

Description: When fear, not based on evidence or reason, is being used as the primary motivator to get others to accept an idea, proposition, or conclusion.

Logical Form:

If you don't accept X as true, something terrible will happen to you.

Therefore, X must be true.

Example #1:

If we don't bail out the big automakers, the US economy will collapse. Therefore, we need to bail out the automakers.

Explanation: The idea of a collapsed economy is frightening enough for many people to overlook the fact that this is a premise without justification, resulting in them just accepting the conclusion. There is no evidence or reason provided for the claim that if we don't bail out the big automakers, the US economy will collapse.

Example #2:

Timmy: Mom, what if I don't believe in God?

Mom: Then you burn in Hell forever. Why do you ask?

Timmy: No reason.

Explanation: Timmy's faith is waning, but Mom, like most moms, is very good at scaring the Hell, in this case, into, Timmy. This is a fallacy because Mom provided no evidence that disbelief in God will lead to an eternity of suffering in Hell, but because the possibility is terrifying to Timmy, he "accepts" the proposition (to believe in God), despite the lack of actual evidence.

Exception: When fear is not the primary motivator, but a supporting one and the probabilities of the fearful event happening are honestly disclosed, it would not be fallacious.

Timmy: Mom, what if I don't believe in God?

Mom: Then I would hope that you don't believe in God for the right reasons, and not because your father and I didn't do a good enough job telling you why you should believe in him, including the possibility of what some believe is eternal suffering in Hell.

Timmy: That's a great answer mom. I love you. You are so much better than my mom in the other example.

Tip: Think in terms of probabilities, not possibilities. Many things are possible, including a lion busting into your home at night and mauling you to death—but it is very, very improbable. People who use fear to manipulate you, count on you to be irrational and emotional rather than reasonable and calculating. Prove them wrong.

References:

Garden, F. (1878). *A Dictionary of English Philosophical Terms.* Rivingtons.

Appeal to Flattery

(also known as: apple polishing, wheel greasing, brown nosing, appeal to pride/argumentum ad superbiam, appeal to vanity)

Description: When an attempt is made to win support for an argument, not by the strength of the argument, but by using flattery on those whom you want to accept your argument. This fallacy is often the cause of people getting tricked into doing something they don't really want to do.

Logical Form:

> *X is true.*
>
> *(flattery goes here)*
>
> *Therefore, X is true.*

Example #1:

> *You should certainly be the one who washes the dishes—you are just so good at it!*

Explanation: You may be great at washing dishes, but that fact in itself is not a sufficient reason for you being the one to wash the dishes. Is it necessary for someone as skilled at dish-washing as you to do the job, or is it a mindless job that anyone can do just fine?

Example #2:

> *Salesguy: You should definitely buy this car. You look so good in it—you look at least ten years younger behind that wheel.*
>
> *Tamera: I'll take it!*

Explanation: The comment about looking ten years younger just because of the car is obvious flattery and not a fact. This would not qualify as a valid reason for making such a purchase.

Exception: Sincere praise is not flattery and is universally appreciated[1]. However, even sincere praise in place of reason in an argument is a fallacy, unless the argument is directly related to the sincere praise.

---

[1] There are exceptions: Women you don't know very well don't usually appreciate praise about their breasts or buttocks—especially in a professional situation.

You are a stunningly beautiful girl—you should be a model.

Fun Fact: Flattery might get you somewhere, but it's usually a place you don't want to be.

References:

LaBossiere, M. C. (1995). Fallacies. *Journal.*

Appeal to Force
argumentum ad baculum

(also known as: argument to the cudgel, appeal to the stick)

Description: When force, coercion, or even a threat of force is used in place of a reason in an attempt to justify a conclusion.

Logical Form:

If you don't accept X as true, I will hurt you.

Example #1:

Melvin: Boss, why do I have to work weekends when nobody else in the company does?

Boss: Am I sensing insubordination? I can find another employee very quickly, thanks to Craigslist, you know.

Explanation: Melvin has asked a legitimate question to which he did not get a legitimate answer, rather his question was deflected by a threat of force (as being forced out of his job).

Example #2:

Jordan: Dad, why do I have to spend my summer at Jesus camp?

Dad: Because if you don't, you will spend your entire summer in your room with nothing but your Bible!

Explanation: Instead of a reason, dad gave Jordan a description of a punishment that would happen.

Exception: If the force, coercion, or threat of force is not being used as a reason but as a fact or consequence, then it would not be fallacious, especially when a legitimate reason is given with the "threat," direct or implied.

> *Melvin: Boss, why do I have to wear this goofy-looking hardhat?*
>
> *Boss: It is state law; therefore, company policy. No hat, no job.*

Tip: Unless you are an indentured servant (slave) or still living with your parents (slave), do not allow others to force you into accepting something as true.

References:

Jason, G. (1987). The nature of the argumentum ad baculum. *PhilosophiaAr, 17*(4), 491–499. https://doi.org/10.1007/BF02381067

Appeal to Heaven
deus vult

(also known as: gott mit uns, manifest destiny, special covenant)

Description: Asserting the conclusion must be accepted because it is the "will of God" or "the will of the gods." In the mind of those committing the fallacy, and those allowing it to pass as a valid reason, the will of God is not only knowable, but the person making the argument knows it, and no other reason is necessary.

Logical Form:

> *God wants us to X.*
>
> *Therefore, we should X.*

Example #1:

Judge: So why did you chop those people into little pieces and put the pieces in a blender?

Crazy Larry: Because God told me to do it.

Judge: Good enough for me. Next case!

Explanation: We should all be thankful that our legal system does not work this way, but human thinking does. Every day, people do things or don't do things according to what they believe is the will of their god. Fortunately, most of the time, this does not include a blender.

Example #2:

Ian: Why is the story of Abraham and Isaac regarded as such a "beautiful" Christian story? The guy was about to burn his son alive as a human sacrifice!

Wallace: Because it was the will of God that Abraham was following, no matter how difficult it was for him. Isn't that beautiful?

Ian: I guess as long as it was the will of God, being asked to burn children alive is a beautiful thing.

Explanation: One needs to ask, how do you know it is the will of God? Satan is said to be the great deceiver—he would only be great if those being deceived couldn't tell the difference between God and Satan. In reality, appealing to Heaven, or God, is an abandonment of logic and reason, and as we have seen, potentially extremely dangerous.

Exception: When the supposed, "will of God," is in line with what someone would already do or believe based on reason, no fallacy is committed.

I choose not to kill other people because I would not want them choosing to kill me, plus, I believe that God wouldn't like it if I did.

Fun Fact: Sometimes the only difference between faithfulness and insanity is adherence to the law.

References:

This is a logical fallacy frequently used on the Internet. No academic sources could be found.

Appeal to Intuition

(also known as: appeal to the gut)

Description: Evaluating an argument based on "intuition" or "gut feeling" that is unable to be articulated, rather than evaluating the argument using reason.

Logical Forms:

Evidence is given for argument X.

X doesn't match person 1's intuition or gut feeling.

Therefore, argument X is rejected.

Person 1 has a gut feeling about claim X.

Therefore, claim X is true.

Example #1:

Nick: Did you know that if the sun were just a few miles closer to Earth, we would burn up, or if it were just a few miles further away we would all freeze? It is like someone put the sun there just for us!

Suzy: Actually, the distance of the sun from Earth varies from about 91 million miles to 94.5 million miles, depending on the time of year.

Nick: That can't be right. The sun never appears a few million miles further away!

Explanation: Besides Nick's flat out rejection of a fact, Nick is evaluating Suzy's refutation based on what feels wrong to him. Nick is abandoning the reasoning process.

Example #2:

Maura: Stop wasting your money on those scratch-off lottery tickets. You know the odds are seriously stacked against you, don't you?

Philip: I do, but I have a really good feeling about this next batch!

Explanation: Maura makes a good argument as to why Phillip should not buy any more tickets, but Philip abandons the reasoning process and makes an appeal to his intuition.

Exception: This doesn't include arguments where subjective feeling plays a significant role.

Maureen: So who are you going to marry?

Joanne: Martin. I have a much better feeling about my future with him than with Tony.

Tip: Intuition can be defined as the sum of our experiences reflected in the feeling of knowledge that cannot be articulated. For example, if one has 30 years of experience as a firefighter, they may "know" when not to open a door in a burning building but not be able to explain why rationally. The problem is, in the moment, intuition is indistinguishable from imagination. When we get these feelings, if time permits, we should do what we can to back them up rationally.

References:

This is a logical fallacy frequently used on the Internet. No academic sources could be found.

Appeal to Loyalty

(also known as: appeal to patriotism [form of])

Description: When one is either implicitly or explicitly encouraged to consider loyalty when evaluating the argument when the truth of the argument is independent of loyalty. Alternatively, one considers loyalty in concluding that the argument is true, false, or not worth investigating.

Logical Forms:

X is loyal to Y.

Y makes false claim Z.

Therefore, X accepts Z as true due to X's loyalty to Y.

Y makes false claim Z.

It is implied that disagreeing with Y is disloyal.

Therefore, X does not question claim Z out of loyalty.

Example #1: Cult leaders appear to have a magical level of influence over their followers. They can do no wrong, and anything they say must be true. This mindset is enforced by rewards and punishments related to loyalty. When Jim Jones claimed that hostile forces would convert captured children of the cult to fascism, no fact-checking was involved. Out of loyalty to the leader, Jones' followers reasoned that suicide was a better alternative and "drank the Kool-Aid" (Flavor Aid).

Nine hundred and nine inhabitants of Jonestown died of apparent cyanide poisoning. Three hundred and four of them were children.

Example #2:

Liberal Friend: Posts fake quote allegedly by a conservative.

Me: Asks for a source because the quote is unbelievable.

Liberal Friend: Refuses to seek the source because it "sounds like something [this conservative] would say."

Explanation: While my liberal friend did not insist the quote was true, he did refuse to investigate it further out of loyalty to his ideological position.

In both politics and religion, people on social media uncritically accept or reject information based on loyalty to their ideology. These are implied arguments rather than explicit arguments. The implication is that because the information is in-line with/ goes against the person's ideology, it must be true/false. This is a form of confirmation bias that is applied to a specific argument.

Exception: There is no fallacy when one claims to follow someone or support them out of loyalty; the fallacy is committed when loyalty is considered in their evaluation of a truth claim.

Variation: The *appeal to patriotism* is a specific form of the *appeal to loyalty* where the object of loyalty is one's country. Disagreement with claims are often met with accusations of being "unpatriotic" or even "treasonous."

Tip: Be loyal to truth and reason, even if it is seen as disloyalty to an ideology.

References:

This is a logical fallacy frequently used on the Internet. No academic sources could be found.

Appeal to Nature
argumentum ad naturam

Description: When used as a fallacy, the belief or suggestion that "natural" is better than "unnatural" based on its naturalness. Many people adopt this as a default belief. It is the belief that is what is natural must be good (or any other positive, evaluative judgment) and that which is unnatural must be bad (or any other negative, evaluative judgment).

The *appeal to nature* fallacy is often confused with the *naturalistic* and the *moralistic fallacies* because they are quite similar. The *appeal to nature*, however, specifically references "natural" or "unnatural" and can also make a non-moral judgment such as "beautiful" or "destructive."

Logical Forms:

X is natural.

Y is not natural.

Therefore, X is better than Y.

100

That which is natural is good, right, beautiful, etc.

X is natural.

Therefore, X is good, right, beautiful, etc.

That which is unnatural is bad, wrong, destructive, etc.

X is unnatural.

Therefore, X is bad, wrong, destructive, etc.

Example #1:

I shop at Natural Happy Sunshine Store (NHSS), which is much better than your grocery store because at NHSS everything is natural including the 38-year-old store manager's long gray hair and saggy breasts.

Explanation: I can appreciate natural food and products as much as the next granola-eating guy, but to make any claim of "betterness," one needs to establish criteria by which to judge. Perhaps not paying almost twice as much for the same general foods is "better" for me. Perhaps I prefer a little insecticide on my apple to insects inside my apple, and maybe I like faux brunettes with perky breasts due to "unnatural" bra support.

Natural is not always "better."

Example #2:

Cocaine is all natural; therefore, it is good for you.

Explanation: There are very many things in this world that are "all natural" and very bad for you besides cocaine, including, earthquakes, monsoons, and viruses, just to name a few. Whereas "unnatural" things such as aspirin, pacemakers, and surgery can be very good things.

Exception: There are many natural things that are better than unnatural, but they must be evaluated based on other criteria besides the "naturalness."

Fun Fact: Mother Nature is the kind of mother who wouldn't hesitate to throw you in a dumpster and leave you there to die.

References:

Moore, G. E., & Baldwin, T. (1993). *Principia Ethica*. Cambridge University Press.

Appeal to Normality

Description: Using social norms to determine what is good or bad. It is the idea that normality is the standard of goodness. This is fallacious because social norms are not the same as norms found in nature or norms that are synonymous with the ideal function of a created system. The conclusion, "therefore, it is good" is often unspoken, but clearly implied.

Logical Forms:

X is considered normal behavior.

Therefore, X is good behavior.

X is not considered normal behavior.

Therefore, X is bad behavior.

X is considered normal behavior.

Therefore, we should strive for X (normality).

Example #1:

I am only slightly obese. That is perfectly normal here in America.

Explanation: The person is correct in that being slightly obese is considered normal in America. In no way is this a good thing by virtually any measure of goodness. Athletes and those who make their health and fitness a priority are far from normal, but viewing that level of health and fitness as bad is clearly fallacious.

Example #2:

Why doesn't Tim get a real job like normal people instead of trying to launch that Internet business from home?

Explanation: Tim is not like normal people when it comes to work—he is part of the minority who dream big and follow their dreams. Tim might make it big, or he might not. Without the Tim's of the world, the normal people would have no place to get a "real job."

Exception: There are circumstances where eccentric or unusual behavior is clearly problematic. These are situations where even slight deviations from the norm have been demonstrated to have negative results, and the implied "badness" of the behavior needs no justification.

My dad got arrested again sunbathing naked in a public park while tripping on acid... during a snowstorm. That's not normal.

Another exception is when "normal" is used in such a way to balance negative social behavior. For example, a mother may yell at her misbehaving child to "act normal" at a school open house. There is no implication here that being "normal" is the ideal behavior, just an immediate and realistic improvement from the current behavior.

Tip: For the most part, being "normal" or "average" is nothing to be proud of. Be better than average.

References:

This is an original logical fallacy named by the author.

Appeal to Novelty
argumentum ad novitatem

(also known as: appeal to the new, ad novitam [sometimes spelled as])

Description: Claiming that something that is new or modern is superior to the status quo, based exclusively on its newness.

Logical Form:

X has been around for years now.

Y is new.

Therefore, Y is better than X.

Example #1: Two words: New Coke.

Explanation: Those who lived through the Coca-Cola identity crises of the mid-eighties know what a mess it was for the company. In fact, the "New Coke Disaster," as it is commonly referred to, is literally a textbook example of attempting to fix what isn't broken. Coke's main marketing ploy was appealing to the novelty, and it failed miserably—even though more people (55%) actually preferred the taste of New Coke, the old was "better."

Example #2:

Bill: Hey, did you hear we have a new operating system out now? It is better than anything else out there because we just released it!

Steve: What's it called?

Bill: Windows Vista!

Steve: Sounds wonderful! I can't wait until all of your users install it on all their computers!

Explanation: For anyone who went through the experience of Vista, this fallacy should hit very close to home. You were most likely assuming that you were getting a superior product to your old operating system—you were thinking "upgrade" when, in fact, those who stuck with the status quo (Windows XP) were much better off.

Exception: There are obvious exceptions, like in claiming that your fresh milk is better than your month old milk that is now growing legs in your refrigerator.

Tip: Diets and exercise programs/gadgets are notorious for preying on our desire for novelty. Don't be swayed by the "latest research" or latest fads. Just remember this: burn more calories than you take in, *and you will lose weight.*

References:

Sternberg, R. J., III, H. L. R., & Halpern, D. F. (2007). *Critical Thinking in Psychology*. Cambridge University Press.

Appeal to Pity
ad misericordiam

(also known as: appeal to sympathy, appeal to victimhood [form of])

Description: The attempt to distract from the truth of the conclusion by the use of pity.

Logical Forms:

Person 1 is accused of Y, but person 1 is pathetic.

Therefore, person 1 is innocent.

X is true because person 1 worked really hard at making X true.

Example #1:

I really deserve an "A" on this paper, professor. Not only did I study during my grandmother's funeral, but I also passed up the heart transplant surgery, even though that was the first matching donor in 3 years.

Explanation: The student deserves an "A" for effort and dedication but, unfortunately, papers are not graded that way. The fact that we should pity her has nothing to do with the quality of the paper written, and if we were to adjust the grade because of the sob stories, we would have fallen victim to the *appeal to pity.*

Example #2:

Ginger: Your dog just ran into our house and ransacked our kitchen!

Mary: He would never do that, look at how adorable he is with those puppy eyes!

Explanation: Being pathetic does not absolve one from his or her crimes, even when he or she is a ridiculously-adorable puppy.

Exception: Like any argument, if it is agreed that logic and reason should take a backseat to emotion, and there is no objective truth claim being made, but rather an opinion of something that should or should not be done, then it could escape the fallacy.

Let's not smack Spot for ransacking the neighbor's kitchen—he's just too damn cute!

Variation: The *appeal to victimhood* uses a form of pity to either establish the innocence of the victim or suggest the victim has the truth on their side. This is an application of the *halo effect,* where victims tend to be seen positively, therefore that which is associated with the victim (e.g., their innocence, or their claims) is also seen as positive (unreasonably and without evidence).

Tip: Avoid pity in argumentation. It is a clear indicator that you have weak evidence for your argument.

References:

Walton, D. (2006). Fundamentals of Critical Argumentation. Cambridge University Press.

Appeal to Popularity
argumentum ad numeram

(also see: appeal to common belief)

Description: Using the popularity of a premise or proposition as evidence for its truthfulness. This is a fallacy which is very difficult to spot because our "common sense" tells us that if something is popular, it must be good/true/valid, but this is not so, especially in a society where clever marketing, social and political weight, and money can buy popularity.

Logical Form:

Everybody is doing X.

Therefore, X must be the right thing to do.

Example #1:

Mormonism is one of the fastest growing sects of Christianity today so that whole story about Joseph Smith getting the golden plates that, unfortunately, disappeared back into heaven, must be true!

Explanation: Mormonism is indeed rapidly growing, but that fact does not prove the truth claims made by Mormonism in any way.

Example #2:

A 2005 Gallup Poll found that an estimated 25% of Americans over the age of 18 believe in astrology—or that the position of the stars and planets can affect people's lives. That is roughly 75,000,000 people. Therefore, there must be some truth to astrology!

Explanation: No, the popularity of the belief in astrology is not related to the truthfulness of astrological claims. Beliefs are often *cultural memes* that get passed on from person to person based on many factors other than truth.

Exception: When the claim being made is about the popularity or some related attribute that is a direct result of its popularity.

People seem to love the movie, The Shawshank Redemption. In fact, it is currently ranked #1 at IMDB.com, based on viewer ratings.

Tip: Avoid this fallacy like you avoid a kiss from your great aunt with the big cold sore on her lip.

References:

Walton, D. N. (1999). *Appeal to Popular Opinion*. Penn State Press.

Appeal to Possibility

Description: When a conclusion is assumed not because it is probably true, but because it is *possible* that it is true or it has not been demonstrated to be impossible, no matter how improbable.

Logical Forms:

> X is possible.
>
> Therefore, X is true.

> X is possible.
>
> Therefore, X is probably true.

Example #1:

> Brittany: I haven't applied to any other schools besides Harvard.
>
> Casey: You think that is a good idea? After all, you only have a 2.0 GPA, your SAT scores were pretty bad, and frankly, most people think you are not playing with a full deck.
>
> Brittany: Are you telling me that it is impossible for me to get in?
>
> Casey: Not *impossible*, but...
>
> Brittany: Then shut your trap.

Explanation: Yes, it is possible that Harvard will accept Brittany to fill some sympathy quota, or perhaps someone at admissions will mix Brittany up with "Britney," the 16-year-old Asian with the 4.0 average who also discovered a vaccine for a rare flu in her spare time, but because Brittany is *appealing to possibility*, she is committing this fallacy.

Example #2:

> Dave: Did you know that Jesus liked to dress up as a woman and sing show tunes?
>
> Tim: And why do you say that?
>
> Dave: You have to admit, it is possible!
>
> Tim: So is the fact that you are a moron.

Explanation: We cannot assume Jesus liked to dress like a woman while belting out 2000-year-old show tunes based on the possibility alone. This also includes the *argument from ignorance* fallacy—concluding a possibility based on missing information (an outright statement that Jesus did not do these things).

Exception: There are no exceptions. Possibility alone never justifies probability.

Tip: Catch yourself every time you are about to use the word "impossible." Yes, there are many things that are logically and physically impossible, and it is a valid concept and word, but so often we use that word when we really mean "improbable." Confusing the impossible with the improbable or unlikely, could, in many cases, destroy the possibility of great success.

References:

This is a logical fallacy frequently used on the Internet. No academic sources could be found.

Appeal to Ridicule
reductio ad ridiculum

(also known as: appeal to mockery, the horse laugh)

Description: Presenting the argument in such a way that makes the argument look ridiculous, usually by misrepresenting the argument or the use of exaggeration.

Logical Form:

Person 1 claims that X is true.

Person 2 makes X look ridiculous by misrepresenting X.

Therefore, X is false.

Example #1:

It takes faith to believe in God just like it takes faith to believe in the Easter Bunny—but at least the Easter Bunny is based on a creature that actually exists!

Explanation: Comparing the belief in God to belief in the Easter Bunny is an attempt at ridicule and not a good argument. In fact, this type of fallacy usually shows desperation in the one committing the fallacy.

Example #2:

Evolution is the idea that humans come from pond scum.

Explanation: It is ridiculous to think that we come from pond scum, and it is not true. It is more accurate to say that we come from exploding stars as every atom in our bodies was once in a star. By creating a ridiculous and misleading image, the truth claim of the argument is overlooked.

Exception: It is legitimate to use ridicule when a position is worthy of ridicule. This is a risky proposition, however, because of the subjectiveness of what kind of argument is actually ridicule worthy. As we have seen, misplaced ridicule can appear as a sign of desperation, but carefully placed ridicule can be a witty move that can work logically and win over an audience emotionally, as well.

Matt: You close-minded fool! Seeing isn't believing, believing is seeing!

Cindy: Does that go for the Easter Bunny as well, or just the imaginary beings of your choice?

Tip: Do your best to maintain your composure when someone commits this fallacy at your expense. Remember, they are the ones who have committed the error in reasoning. Tactfully point it out to them.

References:

Moore, B. N., & Parker, R. (1989). *Critical thinking: Evaluating claims and arguments in everyday life*. Mayfield Pub. Co.

Appeal to Self-evident Truth

Description: Making the claim that something is "self-evident" when it is not self-evident in place of arguing a claim with reason. In everyday terms, something is "self-evident" when understanding what it means immediately results in knowing that it is true, such as 2+2=4. The concept of self-evidence is contentions and argued among philosophers based on their ideas of epistemology. This means that what is "self-evident" to one person is not necessarily self-evident to another. However, some ideas are clearly self-evident and some are not.

Logical Form:

Person 1 claims Y without evidence.

Person 2 asks for evidence.

Person 1 claims that Y is self-evident.

Example #1:

Richie: Lord Xylon is the one true ruler of the universe.

Toby: Why do you think that?

Richie: It is self-evident.

Explanation: People often confuse their own subjective feelings and interpretations with self-evidence. Richie may believe that Lord Xylon is the one true ruler of the universe, but his belief cannot be used in place of evidence.

Example #2:

Sara: No human should ever kill another human being.

111

Dottie: Why not?

Sara: It's self-evident.

Explanation: The fallacy is in the implied claim that the argument needs no evidence or explanation because it is "self-evident."

Exception: This fallacy depends on the claim of "self-evidence" not being self-evident. A claim that it reasonably self-evident would not be fallacious:

Richie: I exist.

Toby: Why do you think that?

Richie: It is self-evident.

Tip: If you can't explain something, that doesn't mean you are dealing with something that is self-evident; it could just be your failure to explain something.

References:

This is a logical fallacy frequently used on the Internet. No academic sources could be found. For the concept of self-evidence, the following reference was used:

Kelly, T. (2016). Evidence. In E. N. Zalta (Ed.), *The Stanford Encyclopedia of Philosophy* (Winter 2016). Metaphysics Research Lab, Stanford University. Retrieved from https://plato.stanford.edu/archives/win2016/entries/evidence/

Appeal to Spite
argumentum ad odium

Description: Substituting spite (petty ill will or hatred with the disposition to irritate, annoy, or thwart) for evidence in an argument, or as a reason to support or reject a claim.

Logical Form:

Claim X is made.

Claim X is associated with thing Y that people feel spite towards.

Therefore, X is true/false.

Example #1:

Aren't you tired of the political divisiveness in this country? Republicans know what they are talking about when it comes to immigration. Don't you agree?

Explanation: This is a slick way of having someone agree with your claim. The arguer began by introducing a common idea that many people despise—political divisiveness (thing Y). Then, made a claim (claim X) in which the person would have to show political divisiveness to reject, in effect, causing the person to substitute spite in the idea of political divisiveness for reason.

Example #2:

Jon: Why should I bother exercising while my spouse is on vacation stuffing her face with food.

Explanation: The reasons for exercising are independent of the Jon's wife's actions. The claim here is that Jon should not bother exercising. The claim is associated with the idea that his wife is "stuffing her face with food" (something Jon feels spite towards). Jon concludes that he shouldn't exercise. If Jon were using reason rather than the emotion of spite, he would find another reason not to exercise—like the fact that he is too far behind on *The Golden Girls* reruns.

Exception: This doesn't apply to emotional, relatively insignificant arguments.

Sib: Dude, can you give me a ride to the mall?

Eddie: You mean in my car about which you said it was "just slightly better than getting around on a drunk donkey"?

Sib: Yea.

Eddie. No. You are not worthy of a ride in my fine automobile.

The claim is that Sib is not worthy of a ride in Eddie's car (an emotional/subjective claim). Although Eddie appeals to spite in his reason, he has the right to in this case.

Tip: Be happy. Avoid spite in all of its forms.

References:

Moore, B. N., & Parker, R. (1997). *Critical Thinking Instructor's Manual: The Logical Accessory.* Mayfield Publishing Company.

Appeal to Stupidity

Description: Attempting to get the audience to devalue reason and intellectual discourse, or devaluing reason and intellectual discourse based on the rhetoric of an arguer.

Logical Form:

> *Person 1 downplays the importance of reason, logic, or science.*
>
> *Person 1 makes a claim, argument, or assertion.*
>
> *Audience is more likely to accept claim, argument, or assertion.*

Example #1:

> *Anthony: You know what's wrong with us today? We think too much! We need to act more with our heart and gut! Today is the first day of the rest of your life! Sign up for my 30-day program now for just $999.99!*
>
> *Audience: (Cheers uncontrollably).*

Explanation: It is a common persuasion technique to get people in an emotional state and have them make an emotional decision while in that state. This is exactly what Anthony is doing here while undermining the importance of critical thinking.

Example #2:

Politician: The other guy likes to throw statistics and data at us showing how much the economy has improved. But data and statistics don't feed our children. You feel it. The economy has gotten worse! Feelings are more important than facts.

Explanation: There is a strong emotional appeal here accompanied by the devaluation of statistics and data (i.e., facts) in favor of feelings in order to answer an objective question: has the economy improved?

Exception: Don't confuse the *appeal to stupidity* with an arational argument. Arational arguments are not subject to reason and are properly feeling-based. Thus, asking people to put aside "reason" is not fallacious.

Mom: Which puppy do you want?

Kid: They are all so cute and lovable. They all look healthy... I can't decide!

Mom: Go with your gut. Which one do you have the strongest feelings for?

Tip: If picking from a liter of puppies, don't choose the craziest one.

References:

This is a logical fallacy frequently used on the Internet. No academic sources could be found.

Appeal to the Law

Description: When following the law is assumed to be the morally correct thing to do, without justification, or when breaking the law is assumed to be the morally wrong thing to do, without justification.

Logical Forms:

X is illegal. Therefore, it is immoral.

Y is legal. Therefore, it is moral.

Example #1:

Tom: I plan on chaining myself to the bulldozer so they can't knock down the senior center.

Judy: That's just wrong. You'll get arrested. Don't be a bad person!

Explanation: Civil disobedience is just one example of something that is illegal but does not have to be immoral. Laws are created for many reasons, and only some are created for "moral" reasons (according to someone's moral code).

Example #2:

Lucy: I cheated on my husband the other night.

Rob: Why did you do that!?

Lucy: Calm down! It's not like cheating is illegal or anything.

Explanation: Again, the law and one's moral code are not the same things. While there does tend to be overlap, assuming illegal is immoral or legal is moral without a rational argument connecting the two concepts, is fallacious.

Exception: Sometimes what is illegal is clearly immoral, and no justification is required. For example, if someone were to say, "How could you kick that old lady while laughing? That is a horrible thing to do, and you can go to jail!"

Tip: Laws become archaic when they do not keep up with social norms and cultural changes. What was once deemed "immoral" could easily change to "moral" within a few years and vice versa. Never simply assume that laws are good and right; demand justification.

References:

This is an original logical fallacy named by the author.

Appeal to the Moon

(also known as: argumentum ad lunam)

Description: Using the argument, "If we can put a man on the moon, we could…" as evidence for the argument. This is a specific form of the *weak analogy*.

Logical Form:

> *If we can put a man on the moon, we can X.*

Example #1:

> *If we can put a man on the moon, we can cure all forms of cancer.*

Explanation: Putting a man on the moon is seen to be a virtually impossible task, but since we did it, the (faulty) reasoning is we can then do any virtually impossible task. Remember that mere possibility is not the same as probability. These kinds of arguments are not suggesting the mere possibility, but probability, based on the fact that we succeeded getting a man on the moon.

Example #2:

> *If NASA can put a man on the moon, you can certainly sleep with me tonight.*

Explanation: This is an even worse analogy. The accomplishments of NASA are independent of our personal accomplishments.

Exception: If the argument is for getting a man on the moon again, then this would work.

> *If we can put a man on the moon in 1969, we can do it today.*

Tip: Believe in the possible just don't count on it unless it is probable.

References:

This is a logical fallacy frequently used on the Internet. No academic sources could be found.

Appeal to Tradition
argumentum ad antiquitatem

(also known as: appeal to common practice, appeal to antiquity, appeal to traditional wisdom, proof from tradition, appeal to past practice, traditional wisdom)

Description: Using historical preferences of the people (tradition), either in general or as specific as the historical preferences of a single individual, as evidence that the historical preference is correct. Traditions are often passed from generation to generation with no other explanation besides, "this is the way it has always been done"—which is not a reason, *it is an absence of a reason.*

Logical Forms:

We have been doing X for generations.

Therefore, we should keep doing X.

Our ancestors thought X was right.

Therefore, X is right.

Example #1:

Dave: For five generations, the men in our family went to Stanford and became doctors, while the women got married and raised children. Therefore, it is my duty to become a doctor.

Kaitlin: Do you want to become a doctor?

Dave: It doesn't matter—it is our family tradition. Who am I to break it?

Explanation: Just as it takes people to start traditions, it takes people to end them. A tradition is not a reason for action

—it is like watching the same movie over and over again but never asking why you should keep watching it.

Example #2:

> *Marriage has traditionally been between a man and a woman; therefore, gay marriage should not be allowed.*

Explanation: Very often traditions stem from religious and/or archaic beliefs, and until people question the logic and reasoning behind such traditions, people who are negatively affected by such traditions will continue to suffer. Just because it was acceptable in past cultures and times, does not mean it is acceptable today. Think racism, sexism, slavery, and corporal punishment.

Exception: Victimless traditions that are preserved for the sake of preserving the traditions themselves do not require any other reason.

Tip: If it weren't for the creativity of our ancestors, we would have no traditions. Be creative and start your own traditions that somehow make the world a better place.

References:

Harpine, W. D. (1993). The Appeal to Tradition: Cultural Evolution and Logical Soundness. *Informal Logic, 15*(3).

Appeal to Trust

(also known as: appeal to distrust [opposite], appeal to trustworthiness)

Description: The belief that if a source is considered trustworthy or untrustworthy, then any information from that source must be true or false, respectively. This is problematic because each argument, claim, or proposition should be evaluated on its own merits.

This doesn't include trusting **in** someone or something. For example, when we trust our children that they will make the right decisions in a certain situation, we are not using fallacious reasoning. When we trust that our seat belts will work when they need to, we are not using fallacious reasoning. When we trust that our puppy will leave us a gift on the carpet if we don't let him out by 7:00 AM, we are not using fallacious reasoning. When we express trust in someone, we are essentially expressing a degree of confidence, **not making an absolute claim of something being true or false**.

Logical Forms:

Source X is a trusted source of information.

Claim Y was made by source X.

Therefore, claim Y must be true.

Source X is a distrusted source of information.

Claim Y was made by source X.

Therefore, claim Y must be false.

Example #1:

I read in the Wall Street Journal that pork bellies are a good investment. So could I borrow a million dollars to invest?

Explanation: The *Wall Street Journal* could reasonably be seen as a trusted source (it doesn't matter if you agree or not, as long as the arguer thinks it is). In this case, the information appears to be more of an opinion than a fact—and an investment prediction, which by its nature is risky and therefore its truth value is questionable.

Example #2:

Cindy: I read in the Global Enquirer that Bingo Kelly, the famous movie star, is in rehab.

Jack: That's poppycock! You can't trust the Global Enquirer any more than you can trust a toddler with a nail gun.

Explanation: The *Global Enquirer* might not be known for its high-quality journalism and truthful reporting. However, even the most untrustworthy sources sometimes share true information. While it might be a good heuristic (rule of thumb) to be highly skeptical of any claims from such an untrustworthy source, such claims cannot be so confidently dismissed without a good reason.

Exception: As long as one is claiming a degree of confidence instead of assuming true or false, there is no fallacy. Trustworthiness does impact the level of confidence one should have, but not certainty.

Tip: Try to keep your level of confidence proportionate to your level of trust.

References:

This is a logical fallacy frequently used on the Internet. No academic sources could be found.

Argument by Emotive Language

(also known as: loaded words, loaded language, euphemisms)

Description: Substituting facts and evidence with words that stir up emotion, with the attempt to manipulate others into accepting the truth of the argument.

Logical Form:

Person A claims that X is true.

Person A uses very powerful and emotive language in the claim.

Therefore, X is true.

Example #1:

By rejecting God, you are rejecting goodness, kindness, and love itself.

Explanation: Instead of just "not believing" in God, we are "rejecting" God, which is a much stronger term—especially when God is associated with "goodness."

Example #2:

The Bible is filled with stories of God's magic.

Explanation: Instead of using the more accepted term "miracles," the word "magic" is used that connotes powers associated with fantasy and make-believe in an attempt to make the stories in the Bible seem foolish.

Example #3:

I don't see what's wrong with engaging the services of a professional escort.

Explanation: That's just a nice way of saying, "soliciting a hooker." No matter what you call it unless you live in certain parts of Nevada (or other parts of the world), it is still legally wrong (not necessarily morally wrong).

Exception: Language is powerful and should be used to draw in emotions, but never at the expense of valid reasoning and evidence.

Tip: *Euphemisms,* when used correctly, reflect good social intelligence. When in a business meeting, say, "Pardon me for a moment, I have to use the restroom," rather than "Pardon me for a moment, I have to move my bowels."

References:

Walton, D. (2006). Fundamentals of Critical Argumentation. Cambridge University Press.

Argument by Fast Talking

Description: When fast talking is seen as intelligence and/or confidence in the truth of one's argument; therefore, seen as evidence of the truth of the argument itself.

Logical Form:

According to person 1, Y is true.

Person 1 speaks very fast.

Therefore, Y is true.

Example #1: (to be read extremely fast)

I hereby submit that it is crystal clear that there is only one true God, without question, without reserve, without hesitation I can say this because I know the truth and I am here to share it with you. Praise Allah!

Explanation: There is absolutely no evidence in the above claim, and if you read it quickly and clearly, you would persuade more people than if you read it like one of the Beverly Hillbillies. If your intent was to persuade others by not giving them time to process what you have said, then you would be guilty of this fallacious tactic.

Example #2: (same example - to be read extremely fast)

I hereby submit that it is crystal clear that there is only one true God, without question, without reserve, without hesitation I can say this because I know the truth and I am here to share it with you. Praise Allah!

Explanation: This time, as the one evaluating the argument, if you allow the rapid pace of the delivery of the argument to serve as evidence for the claim, you are committing the fallacy. Perhaps the arguer does sound confident, and perhaps you are embarrassed to ask him to repeat the argument or slow down; therefore, you just accept it. Either way, that is fallacious reasoning.

Exception: Naturally fast talkers most likely have no intent to deceive, and if you consciously give no undue weight to the claims of a natural fast talker, then no fallacy has been committed.

Tip: Work on your pace as a part of your speaking. It should be just slow enough where you do not lose your audience, and no slower, unless going for a dramatic effect.

References:

Wormeli, R. (2001). *Meet Me in the Middle: Becoming an Accomplished Middle-level Teacher*. Stenhouse Publishers.

Argument by Gibberish

(also known as: bafflement, argument by [prestigious] jargon)

Description: When incomprehensible jargon or plain incoherent gibberish is used to give the appearance of a strong argument, in place of evidence or valid reasons to accept the argument.

The more common form of this argument is when the person making the argument defaults to highly technical jargon or details not directly related to the argument, then restates the conclusion.

Logical Form:

> Person 1 claims that X is true.
>
> Person 1 backs up this claim by gibberish.
>
> Therefore, X is true.

Example #1:

> Fortifying the dextrose coherence leads to applicable inherent of explicable tolerance; therefore, we should not accept this proposal.

Explanation: I have no idea what I just wrote, and the audience will have no idea either—but the audience (depending on who the audience is) will most likely make the assumption that I do know what I am talking about, believe that they are incapable of understanding the argument and therefore, agree with my conclusion since they think I do understand it. This is fallacious reasoning.

Example #2: (The following was taken from the movie *Spies Like Us* where Emmett Fitz-Hume, played by Chevy Chase, was addressing the press.)

> Well, of course, their requests for subsidies was not Paraguayan in and of it is as it were the United States government would never have if the president, our president,

had not and as far as I know that's the way it will always be. Is that clear?

Explanation: Emmett Fitz-Hume was clearly avoiding having to answer the question, and substituted gibberish for an answer. While the press was metaphorically scratching their heads to figure what what was just said, Emmett moved on without answering the question.

Exception: Some arguments require some jargon or technical explanations.

Tip: Remember that good communication is not about confusing people; it's about mutual understanding. Don't try to impress people with fancy words and jargon, when simpler words will do just fine.

References:

This is a logical fallacy frequently used on the Internet. No academic sources could be found.

Argument by Personal Charm

(also known as: sex appeal, flamboyance, eloquence)

Description: When an argument is made stronger by the personal characteristics of the person making the argument, often referred to as "charm."

Logical Form:

> *Person 1 says that Y is true.*
>
> *Person 1 is very charming.*
>
> *Therefore, Y is true.*

Example #1:

> *Hi there, ladies (wink - teeth sparkle). I just want to say that all of you have the right to do what you will with your bodies, including the right to abortion.*

Explanation: The charm of the arguer is irrelevant to the issue of abortion.

Example #2:

> Let me start by thanking the wonderful people of this town for hosting this great event. I would be honored to call you all my friends. As friends, I want to tell you that streaking should be legalized.

Explanation: Buttering up the audience is actually a technique that is suggested—because it is effective. If you know your argument is weak, and compensate by laying on the charm, you are guilty of this fallacious tactic. If you are letting the charm affect your decision, you are also committing the fallacy.

Exception: If the argument being made is directly related to the charm of the arguer, as in arguing that he or she would be the better host for a new show where charm does matter, then no fallacy has been committed.

Tip: If you are a natural charmer don't be afraid to use it—just not at the expense of valid claims and strong evidence.

References:

This is a logical fallacy frequently used on the Internet. No academic sources could be found.

Argument by Pigheadedness

(also known as: argument by stubbornness, invincible ignorance fallacy)

Description: This is a refusal to accept a well-proven argument for one of many reasons related to stubbornness. It can also be the refusal to argue about a claim that one supports.

Logical Form:

> Argument X is well-argued.

Person 1 has no objections to the argument, besides just refusing to accept the conclusion.

Therefore, argument X is not true.

Example #1:

Dad: You are failing math since you moved the Xbox to your room. You have been playing video games for at least 6 hours each day since. Before that, you consistently got A's and B's. Don't you think that the video games are the real problem here?

Blake: No.

Explanation: Blake is offering no counter argument or reasoning for rejecting his dad's well-articulated argument. He is simply being stubborn.

Example #2:

Cathy: I hate everything about Michelle Obama!

Jorge: Do you hate that she launched the national campaign, "Let's Move!," to reduce childhood obesity?

Cathy: Yes.

Jorge: Do you hate that she launched the national veterans' campaign, "Joining Forces," with Dr. Jill Biden?

Cathy: Yes.

Jorge: Do you hate that she traveled to Africa for a week to focus on youth leadership, education, health, and wellness?

Cathy: Yes.

Jorge: Do you hate that she launched the national campaign, "Reach Higher," a higher education initiative?

Cathy: Yes.

Jorge: Do you hate that she launched the national campaign, "Let Girls Learn," a global focus on girls' education?

Cathy: Yes.

Jorge: Do you hate her well-toned triceps and biceps?

Cathy: Yes, especially those!

Explanation: Unreasonable people tend to engage in black-and-white thinking and are committed to an ideological position at any expense—including reason. Cathy is one of those people.

Exception: Don't confuse unwillingness to engage with the *argument by pigheadedness.*

> *Street Preacher (to a woman walking by wearing a t-shirt that reads "Thank God I am an atheist!"): You are going to burn in hell!*
>
> *Woman: (keeps walking)*
>
> *Street Preacher: (frantically quoting Bible verses that support his claim).*
>
> *Woman: Yeah, I don't think so.*
>
> *Street Preacher: (Yelling Bible verses louder as the woman gets farther away, while trying to keep up with her).*
>
> *Woman: I don't buy it, sorry! By the way, you just stepped in dog poop.*

In this example, the woman is not sincerely engaging in the argument. She might have no interest, no time, or simply sees using the Bible to support claims in the Bible as *circular reasoning*, and not see the street preacher as a worthy interlocutor.

Tip: As a reminder, avoid absolutes. Instead of saying that you "hate everything" about someone, say something such as, "there's not much I like about..."

References:

This is a logical fallacy frequently used on the Internet. No academic sources could be found.

Argument by Repetition
argumentum ad nauseam

(also known as: argument from nagging, proof by assertion)

Description: Repeating an argument or a premise over and over again in place of better supporting evidence.

Logical Form:

X is true. X is true. X is true. X is true. X is true. X is true... etc.

Example #1:

That movie, "Kill, Blood, Gore" deserves the Oscar for best picture. There are other good movies, but not like that one. Others may deserve an honorable mention, but not the Oscar, because "Kill, Blood, Gore" deserves the Oscar.

Explanation: There are no reasons given for why, *Kill, Blood, Gore* deserves the Oscar, not even any opinion shared. All we have is a repeated claim stated slightly differently each time.

Example #2:

Saul: At one time, all humans spoke the same language. Then because of the Tower of Babel, God got angry and created all the different languages we have today—or at least some form of them.

Kevin: I studied linguistics in college, and I can pretty much guarantee you that's not what happened. Besides the short story in the Bible, what other evidence do you have to support this theory?

Saul: We know, because of the Word of God, that God got angry and created all the different languages we have today —or at least some form of them.

Kevin: You said that already. What other evidence do you have to support this theory?

Saul: In the Bible, it says that all humans once spoke the same language. Then because of the Tower of Babel, God got angry and created all the different languages we have today —or at least some form of them.

Kevin: (nauseated from the repetition, hurls all over Saul's slacks)

Explanation: Restating the same claims, even rearranging the words or substituting words, is not the same as making new claims, and certainly does not make the claims any more true.

Exception: When an interlocutor is attempting to misdirect the argument, repeating the argument to get back on track is a wise play.

Tip: Repetition can be a good strategy when your interlocutor does not seem to be acknowledging your point. Rather than repeat yourself, rephrase and repeat. Make your same point but in a different way.

References:

This is a logical fallacy frequently used on the Internet. No academic sources could be found.

Argument by Selective Reading

Description: When a series of arguments or claims is made and the interlocutor acts as if the weakest argument was the best one made. This is a form of *cherry picking* and very similar to the *selective attention fallacy*.

Logical Form:

Person 1 makes arguments X, Y, and Z.

Argument Z is the weakest.

Person 2 responds as if argument Z was the best person 1 has made.

Example #1:

Kevin: I think there is good evidence that God exists because of the fine-tuning argument, the teleological argument, and perhaps because over 2 billion believe it as well.

Sydney: It is ridiculous to believe in God just because a lot of other people do too!

Explanation: Kevin gave three reasons for his belief in God, two are worthy of debate, and one is not. Sydney focused on the one that is not and responded as if that were the only one he made.

Example #2:

Jona: Yes, man did walk on the moon. There is overwhelming evidence that does not come from either NASA or the United States government². Besides, I personally know one of the astronauts involved in one of the Apollo missions, and he confirms that they really did send men to the moon.

Biff: Your friend is just being paid to perpetuate the lie.

Explanation: Biff focused on the weaker of the two arguments and ignored the other.

Exception: One can start by dismissing the weakest arguments first, as long as they get to the strongest one.

Tip: If your interlocutor begins rattling off several arguments, politely interrupt them and request that they begin with their strongest argument, and allow you to address that one before proceeding to the next argument.

References:

This is a logical fallacy frequently used on the Internet. No academic sources could be found.

Argument from Age

(also known as: wisdom of the ancients)

---

² https://en.wikipedia.org/wiki/Third-party_evidence_for_Apollo_Moon_landings

Description: The misconception that previous generations had superior wisdom to modern man, thus conclusions that rely on this wisdom are seen accepted as true or more true than they actually are.

Logical Form:

Person 1 says that Y is true.

Person 1 was an ancient mystic.

Therefore, Y is true.

Example #1:

Swami Patooty wrote, back in the 6th century, "To know oneself, is to one day self know." You don't find pearls like that today!

Explanation: There are many sayings today that are just as ambiguous, obscure, and nonsensical as the ones carved in stone 1500 years ago—the difference is perception. Especially with "aged wisdom," we tend to read in meaning to ambiguity where none exists or where the author's intended meaning is impossible to know.

Example #2:

My Grammy told me that to be healthy I should have bacon and eggs every morning for breakfast.

Explanation: It seems politically incorrect to suggest that older generations are not "wise," but the fact is, wisdom is not necessarily a function of age. We have two generations of scientific knowledge that our grandparents did not have, and the world has changed quite a bit in the last two generations. While some advice may be timeless, other advice, such as the advice in the example, was based on the beliefs of the day and should be discarded like a container of chunky milk.

Exception: When the age is directly related to the truth of the claim as in, "Wine tastes better with age."

Fun Fact: Even ancient Greeks said stupid things.

References:

This is a logical fallacy frequently used on the Internet. No academic sources could be found.

Argument from Fallacy
argumentum ad logicam

(also known as: disproof by fallacy, argument to logic, fallacy fallacy, fallacist's fallacy, bad reasons fallacy [form of])

Description: Concluding that the truth value of an argument is false based on the fact that the argument contains a fallacy.

Logical Form:

Argument X is fallacious.

Therefore, the conclusion or truth claim of argument X is false.

Example #1:

Ivan: You cannot borrow my car because it turns back into a pumpkin at midnight.

Sidney: If you really think that, you're an idiot.

Ivan: That is an ad hominem; therefore, I can't be an idiot.

Sidney: I beg to differ.

Explanation: While it is true that Sidney has committed the *ad hominem fallacy* by calling Ivan an idiot rather than providing reasons why Ivan's car won't turn into a pumpkin at midnight, that fallacy is not evidence against the claim.

Example #2:

Karen: I am sorry, but if you think man used to ride dinosaurs, then you are obviously not very well educated.

Kent: First of all, I hold a PhD in creation science, so I am well-educated. Second of all, your ad hominem attack shows that you are wrong, and man did use to ride dinosaurs.

Karen: Getting your PhD in a couple of months, from a "college" in a trailer park, is not being well-educated. My fallacy in no way is evidence for man riding on dinosaurs, and despite what you may think, the Flintstone's was not a documentary!

Explanation: Karen's *ad hominem fallacy* in her initial statement has nothing to do with the truth value of the argument that man used to ride dinosaurs.

Exception: At times, fallacies are used by those who can't find a better way to support the truth claims of their argument—it could be a sign of desperation. This can be evidence for *them not being able to defend their claim*, but not against the claim itself.

Variation: The *Bad Reasons Fallacy* is similar, but the argument does not have to contain a fallacy—it could just be a bad argument with bad evidence or reasons. Bad arguments do not automatically mean that the conclusion is false; there can be much better arguments and reasons that support the truth of the conclusion.

I have never seen God; therefore, he does not exist.

This is a terrible reason to support a very strong conclusion, but this doesn't mean that God does exist; it simply means the argument is weak.

Tip: It may be futile dealing with people who consistently present fallacious arguments. If you find they are simply not very good at reasoning, you can help them learn. However, if they are using fallacious arguments as a form of deception, this is a strong indicator of acting in bad faith.

References:

Logical Fallacies in Psychology. (n.d.). Retrieved from http://kspope.com/fallacies/fallacies.php

Argument from Hearsay

(also known as: the telephone game, Chinese whispers, anecdotal evidence, anecdotal fallacy/Volvo fallacy [form of])

Description: Presenting the testimony of a source that is not an eyewitness to the event in question. It has been conclusively demonstrated that with each passing of information, via analog transmission, the message content is likely to change. Each small change can and often does lead to many more significant changes, as in the *butterfly effect* in *chaos theory*.

Hearsay is generally considered very weak evidence if it is considered evidence at all. Especially when such evidence is *unfalsifiable* (not able to be proven false).

Logical Form:

Person 1 told me that he saw Y.

Therefore, I must accept that Y is true.

Example #1:

Lolita: Bill stole the money from the company petty cash fund.

Byron: How do you know?

Lolita: Because Diane told me.

Byron: How does she know?

Lolita: Julian told her.

Byron: Did anyone actually see Bill steal the money?

Lolita: I don't know, we could ask Morris.

Byron: Who's he?

Lolita: The guy who told Julian.

Explanation: Lolita is making a bold claim about Bill, based on hearsay. Not only did Lolita not see Bill steal the money, but neither did Diane, Julian, and who knows about Morris.

Example #2:

There is life after death! I once heard this story from my friend's sister, that her maid of honor's niece knew this guy who had a friend who heard from his camp counselor a story where some guy was in a coma and saw his grandparents in a tunnel of light, and they told him the winning lottery numbers! I swear to God it's true!

Explanation: The validity of the testimony of a coma patient aside, in all likelihood, stories like these are either pure fabrications or exaggerations of some much less interesting story. Due to something called the *confirmation bias* and the *wishful thinking fallacy*, those who already believe in such phenomena are likely to accept such stories as evidence for their truthfulness when, in fact, such stories are not evidence.

Exception: When you trust the source, and trust that the source is accurately representing the facts, you can at least partially accept the claim, depending on the consequences of accepting or rejecting the claim. For example, if your best friend told you that her best friend told her about an amazing one day sale at the mall, risking a 10-minute drive to the mall might be justified based on the sources.

Variation: The *anecdotal fallacy*, or *volvo fallacy*, is allowing a specific instance of anecdotal evidence to lend much more weight to an argument than it should.

Fun Fact: People are often egregiously wrong in their interpretation of events. As time passes, imagination is confused with actual events. You might be able to trust that your best friend is telling you the truth, but only the truth so far as she recalls from her initial interpretation.

References:

This is a logical fallacy frequently used on the Internet. No academic sources could be found.

Argument from Ignorance
ad ignorantiam

(also known as: appeal to ignorance, appeal to mystery [form of], black swan fallacy [form of], toupee fallacy [form of])

Description: The assumption of a conclusion or fact based primarily on lack of evidence to the contrary. Usually best described by, "absence of evidence is not evidence of absence."

Logical Forms:

X is true because you cannot prove that X is false.

X is false because you cannot prove that X is true.

Example #1:

Although we have proven that the moon is not made of spare ribs, we have not proven that its core cannot be filled with them; therefore, the moon's core is filled with spare ribs.

Explanation: There is an infinity of things we cannot prove—the moon being filled with spare ribs is one of them. Now you might expect that any "reasonable" person would know that the moon can't be filled with spare ribs, but you would be expecting too much. People make wild claims, and get away with them, simply on the fact that the converse cannot otherwise be proven.

Example #2:

To this very day (at the time of this writing), science has been unable to create life from non-life; therefore, life must be a result of divine intervention.

Explanation: Ignoring the *false dilemma*, the fact that we have not found a way to create life from non-life is not evidence that there is no way to create life from non-life, nor is it evidence that we will some day be able to; it is just evidence that we do not know how to do it. Confusing ignorance with impossibility (or possibility) is fallacious.

Exception: The assumption of a conclusion or fact deduced from evidence of absence, is not considered a fallacy, but valid reasoning.

Jimbo: Dude, did you spit your gum out in my drink?

Dick: No comment.

Jimbo: (after carefully pouring his drink down the sink looking for gum but finding none...) Jackass!

Tip: Look at all your existing major beliefs and see if they are based more on the lack of evidence than evidence. You might be surprised as to how many actually are.

Variations: The *black swan fallacy* is committed when one claims, based on past experience, contradictory evidence or claims must be rejected. It is treating the heuristic of induction like an algorithm. The name comes from the claim that "all swans are white" because nobody has ever seen a black swan before... until they did. The reasonable position to hold, assuming you existed in a pre-black-swan world, would be that "all swans *that we currently know of* are white." Leave room for discovery unless it has been demonstrated that the contradictory evidence, or claims cannot possibly exist or such claims would be impossible. For example, claiming "all triangles have three sides" is both accurate and reasonable.

The *toupee fallacy* is a cleverly-named variation of the *argument from ignorance* where the absence of evidence is the result of the claim made being false. Consider the argument, "all toupées look fake; I've never seen one that I couldn't tell was fake." The reason the person has never seen one they couldn't tell was fake is because when they did see one they couldn't tell was fake, they couldn't tell was fake. The same goes for penile enlargements and boob jobs.

The *appeal to mystery* is a specific claim stating that the reason we cannot prove something is because "it is a mystery." Rather than question if the claim is true, we accept that it is true and forego any more investigation by writing it off as a mystery. Why is it that I smell just fine after working out, but everyone else thinks I stink? It's a mystery!

References:

Walton, D. (2010). *Arguments from Ignorance*. Penn State Press.

Argument from Incredulity

(also known as: argument from personal astonishment, argument from personal incredulity, personal incredulity)

Description: Concluding that because you can't or refuse to believe something, it must not be true, improbable, or the argument must be flawed. This is a specific form of the *argument from ignorance*.

Logical Form:

> *Person 1 makes a claim.*
>
> *Person 2 cannot believe the claim.*
>
> *Person 2 concludes, without any reason besides he or she cannot believe or refuses to believe it, that the claim is false or improbable.*

Example #1:

> *Marty: Doc, I'm from the future. I came here in a time machine that you invented. Now, I need your help to get back to the year 1985.*
>
> *Doc: I've had enough practical jokes for one evening. Good night, future boy!*

Explanation: Clearly Marty is making an extraordinary claim, but the doc's dismissal of Marty's claim is based on pure incredulity. It isn't until Marty provides the Doc with extraordinary evidence (how he came up with the Flux Capacitor) that the Doc accepts Marty's claim. Given the nature of Marty's claim, it could be argued that Doc's dismissal of Marty's claim (although technically fallacious) was the more reasonable thing to do than entertain its possibility with good questions.

Example #2:

> *NASA: Yes, we really did successfully land men on the moon.*
>
> *TinFoilHatGuy1969: Yeah, right. And Elvis is really dead.*

Explanation: The unwillingness to entertain ideas that one finds unbelievable when the ideas are mainstream ideas made by a reputable source, such as a NASA and the truthfulness of the moon landings, is fallacious.

Exception: We can't possibly entertain every crackpot with crackpot ideas. People with little credibility or those pushing fringe ideas need to provide more compelling evidence to get the attention of others.

Fun Fact: YouTube is not a reliable source. But this doesn't mean that very reputable sources don't use YouTube for content distribution. The problem is, so does TinFoilHatGuy1969.

References:

Bebbington, D. (2011). Argument from personal incredulity. *Think*, *10*(28), 27–28. https://doi.org/10.1017/S1477175611000030

Argument from Silence
argumentum e silentio

Description: Drawing a conclusion based on the silence of the interlocutor, when the interlocutor is refusing to give evidence for any reason.

Logical Form:

> Person 1 claims X is true, then remains silent.
>
> Person 2 then concludes that X must be true.

Example #1:

> Jay: Dude, where are my car keys?
>
> Silent Bob: (says nothing)
>
> Jay: I KNEW you took them!

Explanation: Refusal to share evidence is not necessarily evidence for or against the argument. Silent Bob's silence does not mean he took the keys. Perhaps he did, or perhaps he knows who did, or perhaps he saw a Tyrannosaurus eat them and was threatened by the king of the pixies not to say anything, or perhaps he just felt like not answering.

Example #2:

> Morris: Oh youthful spirit, you have so much to learn. I know for a fact that there are multiple dimensions that beings occupy.
>
> Clifton: How can you possibly *know* that for a fact?
>
> Morris: (raises one eyebrow, stares deeply into the eyes of Clifton and says nothing)
>
> Clifton: Wow. You convinced me!

Explanation: The reason this technique works so well, is because *imagined reasons are often more persuasive than real reasons.* If someone wants to be convinced, this technique works like a charm. However, to the critical thinker, this will not fly. Silence is not a valid substitute for reason or evidence.

Exception: Generally speaking, absence of evidence is not evidence; however, there are many cases where the *reason* evidence is being held back can be seen as evidence. In the first example, prompting Silent Bob to share a reason for his silence could result in a statement from Silent Bob that can be used as evidence.

Tip: Silence can be very powerful. In public speaking, knowing when to pause and let the audience digest what you said helps them comprehend your message. In argumentation, a pause after making a solid point can increase the odds your interlocutor(s) will accept the point.

References:

Bernecker, S., & Pritchard, D. (2011). *The Routledge Companion to Epistemology*. Routledge.

Argument of the Beard

(also known as: fallacy of the beard, heap fallacy, heap paradox fallacy, bald man fallacy, continuum fallacy, line drawing fallacy, sorites fallacy)

Description: When one argues that no useful distinction can be made between two extremes, just because there is no definable moment or point on the spectrum where the two extremes meet. The name comes from the heap paradox in philosophy, using a man's beard as an example. At what point does a man go from clean-shaven to having a beard?

Logical Form:

> *X is one extreme, and Y is another extreme.*
>
> *There is no definable point where X becomes Y.*
>
> *Therefore, there is no difference between X and Y.*

Example #1:

> *Why does the law state that you have to be 21 years old to drink? Does it really make any difference if you are 20 years and 364 days old? That is absurd. Therefore, if a single day makes no difference, then a collection of 1095 single days won't make any difference. Therefore, changing the drinking age to 18 will not make any difference.*

Explanation: Although this does appear to be typical 18-year-old thinking (sorry 18 year-olds), it is quite a common fallacy. Just because any single step makes no *apparent* difference, there is a difference that becomes more noticeable as the number of those steps increase.

Example #2:

> *Willard: I just realized that I will probably never go bald!*
>
> *Fanny: Why is that?*
>
> *Willard: Well, if I lose just one hair, I will not be bald, correct?*
>
> *Fanny: Of course.*

Willard: If I lose two hairs?

Fanny: No.

Willard: Every time I lose a hair, the loss of that one hair will not make me bald; therefore, I will never go bald.

Fanny: Congratulations, you found the cure to baldness— stupidity!

Explanation: What Willard did not take into consideration is "baldness" is a term used to define a state along a continuum, and although there is no clear point between bald and not bald, the extremes are both clearly recognizable and achievable.

Exception: The larger the spread, the more fallacious the argument, the smaller the spread, the less fallacious.

Fun Fact: There are very few clear lines we can draw between categories in any area of life. Categories are human constructs that we create to help us make sense of things, yet they often end up creating more confusion by tricking us into thinking abstract concepts actually exist.

References:

Murray, M., Murray, R. M., & Kujundzic, N. (2005). *Critical Reflection: A Textbook for Critical Thinking*. McGill-Queen's Press - MQUP.

Argument to Moderation
argumentum ad temperantiam

(also known as: appeal to moderation, middle ground, false compromise, gray fallacy, golden mean fallacy, fallacy of the mean, splitting the difference)

Description: Asserting that given any two positions, there exists a compromise between them that must be correct.

Logical Form:

Person 1 says A.

Person 2 says Z.

Therefore, somewhere around M must be correct.

Example #1:

So you are saying your car is worth $20k. I think it is worth $1, so let's just compromise and say it is worth $10k. (Assuming the car is worth $20k)

Explanation: The price of $20k was a reasonable book value for the car, where the price of $1 was an unreasonable extreme. The fact is the car is worth about $20k—thinking the car is worth $1 or $1,000,000, won't change that fact[3].

Example #2:

Ok, I am willing to grant that there might not be angels and demons really floating around Heaven or hanging out in Hell, but you must grant that there has to be at least one God. Is that a fair compromise?

Explanation: There is no compromise when it comes to truth. Truth is truth. If there are angels, demons, and God, there are angels, demons, and God. If there aren't, there aren't. Compromise and splitting the difference work fine in some cases, but not in determining truth.

Exception: When the two extremes are equally distanced from the "correct" value—and there actually *is* a correct, or fair, value between the two proposed values.

So you are saying your car is worth $40k. I think it is worth $1, so let's just compromise and say it is worth $20k. (Assuming the car is worth $20k)

Tip: If you know you are entering into a negotiation, be prepared to be low-balled, and don't let those figures change your target figure going into the negotiation.

---

[3] Worth, in this sense, has much to do with what someone is willing to pay, but for this example, let's just ignore that detail—otherwise I would need to come up with another example.

References:

This is a logical fallacy frequently used on the Internet. No academic sources could be found.

Argument to the Purse
argumentum ad crumenam

(also known as: appeal to poverty or argumentum ad lazarum, appeal to wealth, appeal to money)

Description: Concluding that the truth value of the argument is true or false based on the financial status of the author of the argument or the money value associated with the truth. The *appeal to poverty* is when the truth is assumed based on a lack of wealth whereas the *appeal to wealth* is when the truth is assumed based on an excess of wealth.

Logical Form:

> *Person 1 says Y is true.*
>
> *Person 1 is very rich.*
>
> *Therefore, Y must be true (appeal to wealth)/false (appeal to poverty).*

Example #1:

> *Mike: Did you know that the author of the book, "Logically Fallacious," made a fortune on the Internet?*
>
> *Jon: So?*
>
> *Mike: That means that this book must be awesome!*

Explanation: While my financial status might impress the participants at an Amway conference, it has little to do with my knowledge of fallacies. However, remember the *argument from fallacy*; just because the argument is fallacious, does not mean the conclusion is not true, dammit.

Example #2:

Simon is very poor. Simon says that the secret to life is giving up all your material possessions, and living off the government's material possessions. Simon must be very enlightened.

Explanation: Just like people tend to associate wealth with wisdom, they also associate extreme poverty with wisdom. Rich people are rich and poor people are poor—which members of those groups have wisdom does not depend on their financial status.

Exception: If one's wealth, or lack thereof, is directly related to the truth value of an argument, then it is not a fallacy.

Mike: Did you know that the author of this book, who does extremely well financially in business, also wrote the book, "Year To Success" that was endorsed by Arnold Schwarzenegger?

Jon: I did not know that.

Mike: That means that his book on success is probably worth looking into!

Jon: I agree, and I am sure Bo will thank you for the cheap plug.

Tip: There is nothing wrong with a little self-promotion.

References:

This is a logical fallacy frequently used on the Internet. No academic sources could be found.

Avoiding the Issue

(also known as: avoiding the question [form of], missing the point, straying off the subject, digressing, distraction [form of])

Description: When an arguer responds to an argument by not addressing the points of the argument. Unlike the *strawman fallacy*, avoiding the issue does not create an unrelated argument to divert attention, it simply avoids the argument.

Logical Form:

Person 1 makes claim X.

Person 2 makes unrelated statement.

Audience and/or person 1 forgets about claim X.

Example #1:

Daryl: Answer honestly, do you think if we were born and raised in Iran, by Iranian parents, we would still be Christian, or would we be Muslim?

Ross: I think those of us raised in a place where Christianity is taught are fortunate.

Daryl: I agree, but do you think if we were born and raised in Iran, by Iranian parents, we would still be Christian, or would we be Muslim?

Ross: Your faith is weak—you need to pray to God to make it stronger.

Daryl: I guess you're right. What was I thinking?

Explanation: Some questions are not easy to answer, and some answers are not easy to accept. While it may seem, at the time, like avoiding the question is the best action, it is actually an abandonment of reason and honest inquiry; therefore, fallacious.

Example #2:

Molly: It is 3:00 in the morning, you are drunk, covered in lipstick, and your shirt is on backward! Would you care to explain yourself?

Rick: I was out with the guys.

Molly: And the lipstick?

Rick: You look wonderful tonight, honey!

Molly: (softening) You think so? I got my hair cut today!

Explanation: It is not difficult to digress a line of questioning, so beware of these attempts.

Exception: At times, a digression is a good way to take the pressure off of a highly emotional argument. A funny story, a joke, or anything used as a "break" could be a very good thing at times. As long as the issue is dealt with again.

Tip: Don't avoid questions where you are afraid you won't like the answers. Face them head on, and deal with the truth.

Variation: *Distraction* can be a form of *avoiding the issue*, but does not have to be just verbal. For example, being asked a question you can't answer and pretending your phone rings, saying you need to use the restroom, faking a heart attack, etc.

References:

This is a logical fallacy frequently used on the Internet. No academic sources could be found.

Base Rate Fallacy

(also known as: neglecting base rates, base rate neglect, prosecutor's fallacy [form of])

Description: Ignoring statistical information in favor of using irrelevant information, that one incorrectly believes to be relevant, to make a judgment. This usually stems from the irrational belief that statistics don't apply to a situation, for one reason or another when, in fact, they do.

Example #1:

> Only 6% of applicants make it into this school, but my son is brilliant! They are certainly going to accept him!

Explanation: Statistically speaking, the son may still have a low chance of acceptance. The school is for brilliant kids (and everyone knows this), so the vast majority of kids who apply are brilliant. Of the whole population of brilliant kids who apply, only about 6% get accepted. So even if the son is brilliant, he still has a low chance of being accepted (about 6%).

Example #2: Faith healing "works," but not all the time, especially when one's faith is not strong enough (as generally indicated by the size of one's financial offering). Unbiased, empirical tests, demonstrate that a small but noticeable percentage of people are cured of "incurable" diseases such as cancer.

Explanation: This is true. However, what is not mentioned in the above is the number of cases of cancer that just go away without any kind of faith healing, in other words, the *base rate* of cancer remission. It is a statistical certainty that among those with cancer, there will be a percentage with spontaneous remission. If that percentage is the same as the faith-healing group, then that is what is to be expected, and no magic or divine healing is taking place. The following is from the American Cancer Society:

> *Available scientific evidence does not support claims that faith healing can cure cancer or any other disease. Some scientists suggest that the number of people who attribute their cure to faith healing is lower than the number predicted by calculations based on the historical percentage of spontaneous remissions seen among people with cancer. However, faith healing may promote peace of mind, reduce stress, relieve pain and anxiety, and strengthen the will to live[4].*

Exception: If there are factors that increase one's odds and alter the known statistical probabilities, it would be a reasonable assumption, as long as the variations from the statistical norm are in line with the factors that cause the variation. In other words, perhaps the mother in our first example knows that her son is gifted musically, that counts for something, then it is not unreasonable to expect a better than 6% probability—but assuming a 50%, 80%, or 100% probability, is still committing the fallacy.

Variation: The *prosecutor's fallacy* is a fallacy of statistical reasoning best demonstrated by a prosecutor when exaggerating the likelihood of a defendant's guilt. In

---

[4] The American Cancer Society, http://www.cancer.org/Treatment/ TreatmentsandSideEffects/ComplementaryandAlternativeMedicine/ MindBodyandSpirit/faith-healing

mathematical terms, it is the claim that the probability of A given B is equal to the probability of B given A. For example,

The probability that you have a cervix given that you are pregnant is the same as the probability that you are pregnant given that you have a cervix.

Clearly, this is wrong. The probability that you have a cervix if you are pregnant is close to 100% (leaving room for weird science and magic). The probability that you are pregnant if you have a cervix is dependent on many other factors, but let's just say it is a lot less than 100%. In legal cases, a prosecutor may abuse this fallacy to convince the jury that the chance of the defendant being innocent is very small, when it fact, if the whole population were considered (as it should be), the chance of the defendant being guilty (based on that statistic alone) is very small.

Tip: Take some time in your life to read a book or take a course on probability. Probability affects our lives in so many ways that having a good understanding of it will continually pay off.

References:

Bar-Hillel, M. (1977). *The Base-Rate Fallacy in Probability Judgments.* Defense Technical Information Center.

Begging the Question
petitio principii

(also known as: assuming the initial point, assuming the answer, chicken and the egg argument, circulus in probando)

Description: Any form of argument where the conclusion is assumed in one of the premises. Many people use the phrase "begging the question" incorrectly when they use it to mean, "prompts one to ask the question." That is NOT the correct usage. *Begging the question* is a form of *circular reasoning*.

Logical Form:

Claim X assumes X is true.

Therefore, claim X is true.

Example #1:

Paranormal activity is real because I have experienced what can only be described as paranormal activity.

Explanation: The claim, "paranormal activity is real" is supported by the premise, "I have experienced what can only be described as paranormal activity." The premise presupposes, or assumes, that the claim, "paranormal activity is real" is already true.

Example #2:

The reason everyone wants the new "Slap Me Silly Elmo" doll is because this is the hottest toy of the season!

Explanation: Everyone wanting the toy is the same thing as it being "hot," so the reason given is no reason at all—it is simply rewording the claim and trying to pass it off as support for the claim.

Exception: Some assumptions that are universally accepted could pass as not being fallacious.

People like to eat because we are biologically influenced to eat.

Tip: Remember that *begging the question* doesn't require a question, but the *complex question fallacy* does.

References:

Walton, D. N., & Fallacy, A. A. P. (1991). *Begging the Question.*

Biased Sample Fallacy

(also known as: biased statistics, loaded sample, prejudiced statistics, prejudiced sample, loaded statistics, biased induction, biased generalization, biased generalizing, unrepresentative sample, unrepresentative generalization)

Description: Drawing a conclusion about a population based on a sample that is biased, or chosen in order to make it appear the population on average is different than it actually is.

This differs from the *hasty generalization fallacy*, where the biased sample is specifically chosen from a select group, and the small sample is just a random sample, but too small to get any accurate information.

Logical Form:

Sample S, which is biased, is taken from population P.

Conclusion C is drawn about population P based on S.

Example #1:

Based on a survey of 1000 American homeowners, 99% of those surveyed have two or more automobiles worth on average $100,000 each. Therefore, Americans are very wealthy.

Explanation: Where did these homeowners live? Beverly Hills, CA. If the same survey was taken in Detroit, the results would be quite different. It is fallacious to accept the conclusion about the American population in general based on not just the geographical sample, but also the fact that homeowners were only surveyed.

Example #2:

Pastor Pete: People are turning to God everywhere! 9 out of 10 people I interviewed said that they had a personal relationship with Jesus Christ.

Fred: Where did you find these people you interviewed?

Pastor Pete: In my church.

Explanation: Pastor Pete has drawn a conclusion about religious beliefs from people "everywhere" based on people he has interviewed in his church. That's like concluding that the world likes to dance naked in front of strangers after interviewing a group of strippers.

Exception: What exactly is "biased" is subjective, but some biases are very clear.

Tip: Be very wary of statistics. Look at the source and details of the studies which produced the statistics. Very often you will find some kind of bias.

References:

Halverson, W. H. (1984). *A Concise Logic*. McGraw-Hill Higher Education.

Blind Authority Fallacy

(also known as: blind obedience, the "team player" appeal, Nuremberg defense, divine authority fallacy [form of], appeal to/argument from blind authority)

Description: Asserting that a proposition is true solely on the authority making the claim. It is often the case that those who blindly follow an authority ignore any counter-evidence to the authority's claim, no matter how strong. The authority could be anyone or anything, including parents, a coach, a boss, a military leader, a document, or a god.

Logical Form:

> *Person 1 says Y is true.*
>
> *Person 1 is seen as the ultimate authority.*
>
> *Therefore, Y is true.*

Example #1: During the Nazi war crimes trials at Nuremberg after World War II, Nazi war criminals were charged with genocide, mass murder, torture, and other atrocities. Their defense: "I was only following orders."

Explanation: Most of us begin our lives seeing our parents as the ultimate authority, and we experience their wrath when we question that authority. Unfortunately, this bad habit is carried over into adulthood where we replace our parents with a coach, a boss, a teacher, a commander, or a god. Rather than question, we blindly follow. This fallacy has probably resulted in more deaths, pain, suffering, and misery than all others combined.

Example #2:

> *Your honor, the Bible clearly says that psychics, wizards, and mediums are to be stoned to death and that it is our responsibility to do so (Leviticus 20:27). Therefore, I had every right to try to stone Dianne Warwick, and her psychic friends, to death.*

Explanation: Most Americans do see the Bible as the ultimate authority, but that darn, pesky legal system gets in the way.

Exception: To quote Col. Jessep from *A Few Good Men*, "We follow orders, son. We follow orders or people die. It's that simple. Are we clear?" I have never served in the military, so I cannot say how far I would go when just, "following orders." I wouldn't want anyone to die because I questioned orders, yet I wouldn't want anyone to die because I followed orders blindly. I guess this is why I am not in the military.

Variation: The *divine authority fallacy* is when the authority referenced is specifically said to be divine.

Tip: Moral reasoning is difficult, and the consequences of making poor moral decisions can be traumatic, but the more experience you have with moral reasoning, the better you will get at it. Don't allow an authority to rob you of this growth opportunity.

References:

This is a logical fallacy frequently used on the Internet. No academic sources could be found.

Broken Window Fallacy

(also known as: glazier's fallacy)

Description: The illusion that destruction and money spent in recovery from destruction, is a net-benefit to society. A broader application of this fallacy is the general tendency to overlook opportunity costs or that which is unseen, either in a financial sense or other.

This fallacy goes far beyond just looking for the silver lining, thinking positive, or making the best of a bad situation. It is the incorrect assumption that the net benefit is positive.

Logical Form:

Disaster X occurred, but this is a good thing because Y will come, as a result.

Example #1:

Dad, I actually did America a favor by crashing your car. Now, some auto shop will have more work, their employees will make more money, those employees will spend their money, and who knows, they might just come to your store and buy some of your products!

Explanation: I actually tried a variation of this argument when I was a kid—it didn't work, but not only did it not work, it is fallacious reasoning, and here is why: by crashing the car, a produced good is destroyed, and resources have to go into replacing that good as opposed to creating new goods.

Example #2:

The Holocaust was a good thing overall. It educated future generations about the evils of genocide.

Explanation: This is a real argument, I kid you not. People tend to overvalue their own gain (the education) and devalue the losses that are unseen (the unimaginable suffering of the victims and their families).

Exception: It might be the case when some kind of destruction actually can benefit society—like in lightning striking the local crack house, and a soup kitchen being reconstructed in its place.

Tip: Be sensitive when looking for the best of a bad situation, keeping in mind all those who may have suffered. In your statement of optimism or hope, be sure to show compassion as well.

The Holocaust was a horrible event in human history, and the damage that resulted will never be forgotten. As with most tragedies, they can be used to educate us, helping us to prevent similar future events.

References:

Russell, D. (1969). *Frederic Bastiat: ideas and influence*. Foundation for Economic Education.

Bulverism

Description: This is a combination of *circular reasoning* and the *genetic fallacy*. It is the assumption and assertion that an argument is flawed or false because of the arguer's suspected motives, social identity, or other characteristic associated with the arguer's identity.

Logical Form:

Person 1 makes argument X.

Person 2 assumes person 1 must be wrong because of their suspected motives, social identity, or other characteristic associated with their identity.

Therefore, argument X is flawed or not true.

Example #1:

Martin: All white people are not racists.

Charlie: Yes they are. You just believe that because you are white.

Explanation: Charlie is making two errors: 1) he is assuming that Martin must be wrong and 2) he is basing that assumption on an accidental feature of Martin—the amount of pigmentation in his skin.

Example #2:

> Mom: Remember, dear. Nobody's going to buy the cow if they get the milk for free.
>
> Daughter: You are only saying that because you are my mother.
>
> Daughter: Wait... did you just call me a cow?

Explanation: Mom is doing her best to advise her daughter that she should be a bit more sexually reserved with her male suitors, cautioning her that she is unlikely to get any commitments unless she holds back sex. Although the claim is indeed dubious, the daughter assumes that it is wrong because of the source (her mother) and her mother's suspected motives (to get her married). So the mother must be wrong (assumption) because of her motives, and it is because of her motives that she is wrong (*circular reasoning* and *genetic fallacy*).

Exception: There is no exception; however, in some cases it is fair to *cast doubt* on the argument based on the identity of the person making the argument. This is a heuristic that may be useful, but problematic in critical argumentation.

Tip: If you want a glass of milk, just buy the glass of milk, you don't need the whole cow (wait, did I just support prostitution?)

References:

Root, J., & Martindale, W. (2012). *The Quotable Lewis*. Tyndale House Publishers, Inc.

Causal Reductionism

(also known as: complex cause, fallacy of the single cause, causal oversimplification, reduction fallacy)

Description: Assuming a single cause or reason when there were actually multiple causes or reasons.

Logical Form:

X occurred after Y.

Therefore, Y caused X (although X was also a result of A,B,C... etc.)

Example #1:

Hank: I ran my car off the side of the road because that damn squirrel ran in front of my car.

Officer Sam: You don't think it had anything to do with the fact that you were trying to text your girlfriend, and driving drunk?

Explanation: While if it were not for the squirrel, perhaps Hank wouldn't have totaled his car. However, if it weren't for him texting while driving drunk, he could have almost certainly prevented taking his unauthorized shortcut through the woods and into a tree.

Example #2:

The reason more and more people are giving up belief in ghosts is because of Bo's books.

Explanation: Thank you, but that would be fallacious reasoning. While my books *may have played a role* in *some* people giving up belief in ghosts, I doubt it was the only cause, and am pretty darn sure that overall, my books have very little effect on the population at large.

Exception: Causes and reasons can be debatable, so if you can adequately defend the fact that you believe there was only a single reason, it won't be fallacious.

Tip: Use "contributing factors" more and "the reason" or "the cause" a lot less.

References:

The Journal of Mental Science. (1952). Longman, Green, Longman & Roberts.

Cherry Picking

(also known as: ignoring inconvenient data, suppressed evidence, fallacy of incomplete evidence, argument by selective observation, argument by half-truth, card stacking, fallacy of exclusion, ignoring the counter evidence, one-sided assessment, slanting, one-sidedness)

Description: When only select evidence is presented in order to persuade the audience to accept a position, and evidence that would go against the position is withheld. The stronger the withheld evidence, the more fallacious the argument.

Logical Form:

> *Evidence A and evidence B is available.*
>
> *Evidence A supports the claim of person 1.*
>
> *Evidence B supports the counterclaim of person 2.*
>
> *Therefore, person 1 presents only evidence A.*

Example #1:

> *Employer: It says here on your resume that you are a hard worker, you pay attention to detail, and you don't mind working long hours.*
>
> *Andy: Yes sir.*
>
> *Employer: I spoke to your previous employer. He says that you constantly change things that should not be changed, you could care less about other people's privacy, and you had the lowest score in customer relations.*
>
> *Andy: Yes, that is all true, as well.*
>
> *Employer: Great then. Welcome to our social media team!*

Explanation: Resumes are a classic example of *cherry picking* information. A resume can be seen as an argument as to why you are qualified for the job. Most employers are wise enough to know that resumes are one-sided and look for more evidence in the form of interviews and recommendations to make a decision.

Example #2:

My political candidate gives 10% of his income to the needy, goes to church every Sunday, and volunteers one day a week at a homeless shelter. Therefore, he is honest and morally straight.

Explanation: What information was left out of the example is that this same candidate gives 10% of his income to needy prostitutes in exchange for services, goes to the bar every Sunday after church (and sometimes before), and only works at the homeless shelter to get clients for his drug dealing business.

Exception: If the parts of the truth being suppressed do not affect the truth of the conclusion, or can reasonably be assumed, they could be left out of the argument. For example, political candidates are not committing this fallacy when they leave out the fact that they will need about 8 hours of sleep each night.

Tip: If you suspect people are only telling you a half-truth, don't be afraid to ask, "Is there anything you are not telling me?"

References:

Fallacies | Internet Encyclopedia of Philosophy. (n.d.). Retrieved from http://www.iep.utm.edu/fallacy/#SuppressedEvidence

Circular Definition

Description: A circular definition is defining a term by using the term in the definition. Ironically, that definition is partly guilty by my use of the term "definition" in the definition. Okay, I am using definition way too much. Damn! I just did it again.

Logical Form:

Term 1 is defined by using term 1 in its definition.

Example #1:

Circular definition: a definition that is circular.

Explanation: The definition is not at all helpful because we used the same words in the term to define them.

Example #2:

> *Flippityflu: smarter than a Floppityflip.*
>
> *Floppityflip: dumber than a Flippityflu.*

Explanation: Here we have two definitions that result in a slightly larger circle, but a circle nonetheless.

Exception: Many definitions are circular, but in the process of defining, there might be enough other information to help us understand the term.

> *Ethics: moral principles that govern a person's behavior or the conducting of an activity.*
>
> *Moral Principles: the principles of right and wrong that are accepted by an individual or a social group.*
>
> *Principles of Right and Wrong: moral principles or one's foundation for ethical behavior.*

Tip: Don't be too quick to call "fallacy" with this one. As demonstrated in the definition, some words in the term can be reused if they are commonly understood.

> *Nimbus cloud: A cloud that produces precipitation.*

References:

Lavery, J., & Hughes, W. (2008). *Critical Thinking, fifth edition: An Introduction to the Basic Skills*. Broadview Press.

Circular Reasoning
circulus in demonstrando

(also known as: paradoxical thinking, circular argument, circular cause and consequence, reasoning in a circle, vicious circle)

Description: A type of reasoning in which the proposition is supported by the premises, which is supported by the proposition, creating a circle in reasoning where no useful information is being shared. This fallacy is often quite humorous.

Logical Form:

X is true because of Y.

Y is true because of X.

Example #1:

Pvt. Joe Bowers: What are these electrolytes? Do you even know?

Secretary of State: They're... what they use to make Brawndo!

Pvt. Joe Bowers: But why do they use them to make Brawndo?

Secretary of Defense: [raises hand after a pause] Because Brawndo's got electrolytes.

Explanation: This example is from a favorite movie of mine, *Idiocracy,* where Pvt. Joe Bowers (played by Luke Wilson) is dealing with a bunch of not-very-smart guys from the future. Joe is not getting any useful information about electrolytes, no matter how hard he tries.

Example #2:

The Bible is the Word of God because God tells us it is... in the Bible.

Explanation: This is a very serious circular argument on which many people base their entire lives. This is like getting an e-mail from a Nigerian prince, offering to give you his billion dollar fortune—but only after you wire him a "good will" offering of $50,000. Of course, you are skeptical until you read the final line in the e-mail that reads *"I, prince Nubadola, assure you that this is my message, and it is legitimate. You can trust this e-mail and any others that come from me."* Now you know it is legitimate... because it says so in the e-mail.

Exception: Some philosophies state that we can never escape circular reasoning because the arguments always come back to axioms or first principles, but in those cases, the circles are very large and do manage to share useful information in determining the truth of the proposition.

Tip: Do your best to avoid circular arguments, as it will help you reason better because better reasoning is often a result of avoiding circular arguments.

References:

Fallacies | Internet Encyclopedia of Philosophy. (n.d.). Retrieved from http://www.iep.utm.edu/fallacy

Commutation of Conditionals

(also known as: the fallacy of the consequent, converting a conditional)

Description: Switching the antecedent and the consequent in a logical argument.

Logical Form:

> *If P then Q.*
>
> *Therefore, if Q then P.*

Example #1:

> *If I have a PhD, then I am smart.*
>
> *Therefore, if I am smart, then I have a PhD.*

Explanation: There are many who could, rightly so, disagree with the first premise, but assuming that premise is true, does not guarantee that the conclusion is true. There are many smart people without PhDs.

Example #2:

> *If I have herpes, then I have a strange rash.*

Therefore, if I have a strange rash, then I have herpes.

Explanation: I am glad this is not true. One can have non-herpes rashes.

Exception: If p=q, then it is necessarily true that q=p.

Tip: If you think might herpes, see your doctor.

References:

Pickard, W. A., & Aristotle. (2006). *On Sophistical Refutations*. ReadHowYouWant.com, Limited.

Complex Question Fallacy
plurium interrogationum

(also known as: many questions fallacy, fallacy of presupposition, loaded question, trick question, false question)

Description: A question that has a presupposition built in, which implies something but protects the one asking the question from accusations of false claims. It is a form of misleading discourse, and it is a fallacy when the audience does not detect the assumed information implicit in the question and accepts it as a fact.

Logical Form:

> Question X is asked that requires implied claim Y to be accepted before question X can be answered.

Example #1:

> How many times per day do you beat your wife?

Explanation: Even if the response is an emphatic, "none!" the damage has been done. If you are hearing this question, you are more likely to accept the possibility that the person who was asked this question is a wife-beater, which is fallacious reasoning on your part.

Example #2:

How many school shootings should we tolerate before we change the gun laws?

Explanation: The presupposition is that changing the gun laws will decrease the number of school shootings. This may be the case, but it is a claim that is implied in the statement and hidden by a more complex question. Reactively, when one hears a question such as this, one's mind will attempt to search for an answer to the question—which is actually a distraction from rejecting the implicit claim being made. It is quite brilliant but still fallacious.

Exception: It is not a fallacy if the implied information in the question is known to be an accepted fact.

How long can one survive without water?

Here, it is presumed that we need water to survive, which very few would deny that fact.

Tip: Remember that fallacious techniques don't require the person using them to be lacking in reason; it is the audience or interlocutor that is at risk for falling for the deception.

References:

Menssen, S., & Sullivan, T. D. (2007). *The Agnostic Inquirer: Revelation from a Philosophical Standpoint*. Wm. B. Eerdmans Publishing.

Conflicting Conditions
contradictio in adjecto

(also known as: a self-contradiction, self-refuting idea)

Description: When the argument is self-contradictory and cannot possibly be true.

Logical Form:

Claim X is made, which is impossible as demonstrated by all or part of claim X.

Example #1:

The only thing that is certain is uncertainty.

Explanation: Uncertainty itself cannot be certain by definition. It is a self-contradiction.

Example #2:

I don't care what you believe, as long as your beliefs don't harm others.

Explanation: This is a contradiction. At first glance, "as long as" appears to be a condition for the assertion, "I don't care what you believe," but it's not; the assertion *has to be* false in all cases. *The arguer must always care if the person believes something that will harm others or not.*

Exception: When the self-contradictory statement is not put forth as an argument, but rather as an ironic statement, perhaps with the intent to convey some kind of deeper truth or meaning, but not necessarily to be taken literally, then this fallacy is not committed.

Fun Fact: This sentence is false.

References:

Cicero: Academic Skepticism | Internet Encyclopedia of Philosophy. (n.d.). Retrieved from http://www.iep.utm.edu/cicero-a/

Confusing an Explanation with an Excuse

(also known as: confusing and explanation with justification, confusing elucidation with justification)

Description: Treating an explanation of a fact as if it were a justification of the fact, a valid reason for the fact, or evidence for the fact.

Logical Form:

> *Person 1 wants claim X be justified.*
>
> *Person 2 explains claim X in detail.*
>
> *Therefore, claim X is justified/true.*

Example #1:

> *Barto: If masks don't work, how do you explain the almost perfect correlation between mask-wearing communities and lower transmission rates?*
>
> *Tikki: All this means is that in communities where more people where masks, the virus is less-likely to spread. It is not proof that masks are the reason.*

Explanation: Not only did Tikki not answer the question asked, she created an answer based on elucidation of what Barto had said. Tikki explained what a correlation is (i.e., not "proof") but came no closer to explaining the reason for the correlation.

Example #2:

> *Virgil: How do you justify the claim that Bigfoot is the missing link between the great apes and humans?*
>
> *Marshall: Well, a "missing link" is the intermediary species between the two in the evolutionary process.*

Explanation: Marshall simply explained what a missing link is; he did not give a valid reason for why he believes that Bigfoot is the missing link.

Exception: If it is clear to both parties that no justification attempt is being made, but rather just stating a fact, then this fallacy is not being committed.

Tip: If you are unsure if someone is trying to make an excuse or simply stating a fact, ask them. Don't assume.

References:

This is a logical fallacy frequently used on the Internet. No academic sources could be found.

Confusing Currently Unexplained with Unexplainable

Description: Making the assumption that what cannot currently be explained is, therefore, unexplainable (impossible to explain). This is a problem because we cannot know the future and what conditions might arise that offer an explanation. It is also important to note that we cannot assume the currently unexplained **is** explainable.

Logical Form:

Claim X is currently unexplained.

Therefore, claim X is unexplainable.

Example #1:

Teri: I don't know why that stuffed animal flew off my dresser this morning. I guess some things in life will forever remain a mystery!

Explanation: The fact that Teri could not explain something, does not make it unexplainable. Later, it might be revealed that a family member was playing a trick and tied a string to the stuffed animal. Maybe Teri will read about a slight earthquake that happened at the same time. Maybe Teri will later discover that there is a rat in her room that made a home in her stuffed animals. The point is, what is currently unexplained is not necessarily unexplainable.

Example #2:

While we may be able to explain **how** humans got here, we will never be able to explain **why**.

Explanation: Besides *begging the question* (this assumes there is a "why"), we don't know if we will never be able to explain why. Perhaps aliens created us, and they will tell us one day that created us for one big social experiment. Perhaps they wanted to see, after seeding Earth with life about 3 1/2 billion years ago, if one of the members of the human species, Alfredo, scratched his left ear at precisely 3:46 PM on December 12, 2023. After which time they will hit the reset button and try a different experiment.

Exception: Like other claims, expressing probability is a way around this fallacy.

> *While we may be able to explain **how** humans got here, we **may** never be able to explain **why** (assuming there is a why).*

Tip: Be careful using terms such as "impossible" and "possible." The casual use of both terms is often incorrect within argumentation.

References:

This is a logical fallacy frequently used on the Internet. No academic sources could be found.

Conjunction Fallacy

(also known as: conjunction effect)

Description: Similar to the *disjunction fallacy,* the *conjunction fallacy* occurs when one estimates a conjunctive statement (this *and* that) to be *more* probable than at least one of its component statements. It is the assumption that more specific conditions are more probable than general ones. This fallacy usually stems from thinking the choices are alternatives, rather than members of the same set. The fallacy is further exacerbated by priming the audience with information leading them to choose the subset as the more probable option.

Logical Form:

> *X is a subset of Y.*

Therefore, X is more probable than Y.

Conjunction X and Y (both taken together) is more likely than a constituent X.

Example #1:

While jogging around the neighborhood, you are more likely to get bitten by someone's pet dog, than by any member of the canine species.

Explanation: Actually, that is not the case. "Someone's pet dog," assuming a real dog and not some robot dog, would also be a member of the canine species. Therefore, the canine species includes wolves, coyotes, as well as your neighbor's Shih Tzu, who is likely to bite you just because he's pissed for being so small.

Example #2: Karen is a thirty-something-year-old female who drives a mini-van, lives in the suburbs, and wears mom jeans. Is Karen more likely to be a woman or a mom?

Explanation: It would be fallacious to say that Karen is more likely to be a mom—even if we found out that Karen spent an hour each day at the playground with other moms. There is a 100% chance the Karen is a woman (we know she is female), and a smaller chance that she is a mom.

Exception: When contradicting conditions are implied, but incorrectly stated.

In the example above, the way the question reads, we now know that there is a 100% chance Karen is a woman and a smaller chance that she is a mom. However, if the questioner meant to imply, "not a mom" or "mom" as the choices, then it could be more of a poorly phrased question than a fallacy.

Tip: Read *Thinking, Fast and Slow*, by Daniel Kahneman and Amos Tversky for a deep dive on cognitive errors.

References:

Kahneman, D. (2013). *Thinking, Fast and Slow* (1st edition). New York: Farrar, Straus and Giroux.

Conspiracy Theory

(also known as: canceling hypothesis, canceling hypotheses, cover-ups)

Description: Explaining that your claim cannot be proven or verified because the truth is being hidden and/or evidence destroyed by a group of two or more people. When that reason is challenged as not being true or accurate, the challenge is often presented as just another attempt to cover up the truth and presented as further evidence that the original claim is true.

Logical Form:

> *A is true.*
>
> *B is why the truth cannot be proven.*
>
> *Therefore, A is true.*

Example #1:

> *Noah's ark has been found by the Russian government a long time ago, but because of their hate for religion, they have been covering it up ever since.*

Example #2:

> *Geologists and scientists all over the world are discovering strong evidence for a 6000-year-old earth, yet because of the threat of ruining their reputation, they are suppressing the evidence and keeping quiet.*

Explanation: The psychology behind conspiracy theories is quite complex and involves many different cognitive biases and fallacies discussed in this book. In general, people tend to overlook the incredible improbabilities involved in a large-scale conspiracy, as well as the potential risks for all involved in the alleged cover-up. In the above examples, those who stick with a literal interpretation of the Bible often experience *cognitive dissonance*, or the mental struggle involved when one's beliefs contradict factual claims. This cognitive dissonance causes people to create conspiracy theories, like the ones above, to change facts to match their beliefs, rather than changing their beliefs to match facts.

Exception: Sometimes, there really are conspiracies and cover-ups. The more evidence one can present for a cover-up, the better, but we must remember that possibility does not equal probability.

Tip: Take time to question any conspiracy theories in which you believe are true. Do the research with an open mind.

References:

Barkun, M. (2006). *A Culture of Conspiracy: Apocalyptic Visions in Contemporary America*. University of California Press.

Contextomy

(also known as: fallacy of quoting out of context, quoting out of context)

Description: Removing a passage from its surrounding matter in such a way as to distort its intended meaning.

Logical Form:

Argument X has meaning 1 in context.

Argument X has meaning 2 when taken out of context.

Therefore, meaning 2 is said to be correct.

Example #1:

David: Can you believe that the president said, "fat people are losers"?

Sam: Where did you hear this?

David: I read it in a headline on BrightBert News.

Sam: He actually said, "People who say, 'fat people are losers' are not only cruel, but they are also wrong as well as being irrational."

Explanation: David fell for *click bait*—a technique used by the media to get people to click their links or discuss their article. He did not bother to investigate the context from which the quote was taken, and he perpetuated the lie.

Example #2:

Trisha: In an interview, your candidate admitted that he was a thief!

Derek: He actually said that when he was three years old, he stole a lollipop from a store, and felt so guilty, that he never stole anything again.

Explanation: Trisha managed to twist the meaning of the candidate's story from one showing the candidate's strong moral character, to one where he is a criminal. Clearly, context is important.

Exception: People often use "you're taking that out of context" to soften something that would otherwise be hard to swallow, yet they are unable to explain adequately how it makes sense in any other context.

Tip: A great response for "you're taking that out of context" is "please do explain it to me in context." If they can't or won't, it is likely that context doesn't make the argument any more palatable.

References:

McGlone, M. S. (2005). Contextomy: the art of quoting out of context. *Media, Culture & Society, 27*(4), 511–522. https://doi.org/10.1177/0163443705053974

Deceptive Sharing

Description: Sharing an article, post, or meme on social media with the intent to influence public perception to perceive a statistically rare event as a common event. The cognitive bias behind this fallacy is the *availability heuristic* that causes us to have a skewed perception of reality based on specific examples that easily come to mind.

Like most fallacies, we have the fallacious tactic by the one who shares an article, post, or meme on social media depicting a statistically rare event with the intent to manipulate public perception of the event as a common event. Someone who views an article, post, or meme on social media depicting a statistically rare event and believes it to be a common event, has been a victim of *deceptive sharing* and is using fallacious reasoning. It is also possible for those sharing content to be deceived, themselves.

There is a strong, implied argument with the share that the event is far more common than it actually is. If the content is shared with an explicit argument claiming that the event is more common than it really is, then there is no fallacy; it is a factual error. What makes this fallacious is the implied argument that remains unsaid but clearly implied.

Logical Forms:

[fallacious tactic]

Event X is statistically rare.

Person 1 shares article, post, or meme of an instance of event X with the intent to deceive others in thinking event X is far more common than it is.

[fallacious reasoning]

Event X is statistically rare.

Person 1 shares article, post, or meme of an instance of event X.

Person 2 believes the event is far more common than it is.

Event X is statistically rare.

Person 1 shares article, post, or meme of an instance of event X, believing that event X is far more common than it is.

Example #1: During the COVID-19 pandemic, there was much debate on reopening schools. Like with many issues, there was a strong partisan split where liberals were mostly against sending kids back to school, and conservatives were mostly for sending kids back to school. Several of my liberal friends commonly shared stories about kids getting sick, including this story posted with no comment nor argument:

> *Health officials in Georgia confirmed this week that a 7-year-old boy with no underlying health conditions has died from the coronavirus, the youngest fatality from the pandemic in the state so far.*

The strategy is to let those who comment make the arguments that the one posting is not willing to make nor defend, and the one who shared the article can remain blameless.

Children, especially healthy children with no underlying health conditions, dying from COVID-19 is extremely rare. Sharing stories of this happening gives people the impression that it is far more common than it actually is, causing them to make important decisions based on a poor understanding of the data.

Example #2: Some people who were adamantly against wearing masks shared the story published by the *New York Post* on May 6th, 2020, with the headline "Two Boys Drop Dead in China While Wearing Masks During Gym Class." Ignoring the problem with causation (i.e., it has not been determined that the masks had anything to do with the deaths), the purpose for sharing the article is very clear: To attempt to vindicate the sharer's anti-mask-wearing position. The fact is, recorded instances of people dying from wearing masks are exceptionally rare.

Exception: It may be the case that statistically rare events are also "feel good" events that have no manipulative intent, for example, sharing a story about a local child who saved his family from a gas leak. There is no implication here that kids saving their families from gas leaks is a common occurrence.

A more questionable exception is the statistically rare, "feel good" event that may be shared with the intent to manipulate. An example is FOX News, with their regular posts of "hero cops" who save babies, help old ladies across the street, or save the world from intergalactic invaders. The manipulative intent is debatable. While the public does love these stories, they also counter the police brutality stories commonly posted by mainstream media.

Tip: Remember the *principle of charity*. If you are not confident that the sharer is implying that the event they are sharing is far more common than reality dictates, ask, "what is the reason you are sharing this?"

References:

This is an original logical fallacy named by the author.

Definist Fallacy

(also known as: persuasive definition fallacy, redefinition)

Description: Defining a term in such a way that makes one's position much easier to defend.

Logical Form:

> *A has definition X.*
>
> *X is harmful to my argument.*
>
> *Therefore, A has definition Y.*

Example #1:

> *Before we argue about the truth of creationism, let's define creationism as, "The acceptance of a set of beliefs even more ridiculous than those of flat-earthers."*

Example #2:

Before we argue about the truth of creationism, let's define evolution as, "Faith in a crackpot theory that is impossible to prove with certainty."

Explanation: It should be clear by the two examples who is defending what position. Both interlocutors are taking the opportunity to define a term as a way to take a cheap shot at the interlocutor. In some cases, they might actually hope their definition is accepted, which would make it very easy to defend, compared to the actual definition.

Exception: When a definition used is really an accurate definition from credible sources, regardless of the damage it might do to a position.

Tip: Do not accept definitions put forth by the interlocutor unless you researched your definition on your own, and agree.

References:

Bunnin, N., & Yu, J. (2008). *The Blackwell Dictionary of Western Philosophy.* John Wiley & Sons.

Denying a Conjunct

Description: A formal fallacy in which the first premise states that at least one of the two *conjuncts* (antecedent and consequent) is false and concludes that the other conjunct must be true.

Logical Forms:

Not both P and Q.

Not P.

Therefore, Q.

Not both P and Q.

Not Q.

Therefore, P.

Example #1:

I am not both a moron and an idiot.

I am not a moron.

Therefore, I am an idiot.

Explanation: I might be an idiot, but the truth of both premises does not guarantee that I am; therefore, this argument is invalid—technically, the form of this formal argument is invalid. Being "not both" a moron and an idiot, only means that if I am not one of the two, I am simply not one of the two—we cannot logically conclude that I am the other.

Example #2:

I am not both a Christian and a Satanist.

I am not a Satanist.

Therefore, I am a Christian.

Explanation: The truth of both premises does not guarantee that I am a Christian; therefore, this argument is invalid—the form of this formal argument is invalid. Being "not both" a Satanist and a Christian, only means that if I am not one of the two, I am simply not one of the two—we cannot logically conclude that I am the other.

Fun Fact: Atheists don't eat babies.

References:

Kiersky, J. H., & Caste, N. J. (1995). *Thinking Critically: Techniques for Logical Reasoning*. West Publishing Company.

Denying the Antecedent

(also known as: inverse error, inverse fallacy)

Description: It is a fallacy in formal logic where in a standard if/then premise, the antecedent (what comes after the "if") is made not true, then it is concluded that the consequent (what comes after the "then") is not true.

Logical Form:

If P, then Q.

Not P.

Therefore, not Q.

Example #1:

If it barks, it is a dog.

It doesn't bark.

Therefore, it's not a dog.

Explanation: It is not that clear that a fallacy is being committed, but because this is a formal argument following a strict form, even if the conclusion seems to be true, the argument is still invalid. This is why fallacies can be very tricky and deceptive. Since it doesn't bark, we cannot conclude with certainty that it isn't a dog—it could be a dog who just can't bark.

The arguer has committed a formal fallacy, and the argument is invalid because the truth of the premises does not guarantee the truth of the conclusion.

Example #2:

If I have cable, then I have seen a naked lady.

I don't have cable.

Therefore, I have never seen a naked lady.

Explanation: The fallacy is more obvious here than in the first example. Denying the antecedent (saying that I don't have cable) does not mean we must deny the consequent (that I have seen a naked lady...I have, by the way, in case you were wondering).

The arguer has committed a formal fallacy, and the argument is invalid because the truth of the premises does not guarantee the truth of the conclusion.

Tip: If you ever get confused with formal logic, replace the words with letters, like we do in the logical form, then replace the letters with different phrases and see if it makes sense or not.

References:

Kiersky, J. H., & Caste, N. J. (1995). *Thinking Critically: Techniques for Logical Reasoning*. West Publishing Company.

Denying the Correlative

(also known as: denying the correlative conjunction)

Description: Introducing alternatives when, in fact, there are none. This could happen when you have two mutually exclusive statements (*correlative conjunction*) presented as choices, and instead of picking one or the other, introduce a third—usually as a distraction from having to choose between the two alternatives presented.

Logical Form:

Either X or not X.

Therefore, Y.

Example #1:

Rocco: Do ya have the five grand you owe me or not?

Paulie: I can get it.

Rocco: That means you don't have it?

Paulie: I know someone who does.

Rocco: Read my lips: do you have my money or not?

Paulie: No.

(sound of a baseball bat breaking kneecaps)

Explanation: Rocco was asking a simple question, and out of personal safety, Paulie was committing the fallacy of *denying the correlative* by offering up another option to a choice that only had two. If Paulie were smarter, he could not have committed the fallacy and saved his kneecaps, by honesty and a little negotiation:

> *Rocco: Do ya have the five grand you owe me or not?*
>
> *Paulie: No. I realize I did not hold up my end of the deal, so I will compensate you for that.*
>
> *Rocco: What are you sayin'?*
>
> *Paulie: I can have your $5000 by this time tomorrow, plus an extra $500 for making you have to wait an extra day.*
>
> *Rocco: Deal. I'll be back this time tomorrow.*
>
> *(sound of heart dropping from throat)*

Example #2:

> *Judge: So did you kill your landlord or not?*
>
> *Kirk: I fought with him.*

Explanation: Here is a classic case where a "yes" or "no" answer is expected, and the only acceptable answer to such a question, yet Kirk is deflecting the question by providing a third answer option, that leaves the original question unanswered.

Exception: When non-mutually exclusive choices are presented as mutually exclusive choices, the fallacy lies with the one presenting the choices (*false dilemma*).

Tip: Don't borrow money from anyone named "Rocco."

References:

This is a logical fallacy frequently used on the Internet. No academic sources could be found.

Disjunction Fallacy

Description: Similar to the *conjunction fallacy*, the *disjunction fallacy* occurs when one estimates a disjunctive statement (this *or* that) to be *less* probable than at least one of its component statements.

Logical Forms:

> Disjunction X or Y (both taken together) is less likely than a constituent Y.

Example #1:

> Mr. Pius goes to church every Sunday. He gets most of his information about religion from church and does not really read the Bible too much. Mr. Pius has a figurine of St. Mary at home. Last year, when he went to Rome, he toured the Vatican. From this information, Mr. Pius is more likely to be Catholic than a Catholic or a Muslim.

Explanation: This is incorrect. While it is very likely that Mr. Pius is Catholic based on the information, it is more likely that he is Catholic or Muslim.

Example #2:

> Bill is 6'11" tall, thin, but muscular. We know he either is a pro basketball player or a jockey. We conclude that it is more probable that he is a pro basketball player than a pro basketball player or a jockey.

Explanation: This is incorrect. While it is very likely that Bill plays the B-ball, given that he would probably crush a horse, it is statistically more likely that he is either a pro basketball player or a jockey since that option includes the option of him being just a pro basketball player. Don't let what seems like common sense fool you.

Tip: Go back and read the entry for the *conjunction fallacy* again and make sure you know the difference.

References:

Gilovich, T., Griffin, D., & Kahneman, D. (2002). *Heuristics and Biases: The Psychology of Intuitive Judgment.* Cambridge University Press.

Distinction Without a Difference

Description: The assertion that a position is different from another position based on the language when, in fact, both positions are the same—at least in practice or practical terms.

Logical Form:

Claim X is made where the truth of the claim requires a distinct difference between A and B.

There is no distinct difference between A and B.

Therefore, claim X is true.

Example #1:

Sergio: There is no way I would ever even consider taking dancing lessons.

Kitty: How about I ask my friend from work to teach you?

Sergio: If you know someone who is willing to teach me how to dance, then I am willing to learn, sure.

Explanation: Perhaps it is the stigma of "dancing lessons" that is causing Sergio to hold this view, but the fact is, someone teaching him how to dance is the same thing. Sergio has been duped by language.

Example #2:

We must judge this issue by what the Bible says, not by what we think it says or by what some scholar or theologian thinks it says.

Explanation: Before you say, "Amen!," realize that this is a clear case of *distinction without a difference*. There is absolutely no difference here because the only possible way to read the Bible is through interpretation, in other words, what we think it says. What is being implied here is that one's own interpretation (what he or she thinks the Bible says) is what it really says, and everyone else who has a different interpretation is not really reading the Bible for what it says.

Exception: It is possible that some difference can be very minute, exist in principle only, or made for emphasis, in which case the fallacy could be debatable.

> Coach: I don't want you to try to get the ball; I want you to GET the ball!

In practical usage, this means the same thing, but the effect could be motivating, especially in a non-argumentative context.

Tip: Replace the phrase, "I'll try" in your vocabulary with, "I'll do my best." While the same idea in practice, perceptually it means so much more.

References:

Smart, B. H. (1829). *Practical Logic,: Or Hints to Theme-writers: to which are Now Added Some Prefatory Remarks on Aristotelian Logic, with Particular Reference to a Late Work of Dr. Whatley's.* Whittaker, Treacher, & Company.

Double Standard

Description: Judging two situations by different standards when, in fact, you should be using the same standard. This is used in argumentation to unfairly support or reject an argument.

Logical Form:

> Person 1 makes claim X and gives reason Y.
>
> Person 2 makes claim Z and gives reason Y.
>
> Person 1 unfairly rejects reason Y, but only for claim Z and not claim X.

Example #1:

> *Husband: I forbid you to go to that male strip club! That is a completely inappropriate thing for a wife to do!*
>
> *Wife: What about when you went to the female strip club last year?*
>
> *Husband: That was just for fun, and besides, that's different.*

Explanation: The husband is holding his wife to a different standard without articulating the standard. Most people would also agree that the standard is unfair.

Example #2:

> *Catholic: I know St. Peter answers prayers because when I pray to him, my prayers are sometimes answered. When they are not, it is because St. Peter knows what is best for me.*
>
> *Protestant: Do you realize how foolish that sounds? You can say the same thing about praying to a mailbox.*
>
> *Catholic: How do you know God answers prayers?*
>
> *Protestant: Well... I... that's different.*

Explanation: It often occurs within religion where the standards applied to one religion or denomination to claim "truth" don't apply to arguments from other religions or denominations. In this example, the Protestant is demanding stronger "evidence" for the Catholic's claim than she would demand for herself explaining how God answers prayers.

Exception: The fallacy is in the fact that the standards *should* be the same, but sometimes there are legitimate different standards. For example, a president's remarks are held to a different standard than a reality television star's remarks.

Fun Fact: The default position is equal standards. One should not have to argue for this; the one claiming that standards are not equal has the *burden of proof*.

References:

This is a logical fallacy frequently used on the Internet. No academic sources could be found.

Ecological Fallacy

(also known as: ecological inference fallacy)

Description: The interpretation of statistical data where inferences about the nature of individuals are deduced from inference for the group to which those individuals belong.

Logical Form:

> *Group X has characteristic Y.*
>
> *Person 1 is in group X.*
>
> *Therefore, person 1 has characteristic Y.*

Example #1:

> *Men score better on math than women do. Jerry is a man. Therefore, Jerry is better at math than Sylvia, who is a woman.*

Explanation: The fact that men score better on math than women is a group generalization. This does not mean that any individual man will score better than any individual woman on math. Educated guesses could be made if we knew more about the statistics. For example, if we just knew that men scored an average of 8% higher than women, we could not even say that any given man is likely to be better at math than any given woman. This is because there could be what is referred to as an *uneven distribution*, that is, there could be a small group of women who are really bad at math or a small group of men who are really good at math that throws off the curve.

Example #2: A study was done recently showing that church attendance was positively correlated with marriage longevity, that is, those couples who attended church together more often were more likely to stay married. This really should not be a surprise considering the general view of divorce within religion. What this does not mean is that any given couple who does not attend church is more likely to get divorced than any given couple that does attend church.

Explanation: To make this claim, we would need more information on the raw data used. Perhaps just religious fanatics who go to church daily have a practically non-existent divorce rate of say 2%. Then it is possible that those who never go to church have a lower divorce rate than those who do go to church every Sunday, but because of the fanatics, the distribution is not evenly distributed.

Exception: It is not unreasonable to make a probabilistic claim about any given member of a group if the data warrants such a claim. For example, if 999 jellybeans in a jar are red and one is green, we can say that any given jellybean in the jar is 99.9% likely to be red.

Fun Fact: Although this is a statistical fallacy, it is commonly extended to everyday situations. If you don't mind getting into statistics a bit, understanding statistical fallacies could improve one's overall reasoning ability.

References:

Babbie, E. R. (2016). *The Basics of Social Research*. Cengage Learning.

Etymological Fallacy

Description: The assumption that the present-day meaning of a word should be/is similar to the historical meaning. This fallacy ignores the evolution of language and heart of linguistics. This fallacy is usually committed when one finds the historical meaning of a word more palatable or conducive to his or her argument. This is a more specific form of the *appeal to definition*.

Logical Form:

X is defined as Y.

X used to be defined as Z.

Therefore, X means Z.

Example #1:

> Elba: I can't believe the art critic said my artwork is awful!
>
> Rowena: He must have meant it in the old sense of the word —that your artwork inspired awe!
>
> Elba: Yes! That makes sense now!

Explanation: "Awful" did once mean "to inspire awe," but there are very few, if any, people who continue to use the term in this way. Just because it makes her feel better, it cannot be assumed.

Example #2:

> Steve: I think it is fantastic that you and Sylvia are getting married!
>
> Chuck: I cannot believe you think my getting married only exists in my imagination! That is what fantastic means, after all.

Explanation: Yes, it is true "fantastic" was once most commonly used as existing only in the imagination, but common use of this word has a very different definition.

Exception: If a bogus, "modern," definition is made up by a questionable source, that won't make all other sources "historical."

Tip: Don't call a housewife a "hussy" even though the word "hussy" comes from the word "housewife" and used to refer to the mistress of a household, not the disreputable woman it refers to today. They don't like that.

References:

Wilson, K. G. (1993). *The Columbia Guide to Standard American English*. Columbia University Press.

Equivocation

(also known as: doublespeak)

Description: Using an ambiguous term in more than one sense, thus making an argument misleading.

Logical Form:

> *Term X is used to mean Y in the premise.*
>
> *Term X is used to mean Z in the conclusion.*

Example #1:

> *I want to have myself a merry little Christmas, but I refuse to do as the song suggests and make the yuletide gay. I don't think sexual preference should have anything to do with enjoying the holiday.*

Explanation: The word, "gay" is meant to be in light spirits, joyful, and merry, not in the homosexual sense.

Example #2:

> *The priest told me I should have faith.*
>
> *I have faith that my son will do well in school this year.*
>
> *Therefore, the priest should be happy with me.*

Explanation: The term "faith" used by the priest, was in the religious sense of believing in God without sufficient evidence, which is different from having "faith" in your son in which years of good past performance leads to the "faith" you might have in your son.

Exception: Equivocation works great when deliberate attempts at humor are being made.

Tip: When you suspect equivocation, substitute the word with the same definition for all uses and see if it makes sense.

References:

Parry, W. T., & Hacker, E. A. (n.d.). *Aristotelian Logic*. SUNY Press.

Exclusive Premises

(also known as: fallacy of exclusive premises)

Description: A standard form categorical syllogism that has two negative premises either in the form of "no X are Y" or "some X are not Y."

Logical Forms:

No X are Y.

Some Y are not Z.

Therefore, some Z are not X.

No X are Y.

No Y are Z.

Therefore, no Z are X.

Example #1:

No kangaroos are MMA fighters.

Some MMA fighters are not Mormons.

Therefore, some Mormons are not kangaroos.

Example #2:

No animals are insects.

Some insects are not dogs.

Therefore, some dogs are not animals.

Example #3:

No animals are insects.

No insects are dogs.

Therefore, no dogs are animals.

Explanation: Remember why fallacies are so dangerous: because they appear to be good reasoning. The conclusion in example #1 makes sense, but it does not follow logically—it is an invalid argument. Based on the first two premises, there is no way logically to deduce that conclusion. Now, look at examples #2 and #3. We use the same logical form of the argument, committing the same fallacy, but by changing the terms it is much more clear that something went wrong somewhere, and it did. This kind of argument, the *categorical syllogism*, cannot have two negative premises and still be valid.

Just because the conclusion appears true, it does not mean the argument is valid (or strong, in the case of an informal argument).

Tip: Learn to recognize the forms of formal fallacies, and you will easily spot invalid formal arguments.

References:

Goodman, M. F. (1993). *First Logic*. University Press of America.

Existential Fallacy

(also known as: existential instantiation)

Description: A formal logical fallacy, which is committed when a categorical syllogism employs two universal premises ("all") to arrive at a particular ("some") conclusion.

In a valid categorical syllogism, if the two premises are universal, then the conclusion *must* be universal, as well.

The reasoning behind this fallacy becomes clear when you use classes without any members, and the conclusion states that there are members of this class—which is wrong.

Logical Form:

All X are Y.

All Z are X.

Therefore, some Z are Y.

Example #1:

All babysitters have pimples.

All babysitter club members are babysitters.

Therefore, some babysitter club members have pimples.

Example #2:

All forest creatures live in the woods.

All leprechauns are forest creatures.

Therefore, some leprechauns live in the woods.

Explanation: In both examples, the fallacy is committed because we have two universal premises and a particular conclusion, but our example #1 conclusion makes sense, no? **Just because the conclusion *might* be true, does not mean the logic used to produce it, was valid.** This is how tests like SAT's and GRE's screw us over and, technically, in the above example, *all* babysitter club members have pimples, not just *some*.

Now, look at the second example. Same form, but when we use classes that obviously (to most people) have no members (leprechauns), we can see that it results in a conclusion that is false.

Exception: There actually *is* an exception to this formal fallacy —if we are strictly using Aristotelian logic, then it is permissible because apparently, Aristotle did not see a problem with presupposing that classes have members even when we are not explicitly told that they do.

Tip: When making a claim, be as precise as possible in the scope of the claim. Don't just say "men are bastards," say "*some* men are bastards," or better yet, "12.62% of men are bastards."

References:

Goodman, M. F. (1993). *First Logic*. University Press of America.

Extended Analogy

Description: Suggesting that because two things are alike in some way and one of those things is like something else, then both things must be like that "something else."

In essence, the *ad Hitlerum fallacy* is an extended analogy because it is the attempt to associate someone with Hitler's psychotic behavior by way of a usually much more benign connection.

Logical Form:

> *A is like B in some way.*
>
> *C is like B in a different way.*
>
> *Therefore, A is like C.*

Example #1:

> *Jennie: Anyone who doesn't have a problem with slaughtering animals for food, should not, in principle, have a problem with an advanced alien race slaughtering us for food.*
>
> *Carl: Fruitarians, the crazy people who won't eat anything except for fruit that fell from the tree, are also against slaughtering animals for food. Are you crazy like them?*

Explanation: Although I don't think I can ever give up delicious chicken, Jennie does make a good point via a valid analogy. Ignoring Carl's attempt to *poison the well* by using *loaded language* he is, by *extended analogy*, claiming the "craziness" of the fruitarians must be shared by her, as well, since they both are alike because they share a view on using animals for food.

Example #2:

> *Science often gets things wrong. It wasn't until the early 20th century when particle physics came along that scientists realized that the atom wasn't the smallest particle in existence. So perhaps science will soon realize that it is wrong*

about the age of the universe, the non-existence of a global flood, evolution, and every other science fact that contradicts the Bible when read literally.

Explanation: To see this fallacy, let's put it in the logical form, using just the evolution claim:

P1. Thinking the atom was the smallest particle was a mistake of science.

P2. Evolution is also a mistake of science.

C. Therefore, science thinking the atom was the smallest particle is like science thinking evolution is true.

Premise two (P2) should jump out as a bold assumption, although not fallacious. Remember, the premises don't have to be true for the argument to be valid, but if both premises were true, does the conclusion (C) follow? No, because of the *extended fallacy.* The reason is if evolution were false it would not be for the same reason that science thought the atom was the smallest particle. Science "was wrong" in that case because it did not have access to the whole truth due to discoveries yet to be made at the time. If evolution were wrong, then all the discoveries that have been made, the facts that have been established, the foundation of many sciences that have led to countless advances in medicine, would all be dead wrong. This would be a mistake of unimaginable proportions and consequences that would unravel the very core of scientific understanding and inquiry.

Exception: If one can show evidence that the connection between all the subjects is the same, it is not fallacious.

It is crazy to think that carrots have feelings.

It is crazy to think that cows have feelings.

Therefore, vegetarians are just as crazy as fruitarians[5].

---

[5] For the record, I certainly do not think vegetarians are crazy, and I don't even think fruitarians are crazy. I certainly believe animals have feelings. Carrots? Not so much.

Tip: Don't call people crazy—leave that kind of psychological assessment for the licensed professionals. You can call them, "nutjobs."

References:

This is a logical fallacy frequently used on the Internet. No academic sources could be found.

Fact-to-Fiction Fallacy

Description: Attempting to support a narrative or argument with facts that don't support the narrative or argument. The distinguishing characteristic of the *fact-to-fiction fallacy* is the accusation that those who reject your conclusion are rejecting the facts.

Logical Form:

Facts are stated and made clear they are facts.

Therefore, some conclusion is true that is not supported by the facts.

If you reject the conclusion, you are rejecting the facts.

Example #1:

FACT: On average, 150,000 people die every day around the world. It is crazy to panic about a virus that, at its peak, was killing 8,000 people per day. But what else can be expected from a moron like you who rejects facts?

Explanation: It is a fact that, on average, 150,000 people die every day around the world. It is also a fact that at its peak in the spring of 2020, the Coronavirus was killing about 8,000 people per day. What hasn't been established is what justifies "panic." "Panic," or perhaps more accurately "serious concern," can be justified in many other ways besides the total number of historical deaths. Given this, it doesn't follow that it is "crazy to panic." Further, saying or writing "FACT," followed by an accusation of rejecting the fact, makes this more fallacious than a standard *non-sequitur*.

Example #2: In May of 2020, it was common to hear accusations of "anti-science" hurled at people who wanted the country to reopen after being closed due to the Covid-19 pandemic.

Explanation: "Anti-science" is similar to "anti-fact." There are many facts that point to ways the virus could spread, and reopening the country would unquestionably increase the odds that the virus would spread. Science doesn't make value judgments, however. For example, would an extra X number of deaths per week justify people getting back to work? Science informs political decisions such as these; it doesn't answer them. It can be perfectly consistent to agree with the science (facts) and still reject the argument that we are reopening the country "too soon."

Exception: If there is no accusation of rejecting facts, we might have a *non-sequitur*, but not a *fact-to-fiction fallacy*. It is not unreasonable to state a fact such as the 150,000 deaths per day stat, then ask why we are taking the actions we are for just 8000 deaths? These kinds of questions are likely to lead to answers that expose the nuance of the arguments.

Tip: Be careful not to read too much into facts. Our minds tend to "connect the dots" in order to support the narratives we already accept.

References:

This is an original logical fallacy named by the author.

Failure to Elucidate
obscurum per obscurius

Description: When the definition is made more difficult to understand than the word or concept being defined.

Logical Form:

Person 1 makes a claim.

Person 2 asks for clarification of the claim, or a term being used.

Person 1 restates the claim or term in a more confusing way.

Example #1:

Tracy: I don't like him because of his aura.

TJ: What do you mean by that?

Tracy: I mean that he is projecting a field of subtle, luminous radiation that is negative.

Explanation: This is such a common fallacy, yet rarely detected as one. Usually, out of fear of embarrassment, we accept confusing definitions as legitimate elucidations, that is, we pretend the term that was defined is now clear to us. What exactly is the field? How is it detected? Are there negative and positive ones? How do we know?

Example #2:

Linda: We live in a spirit-filled world; I am certain of that.

Rob: What is a "spirit"?

Linda: A noncorporeal substance.

Explanation: Many times, we fool ourselves into thinking that because we know other words for the term, we better understand what the term *actually represents*. The above example is an illustration of this. We can redefine, "spirit" as many times as we like, but our understanding of what a spirit actually is will still be lacking.

Assuming we did not really understand what was meant by "spirit," the definition, "noncorporeal substance" might or might not shed any light on what is meant by the term. In this case, it might be more clear now that Linda is not referring to alcoholic beverages, but conceptually, what is a non-physical substance? If "substance" is defined as being physical matter or material, does a "non-physical" substance even make sense?

We fallaciously reason that we now understand what the term represents when, in fact, we don't.

Exception: Some may actually just lack the vocabulary needed —this is not your fault, but you should do your best to attempt to elucidate using words understandable to your audience.

Tip: Failure to elucidate often results in endless and pointless debates. Take, for example, the common position that guns are not a problem in the USA. We often see this position presented as an unhelpful meme, such as "Guns don't kill people, people kill people." What this needs is a "therefore," followed by a conclusion. For example, "Guns don't kill people, people kill people. Therefore, we should be focusing more on what makes people use guns violently and less on just banning the use of guns." This is very different from, "Guns don't kill people, people kill people. Therefore, anyone should be allowed to carry any kind of gun with no restrictions." Don't waste your time imagining the argument or point the other person is trying to make—ask for clarification.

References:

Cederblom, J., & Paulsen, D. (2011). *Critical Reasoning* (7 edition). Boston, MA: Wadsworth Publishing.

Fake Precision

(also known as: over-precision, false precision, misplaced precision, spurious accuracy)

Description: Using implausibly precise statistics to give the appearance of truth and certainty, or using a negligible difference in data to draw incorrect inferences.

Logical Forms:

Statistic X is unnecessarily precise and has probability A of being true.

Statistic X is interpreted as having probability A+B as being true.

Statistic X represents position A.

Statistic Y represents position B.

Statistic Y is insignificantly different from statistic X.

Position A is seen as significantly different from position B.

Example #1:

Tour Guide: This fossil right here is 120,000,003 years old.

Guest: How do you know that?

Tour Guide: Because when I started working here three years ago, the experts did some radiometric dating and told me that it was 120,000,000 years old.

Explanation: Although more of a comedy skit than anything else, this demonstrates the fallacious reasoning by the tour guide in her assumption that the dates given to her were precise to the year.

Example #2: The difference between first and second in many cases is negligible, statistically, yet we give those differences artificial meaning. Who was the *second* person to walk on the moon... just minutes after Neil Armstrong? Does anyone remember who the *second* fastest man in the world is, even though he might come in .01 seconds after the first place winner?

Explanation: We often artificially assign significant meaning to tiny statistical differences. It is a fallacy when we infer that the first place runner is "much faster" than the second place runner, even though the difference is .01 seconds.

Exception: In reality, tiny statistical differences can have a significant impact, regardless of our interpretation. For example, jumping out of the way of a car .01 seconds too late can mean the difference between a close call, and death.

Tip: Don't confuse fake precision with real performance.

References:

Huff, D. (1993). *How to Lie with Statistics* (Reissue edition). New York: W. W. Norton & Company.

Fallacy of (the) Undistributed Middle

(also known as: maldistributed middle, undistributed middle term)

Description: A formal fallacy in a categorical syllogism where the *middle term*, or the term that does not appear in the conclusion, is not distributed to the other two terms.

Logical Form:

> All A's are C's.
>
> All B's are C's.
>
> Therefore, all A's are B's.

Example #1:

> All lions are animals.
>
> All cats are animals.
>
> Therefore, all lions are cats.

Explanation: We are tricked because the conclusion makes sense, so out of laziness we accept the argument, but the argument is invalid, and by plugging in new terms, like in the next example, we can see why.

Example #2:

> All ghosts are imaginary.
>
> All unicorns are imaginary.
>
> Therefore, all ghosts are unicorns.

Explanation: While there may be ghosts that are unicorns, it does not follow from the premises: the only thing the premises tell us about ghosts and unicorns is that they are both imaginary—we have no information how they are related to each other.

Fun Fact: I have it on good authority that unicorns do poop rainbows.

References:

Goodman, M. F. (1993). *First Logic*. University Press of America.

Fallacy of Composition

(also known as: composition fallacy, exception fallacy, faulty induction)

Description: Inferring that something is true of the whole from the fact that it is true of some part of the whole. This is the opposite of the *fallacy of division*.

Logical Form:

> A is part of B.
>
> A has property X.
>
> Therefore, B has property X.

Example #1:

> Each brick in that building weighs less than a pound. Therefore, the building weighs less than a pound.

Example #2:

> Hydrogen is not wet. Oxygen is not wet. Therefore, water (H_2O) is not wet.

Example #3:

> Your brain is made of molecules. Molecules are not the source of consciousness. Therefore, your brain cannot be the source of consciousness.

Explanation: I included three examples that demonstrate this fallacy from the very obvious to the less obvious, but equally as flawed. In the first example, it is obvious because weight is cumulative. In the second example, we know that water is wet, but we only experience the property of wetness when the molecules are combined and in large scale. This introduces the concept of *emergent properties*, which when ignored, tends to promote *magical thinking*. The final example is a common argument made for a supernatural explanation for consciousness. On the surface, it is difficult to imagine a collection of molecules resulting in something like consciousness because we are focusing on the properties of the parts (molecules) and not the whole system, which incorporates emergence, motion, the use of energy, temperature (vibration), order, and other *relational properties*.

Exception: If the whole is very close to the similarity of the parts, then more assumptions can be made from the parts to the whole. For example, if we open a small bag of potato chips and discover that the first one is delicious, it is not fallacious to conclude that the whole snack (all the chips, minus the bag) will be just as delicious, but we cannot say the same for one of those giant family size bags because most of us would be hurling after about 10 minutes of our chip-eating frenzy.

Tip: It is worth a few minutes of your time to research the topic of "emergence."

References:

Goodman, M. F. (1993). *First Logic*. University Press of America.

Fallacy of Division

(also known as: false division, faulty deduction, division fallacy)

Description: Inferring that something is true of one or more of the parts from the fact that it is true of the whole. This is the opposite of the *fallacy of composition*.

Logical Form:

A is part of B.

B has property X.

Therefore, A has property X.

Example #1:

His house is about half the size of most houses in the neighborhood; therefore, his doors must all be about 3 1/2 feet high.

Explanation: The size of one's house almost certainly does not mean that the doors will be smaller, especially by the same proportions. The size of the whole (the house) is not directly related to the size of every part of the house.

Example #2:

I heard that the Catholic Church was involved in a sex scandal cover-up. Therefore, my 102-year-old Catholic neighbor, who frequently attends Church, is guilty as well!

Explanation: While it is possible that the 102-year-old granny is guilty for some things, like being way too liberal with her perfume, she would not be guilty in any sex scandals just by her association with the Church alone. Granted, it can be argued that Granny's financial support of the Church makes her morally complicit, but it is clear her "crimes" are in a different category than those behind the cover-ups.

Exception: When a part of the whole has a property that, by definition, causes the part to take on that property.

My 102-year-old neighbor is a card-carrying member of an organization of thugs that requires its members to kick babies. Therefore, my neighbor is a thug... and she wears way too much perfume.

Tip: Review the *fallacy of composition* and see if you understand the difference well-enough to explain it to someone.

References:

Goodman, M. F. (1993). *First Logic*. University Press of America.

Fallacy of Every and All

Description: When an argument contains both universal quantifiers and existential quantifiers (all, some, none, every) with different meanings, and the order of the quantifiers is reversed. This is a specific form of *equivocation*.

Logical Form:

Quantifier X then quantifier Y.

Therefore, quantifier Y then quantifier X.

Example #1:

Everyone should do something nice for someone. I am someone, so everyone should do something nice for me!

Explanation: We have a reversal of the quantifiers.

Everyone (quantifier X) should do something nice for someone (quantifier Y). I am someone (quantifier Y), so everyone (quantifier X) should do something nice for me!

Assuming one accepts the premise that "everyone should do something nice for someone," the word "someone" in that sentence means "some person or another" whereas in the second sentence it means "a specific person." By equivocating the meanings of "someone," we appear to be making a strong argument when in fact we are not.

Example #2:

Everyone loves someone.

I am someone.

Therefore, everyone loves me!

Explanation: "Someone" (quantifier X) referred to "any given person" in the first premise. In the second premise, "someone" is referring specifically to me. In the conclusion, we have a reversal of the quantifiers as they were presented in the premises.

Tip: It really is a good idea to do something nice for someone.

References:

Salmon, M. H. (2012). *Introduction to Logic and Critical Thinking.* Cengage Learning.

Fallacy of Four Terms
quaternio terminorum

(also known as: ambiguous middle term)

Description: This fallacy occurs in a categorical syllogism when the syllogism has four terms rather than the requisite three (in a sense, it cannot be a categorical syllogism to begin with!) If it takes on this form, it is invalid. The *equivocation fallacy* can also fit this fallacy because the same term is used in two different ways, making four distinct terms, although only appearing to be three.

Logical Form: There are many possible forms, this is one example:

All X are Y.

All A are B.

Therefore, all X are B.

Example #1:

All cats are felines.

All dogs are canines.

Therefore, all cats are canines.

Explanation: When you add in a fourth term to a categorical syllogism that can only have three terms to be logically valid, we get nonsense—or at least an invalid argument.

Example #2:

All Greek gods are mythical.

All modern day gods are real.

Therefore, all Greek gods are real.

Explanation: Again, nonsense. If we take away one of the terms, we end up with a valid syllogism:

All Greek gods are mythical.

All mythical gods don't really exist.

Therefore, all Greek gods don't really exist.

Fun Fact: Greek gods may not exist, but Greek yogurt does.

References:

Bunnin, N., & Yu, J. (2008). *The Blackwell Dictionary of Western Philosophy*. John Wiley & Sons.

Fallacy of Opposition

Description: Asserting that those who disagree with you must be wrong and not thinking straight, primarily based on the fact that they are the opposition.

Logical Form:

Person 1 is asserting X.

Person 1 is the opposition.

Therefore, X must be wrong.

Example #1:

President Trump said that he was proud of the children who participated in this year's Special Olympics. Those kids are a bunch of losers.

Explanation: This is an extreme example of a very real example that we have all seen since around early 2016. Those who passionately hate Trump, reflexively disagree with everything he says and does, associating the truth of his statement with the feelings they have for him. This is not reasonable thinking.

Example #2:

The Democrats support more aggressive gun control laws. Can you believe they want to deny repeat offenders and those on the terrorist watch list their rights?

Explanation: Very often we see support for reasonable policies rejected based on the party that proposes such policies. We know this because research has been done in this area.

Exception: There might be a situation where your opposition must say things that are demonstrably wrong, or they wouldn't be your opposition. For example,

Only those who disagree with X are my opposition.

X is demonstrably right.

Bill is my opposition.

Therefore, Bill is wrong.

It seems strange to suggest that because Bill is my opposition, he is wrong, but this is necessarily true if we hold that "Only those who disagree with X are my opposition" and "X is demonstrably right." This wouldn't make logical sense if we didn't set the conditions so that anyone belonging to the group "opposition" would be wrong.

Tip: Rejecting information from an interlocutor known to lie, might be a reasonable heuristic, but it is not a good critical thinking technique.

References:

This is a logical fallacy frequently used on the Internet. No academic sources could be found.

False Attribution

Description: Appealing to an irrelevant, unqualified, unidentified, biased, or fabricated source in support of an argument (modern usage). Historical use of this fallacy was in the attribution of "religious" or "spiritual" experiences to outside "higher" sources rather than internal, psychological processes (see *fantasy projection*).

Logical Form:

> *Claim X is made.*
>
> *Source Y, a fake or unverifiable source, is used to verify claim X.*
>
> *Therefore, claim X is true.*

Example #1:

> *But professor, I got all these facts from a program I saw on TV once... I don't remember the name of it though.*

Explanation: Without a credible, verifiable source, the argument or claim being made is very weak.

Example #2:

> *I had this book that proved that leprechauns are real and have been empirically verified by scientists, but I lost it. I forgot the name of it as well—and who the author was.*

Explanation: A story of "this book" hardly can serve as proof of an event as potentially significant as the discovery of leprechauns that have been empirically verified by scientists. While it might be the case that the person telling this story really does remember reading a convincing argument, it very well could be the case that this person is fabricating this book—it sure sounds like it. In either case, it is fallacious to accept the claim that leprechauns are real and have been empirically verified by scientists based on this argument.

Tip: Don't falsify facts. If you get caught lying, you will almost certainly lose the argument, even if you are right.

References:

The Journal of Philosophy. (1918). Journal of Philosophy, Incorporated.

False Conversion

(also known as: illicit conversion, [illicit] inductive conversion)

New Terminology:

Type "A" Logical Forms: A proposition or premise that uses the word, "all" or "every" (e.g., All P are Q)

Type "E" Logical Forms: A proposition or premise that uses the word, "none" or "no" (e.g., No P are Q)

Type "I" Logical Forms: A proposition or premise that uses the word, "some" (e.g., Some P are Q)

Type "O" Logical Forms: A proposition or premise that uses the terms, "some/not" (e.g., Some P are not Q)

Description: The formal fallacy where the subject and the predicate terms of the proposition are switched (*conversion*) in the conclusion, in a proposition that uses "all" in its premise (type "A" forms), or "some/not" (type "O" forms).

Logical Form:

All P are Q.

Therefore, all Q are P.

Some P are not Q.

Therefore, some Q are not P.

Example #1:

All Hollywood Squares contestants are bad actors.

Therefore, all bad actors are Hollywood Squares contestants.

Example #2:

> *Some people in the film industry do not win Oscars.*
>
> *Therefore, some Oscar winners are not people in the film industry.*

Explanation: It does not follow logically that just because all *Hollywood Squares* contestants are bad actors that all bad actors actually make it on *Hollywood Squares*. Same form problem with the second example—but we used "some" and "are not."

Exception: None, but remember that type "E" and type "I" forms can use conversion and remain valid.

> *No teachers are psychos.*
>
> *Therefore, no psychos are teachers.*

Tip: Remember that formal fallacies are often obscured by unstructured rants. Creating a formal argument from such rants is both an art and a science.

References:

Welton, J. (1896). *A Manual of Logic.* W. B. Clive.

False Dilemma

(also known as: all-or-nothing fallacy, false dichotomy [form of], the either-or fallacy, either-or reasoning, fallacy of false choice, fallacy of false alternatives, black-and-white thinking, the fallacy of exhaustive hypotheses, bifurcation, excluded middle, no middle ground, polarization)

Description: When only two choices are presented yet more exist, or a spectrum of possible choices exists between two extremes. False dilemmas are usually characterized by "either this or that" language, but can also be characterized by omissions of choices. Another variety is the *false trilemma*, which is when three choices are presented when more exist.

Logical Forms:

Either X or Y is true.

Either X, Y, or Z is true.

Example (two choices):

You are either with God or against him.

Explanation: As Obi-Wan Kenobi so eloquently puts it in *Star Wars episode III*, "Only a Sith deals in absolutes!" There are also those who simply don't believe there is a God to be either with or against.

Example (omission):

I thought you were a good person, but you weren't at church today.

Explanation: The assumption here is that bad people don't go to church. Of course, good people exist who don't go to church, and good church-going people could have had a really good reason not to be in church—like a hangover from the swingers' gathering the night before.

Exception: There may be cases when the number of options really is limited. For example, if an ice cream man just has chocolate and vanilla left, it would be a waste of time insisting he has mint chocolate chip.

It is also not a fallacy if other options exist, but you are not offering other options as a possibility. For example:

Mom: Billy, it's time for bed.

Billy: Can I stay up and watch a movie?

Mom: You can either go to bed or stay up for another 30 minutes and read.

Billy: That is a false dilemma!

Mom: No, it's not. Here, read Bo's book and you will see why.

Billy: This is freaky, our exact conversation is used as an example in this book!

Tip: Be conscious of how many times you are presented with false dilemmas, and how many times you present yourself with false dilemmas.

Variation: Staying true to the definitions, the *false dilemma* is different from the *false dichotomy* in that a dilemma implies two equally unattractive options whereas a dichotomy generally comprises two opposites. This is a fine point, however, and is generally ignored in common usage.

References:

Moore, B. N., & Parker, R. (1989). *Critical thinking: evaluating claims and arguments in everyday life.* Mayfield Pub. Co.

False Effect

Description: Claiming that the cause is true or false based on what we know about the effect in a claim of causality that has not been properly established. The cause is often an implied claim, and it is this claim that is being deemed true or false, right or wrong.

Logical Forms:

X apparently causes Y.

Y is wrong.

Therefore, X is wrong.

X apparently causes Y.

Y is right.

Therefore, X is right.

Example #1:

> *Mom: Watching TV that close will make you go blind, so move back!*
>
> *Jonny: That is B.S., Mom. Sorry, I am not moving.*

Explanation: The *false effect* of watching TV too closely is going blind. For the most part, the threat that you will "ruin" your eyesight is an old wives' tale. Almost certainly, nobody is going blind from sitting too close unless they ram their eyes into the protruding knobs. Regardless of the *false effect* (i.e., blindness), watching TV too closely (the cause) has been shown to have some adverse effects on vision, so concluding that one shouldn't "move back" from sitting too close is fallacious.

Example #2:

> *The Church used to claim that giving 10% of your income to the Church will free a child's soul from Limbo into Heaven, so clearly giving money to the Church is a scam!*

Explanation: Centuries ago, the Church did accept "contributions" to get loved ones out of "Limbo," and it wasn't until 2007 when the Church made it clear that Limbo was a theory and not an official doctrine of the Church, separating the Church from that belief. As for the argument, the *false effect* of "freeing a child's soul from Limbo" does not warrant the conclusion that giving your money to the Church is a scam.

Example #3:

> *The presence of police at protests cause an escalation of violence. It was the case that at the protest last night attended by uniformed police, there was an escalation of violence. Therefore, police should not be at protests.*

Explanation: We begin with a causal claim: The presence of police at protests cause an escalation of violence (X apparently causes Y). This is just a claim at this point and has not been established, but because there was an escalation of violence (Y is right), it is concluded that the implied claim (police should not be at protests) is true (therefore, X is right). In reality, we don't know what caused the escalation of violence, so we cannot conclude anything about the claim. In addition, we are assuming we have agreed to the condition:

> *If the presence of police at protests cause an escalation of violence, then there should be no presence of police at protests.*

To which we may not want to agree if we reason that the presence of police at protests results in a greater good.

Exception: It can be difficult to parse the claim that is being said to be wrong or right, in which case the causal link might be what is really being rejected. In our first example, it is fallacious to conclude that there is no reason we shouldn't watch TV close up. We parsed this from "Watching TV that close will make you go blind." If one is claiming that the causal claim is what is false after showing the effect to be false, then there is no fallacy.

> *Mom: Watching TV that close will make you go blind, so move back!*

> *Jonny: That is B.S., Mom. Watching TV too close does NOT make someone go blind.*

Fun Fact: This fallacy is different from the *false cause* fallacy (listed under *questionable cause*).

References:

This is a logical fallacy frequently used on the Internet. No academic sources could be found.

False Equivalence

Description: An argument or claim in which two completely opposing arguments appear to be logically equivalent when in fact they are not. The confusion is often due to one shared characteristic between two or more items of comparison in the argument that is way off in the order of magnitude, oversimplified, or just that important additional factors have been ignored.

Logical Form:

Thing 1 and thing 2 both share characteristic A.

Therefore, things 1 and 2 are equal.

Example #1:

President Petutti ordered a military strike that killed many civilians. He is no different than any other mass murder and he belongs in prison!

Explanation: Both president Petutti and a mass murder share the characteristic that something they did resulted in the death of civilians. However, the circumstances, the level of responsibility, and the intent are significantly different for the president than the typical mass murder and ignoring these factors is unreasonable, thus makes the argument fallacious.

Example #2: Using the second amendment as justification to allow civilians to own nuclear submarines.

Explanation: In this case, the first "thing" is the weapon as understood at the time the second amendment was passed. The second "thing" of comparison is the nuclear submarine, also a weapon, but one of significantly different magnitude. This example also introduces the difference between a legal justification and an argumentative one (see *appeal to the law*).

Exception: Like most fallacies, this is one of degree rather than kind. The order of magnitude can be debated. Some may exaggerate this order of magnitude claiming a fallacy where it would be unreasonable to do so.

Tip: Listen and read carefully. Often, people will make analogies and others will interpret them as claims of equivalence.

References:

This is a logical fallacy frequently used on the Internet. No academic sources could be found.

Fantasy Projection

Description: Confusing subjective experiences, usually very emotionally charged, with objective reality, then suggesting or demanding that others accept the subjective experience as objective reality.

New Terminology: In this context, *subjective experience* is the way one interprets some external stimuli. *Objective reality* is independent of our interpretations; it is a collection of facts about the world we all share.

Logical Form:

> Person 1 has subjective experience X.
>
> Person 1 incorrectly believes that experience X represents objective reality.
>
> Therefore, person 1 insists that others accept that X represents objective reality.

Example #1:

> Freddie: People are mean to me wherever I go. It is clear that we live in a cruel world with people who are mostly nasty. If you don't see that, something is wrong with you!

Explanation: Perhaps people are mean to Freddie because Freddie is mean to others, and it's Freddie's behavior that is resulting in the "mean" behaviors of others (this is known as a *self-fulfilling prophecy*). Freddie is projecting his experience, which is unique to him, onto the world at large. He is insisting that other people see humanity the way he does. We don't deny that Freddie is experiencing the world in the way he is; we just don't accept that Freddie's experience represents objective reality. To accurately determine if the world is, indeed, made up of "people who are mostly nasty," we would need to conduct research using the scientific method.

Example #2:

> I feel that we are all surrounded by Narggles. These are spiritual beings who help us through life. We know they exist

because they are the ones that give us the confidence to move forward in a decision.

Explanation: Ignoring the circular reasoning (how we "know" Narggles exist), one person's fantasy might be their own reality, but not everyone else's.

Exception: One can argue that one's subjective experience is part of objective reality as long as they don't insist that you interpret the stimuli the same way they did.

> *Freddie: It is a fact that this world consists of people who feel like most people they interact with are mean to them.*

Fun Fact: Everyone knows Kerplunkers, not Narggles, are spiritual beings who help us through life.

References:

This is a logical fallacy frequently used on the Internet. No academic sources could be found.

Far-Fetched Hypothesis

Description: Offering a bizarre (far-fetched) hypothesis as the correct explanation without first ruling out more mundane explanations.

Logical Form:

> *Far-fetched hypothesis is proposed.*
>
> *Mundane, probable hypotheses are ignored.*

Example #1:

> *Seth: How did my keys get in your coat pocket?*
>
> *Terrence: Honestly, I don't know, but I have a theory. Last night, a unicorn was walking through the neighborhood. The local leprechauns did not like this intrusion, so they dispatched the fairies to make the unicorn go away. The fairies took your keys and dropped them on the unicorn,*

*scaring the unicorn back from where he came. The fairies
then returned your keys but accidentally put them in my coat
pocket.*

Explanation: When creating a hypothesis, there are infinite possibilities, but far fewer probabilities. Skipping over the probabilities is fallacious reasoning. We should start with the fact that Terrence is lying, then go from there. There are many theories between lying and the mythical creature caper theory.

Example #2:

*The rainbow represents a special covenant or promise of
protection from another worldwide flood. The rainbow's
appearance to Noah may have been its first occurrence in the
sky (Gen. 9:8-17). Typical raindrops of sufficient size to cause
a rainbow require atmosphere instability. Prior to the Flood,
weather conditions were probably very stable. (Donald B.
DeYoung, Weather and The Bible, Grand Rapids, Eerdmans,
1992, pp. 112,113).*

Explanation: This is part of an attempt by a young-earth creationist to make Genesis a literal, historical fact. Of course, the mundane explanation is that Genesis is not meant to be taken as a literal, historical fact—it is not meant to be read as a science book.

Exception: If mundane explanations can be ruled out first, usually through falsification, then we can move on to more bizarre hypotheses.

Fun Fact: The *Principle of Parsimony* states that the most acceptable explanation of an occurrence, phenomenon, or event is the simplest, involving the fewest entities, assumptions, or changes.

References:

Dennett, D. C. (2006). *Breaking the Spell: Religion as a Natural Phenomenon*. Penguin.

Faulty Comparison

(also known as: bad comparison, false comparison, inconsistent comparison [form of])

Description: Comparing one thing to another that is really not related, in order to make one thing look more or less desirable than it really is.

Logical Form:

X is different from Y in way Z.

It is unreasonable to compare X to Y in way Z.

Therefore, X is seen as more/less favorable.

Example #1:

Broccoli has significantly less fat than the leading candy bar!

Explanation: While both broccoli and candy bars can be considered snacks, comparing the two in terms of fat content and ignoring the significant difference in taste, leads to the false comparison.

Example #2:

Religion may have been wrong about a few things, but science has been wrong about many more things!

Explanation: We are comparing a *method of knowledge* (science) to a *system of belief* (faith), which is not known for revising itself based on new evidence. Even when it does, the "wrongs" are blamed on human interpretation. Science is all about improving ideas to get closer to the truth, and, in some cases, completely throwing out theories that have been proven wrong. Furthermore, the claims of religion are virtually all *unfalsifiable*, thus cannot be proven wrong. Therefore, comparing religion and science on the basis of falsifiability is a faulty comparison.

Exception: One can argue what exactly is "really not related."

Variation: An *inconsistent comparison* is when something is compared to multiple things in different ways, giving the impression that what is being compared is far better or worse than it actually is. For example,

> Serial killer Ted Bundy wasn't so bad. He didn't kill children like Luis Garavito, he didn't kill nearly as many people as Hitler, and he is much kinder than Satan.

Tip: Comparisons of any kind almost always are flawed. Think carefully before you accept any kind of comparison as evidence.

References:

Dowden, B. H. (1993). *Logical Reasoning*. Bradley Dowden.

Gadarene Swine Fallacy

Description: The assumption that because an individual is not in formation with the group, that the individual must be the one off course. It is possible that the one who appears off course is the only one on the right course.

Logical Form:

> Person X stands out from the group.
>
> Therefore, person X is wrong.

Example #1:

> Why can't your daughter fall in line like the other girls?

Explanation: The assumption here is that the "other girls" are doing the right thing. This needs to be established or demonstrated through reason and evidence.

Example #2: Many people throughout history started revolutions by taking the morally right action when it was considered morally wrong or even illegal at the time. Consider Rosa Parks.

Exception: It is just as wrong to assume that the one is "out of formation" as it is to assume that all the rest must be "out of formation." While it might be statistically more probable that the one is out of formation, evidence should be sought before making any definitive claim.

Tip: Compare this to the *Galileo fallacy*. You will see that being the oddball neither makes you right nor wrong.

References:

Laing, R. D. (1990). *The Politics of Experience and The Bird of Paradise*. Penguin Books Limited.

Galileo Fallacy

(also known as: Galileo argument, Galileo defense, Galileo gambit, Galileo wannabe)

Description: The claim that because an idea is forbidden, prosecuted, detested, or otherwise mocked, it must be true, or should be given more credibility. This originates from Galileo Galilei's famous persecution by the Roman Catholic Church for his defense of heliocentrism when the commonly accepted belief at the time was an earth-centered universe.

Logical Form:

Claim X is made.

Claim X is ridiculous.

Person A argues that claim Y was seen as ridiculous at the time, and it turned out to be right.

Therefore, claim X is true (or should be given more credibility).

Example #1:

Lindi and Jonah claim that Elvis is still alive and living on the planet Hounddogian, in the constellation Bluesuede. When questioned about their odd beliefs, Lindi and Jonah *confidently reply, "You know, people thought Galileo was nuts, too."*

Explanation: Lindi and Jonah are making an extraordinary claim and offering no evidence to support their claim. They are using Galileo in an attempt to get the audience to doubt their skepticism about the claim.

Example #2:

> Sidney: I am mere weeks away from getting my time machine to work, at which time, I will go back to 1626 and buy Manhattan from the Native Americans before the Dutch West India Company gets their greedy hands on it. I'll be much more generous and give the Native Americans 70 guilders, not a measly 60.
>
> Pete: Is this the time travel kit you bought online for $99.99?
>
> Sidney: Go ahead and mock me. People mocked the Wright brothers too for wanting to fly like birds!

Explanation: Although Sidney did not use the exact example of Galileo, the fallacy is the same. Any reference to a similar story counts.

Exception: Using Galileo or similar success stories to serve as effective inspirational anecdotes to encourage people to reach outside their comfort zone is not fallacious. It does not mean, however, that because they succeeded, that everyone else will or even can.

Tip: Remember that for every Galileo, there are millions of cranks, quacks, and wackos, and statistically speaking, those who use the Galileo defense are one of the latter.

References:

This is a logical fallacy frequently used on the Internet. No academic sources could be found.

Gambler's Fallacy

(also known as: the Monte Carlo fallacy, the doctrine of the maturity of chances)

Description: Reasoning that, in a situation that is pure random chance, the outcome can be affected by previous outcomes.

Logical Form:

> *Situation X is purely random.*
>
> *Situation X resulted in Y.*
>
> *Y is less likely to be result next time.*

Example #1:

> *I have flipped heads five times in a row. As a result, the next flip will probably be tails.*

Explanation: The odds for each and every flip are calculated independently from other flips. The chance for each flip is 50/50, no matter how many times heads came up before.

Example #2:

> *Eric: For my lottery numbers, I chose 6, 14, 22, 35, 38, 40. What did you choose?*
>
> *Steve: I chose 1, 2, 3, 4, 5, 6.*
>
> *Eric: You idiot! Those numbers will never come up!*

Explanation: "Common sense" is contrary to logic and probability, when people think that any possible lottery number is more probable than any other. This is because we see meaning in patterns—but probability doesn't. Because of what is called the *clustering illusion*, we give the numbers 1, 2, 3, 4, 5, and 6 special meaning when arranged in that order, random chance is just as likely to produce a 1 as the first number as it is a 6. Now the second number produced is only affected by the first selection in that the first number is no longer a possible choice, but still, the number 2 has the same odds of being selected as 14, and so on.

Example #3:

Maury: Please put all my chips on red 21.

Dealer: Are you sure you want to do that? Red 21 just came up in the last spin.

Maury: I didn't know that! Thank you! Put it on black 15 instead. I can't believe I almost made that mistake!

Explanation: The dealer (or whatever you call the person spinning the roulette wheel) really should know better—the fact that red 21 just came up is completely irrelevant to the chances that it will come up again for the next spin. If it did, to us, that would seem "weird," but it is simply the inevitable result of probability.

Exception: If you think something is random, but it really isn't—like a loaded die, then previous outcomes can be used as an indicator of future outcomes.

Tip: Gamble for fun, not for the money, and don't wager more than you wouldn't mind losing. Remember, at least as far as casinos go, the odds are against you.

References:

Tversky, A., & Kahneman, D. (1974). Judgment under Uncertainty: Heuristics and Biases. *Science, 185*(4157), 1124–1131. https://doi.org/10.1126/science.185.4157.1124

Genetic Fallacy

(also known as: fallacy of origins, fallacy of virtue)

Description: Basing the truth claim of an argument on the origin of its claims or premises.

Logical Form:

The origin of the claim is presented.

Therefore, the claim is true/false.

Example #1:

Lisa was brainwashed as a child into thinking that people are generally good. Therefore, people are not generally good.

Explanation: That fact that Lisa may have been brainwashed as a child, is irrelevant to the claim that people are generally good.

Example #2:

He was born to Catholic parents and raised as a Catholic until his confirmation in 8th grade. Therefore, he is bound to want to defend some Catholic traditions and, therefore, cannot be taken seriously.

Explanation: I am referring to myself here. While my upbringing was Catholic, and I have long since considered myself a Catholic, that is irrelevant to any defenses I make of Catholicism—like the fact that many local churches do focus on helping the community through charity work. If I make an argument defending anything Catholic, the argument should be evaluated on the argument itself, not on the history of the one making the argument or how I came to hold the claims as true or false.

Exception: At times, the origin of the claim is relevant to the truth of the claim.

I believe in closet monsters because my big sister told me unless I do whatever she tells me, the closet monsters will eat me.

Tip: Remember that considering the source is often a useful heuristic in quickly assessing if the claim is *probably* true or not, but dismissing the claim or accepting it as true based on the source is fallacious.

References:

Engel, S. M., Soldan, A., & Durand, K. (2007). *The Study of Philosophy*. Rowman & Littlefield.

Gish Gallop

Description: Overwhelming an interlocutor with as many arguments as possible, without regard for accuracy or strength of the arguments. This is especially disingenuous when the interlocutor is not allowed to interrupt and address the arguments, as in formal debate or in writing. To the spectator unfamiliar with this strategy, the interlocutor's inability to accurately respond to all the claims in the given time is fallaciously seen as a "win" for the Gish Galloper or appears to lend credibility to the arguments made when in fact it does not.

Logical Form:

> Person 1 presents weak arguments A, B, C, D, E... without Person 2 being given the opportunity to address each argument.

Example #1: The term was coined by Eugenie Scott of the National Center for Science Education in the 1990s. Dr. Scott coined the term based on the behavior of creationist Duane Gish in formal debates. Dr. Scott states:

> *"On the radio, I have been able to stop Gish, et al, and say, 'Wait a minute, if X is so, then wouldn't you expect Y?' or something similar, and show that their 'model' is faulty. But in a debate, the evolutionist has to shut up while the creationist Gallops along, spewing out nonsense with every paragraph."*

Example #2: In a 2012 debate between Mitt Romney and President Obama, Romney overwhelmed Obama with many arguments of questionable strength, resulting in many referring to Romney's strategy as an example of the Gish Gallop.

Exception: The two key characteristics of the Gish Gallop are 1) the number of arguments in uninterrupted succession and 2) the lack of strength of the arguments presented. The number of arguments presented is problematic when the interlocutor doesn't have a reasonable amount of time (or space if in writing and limited by characters) to respond. The strength of the arguments is debatable, so in the case of Romney and Obama, it can be argued that Romney was making strong arguments, in which case Romney's crime was simply presenting too many of these arguments at once.

Fun Fact: A thousand bad arguments don't add up to a single good argument, although many people interpret numerous bad arguments as "strong evidence" (e.g., "they can't all be wrong" - Yes, they can all be wrong.)

References:

https://rationalwiki.org/wiki/Gish_Gallop

Hasty Generalization

(also known as: argument from small numbers, statistics of small numbers, insufficient statistics, argument by generalization, faulty generalization, hasty induction, inductive generalization, insufficient sample, lonely fact fallacy, over generality, overgeneralization, unrepresentative sample)

Description: Drawing a conclusion based on a small sample size, rather than looking at statistics that are much more in line with the typical or average situation.

Logical Form:

Sample S is taken from population P.

Sample S is a very small part of population P.

Conclusion C is drawn from sample S and applied to population P.

Example #1:

My father smoked four packs of cigarettes a day since age fourteen and lived until age sixty-nine. Therefore, smoking really can't be that bad for you.

Explanation: It is extremely unreasonable (and dangerous) to draw a universal conclusion about the health risks of smoking by the case study of one man.

Example #2:

Four out of five dentists recommend Happy Glossy Smiley toothpaste brand. Therefore, it must be great.

Explanation: It turns out that only five dentists were actually asked. When a random sampling of 1000 dentists was polled, only 20% actually recommended the brand. The four out of five result was not necessarily a *biased sample* or a dishonest survey; it just happened to be a statistical anomaly common among small samples.

Exception: When statistics of a larger population are not available, and a decision must be made or opinion formed if the small sample size is all you have to work with, then it is better than nothing. For example, if you are strolling in the desert with a friend, and he goes to pet a cute snake, gets bitten, then dies instantly, it would not be fallacious to assume the snake is poisonous.

Tip: Don't base decisions on small sample sizes when much more reliable data exists.

References:

Hurley, P. J. (2011). *A Concise Introduction to Logic.* Cengage Learning.

Having Your Cake

(also known as: failure to assert, diminished claim, failure to choose sides)

Description: Making an argument, or responding to one, in such a way that it does not make it at all clear what your position is. This puts you in a position to back out of your claim at any time and go in a new direction without penalty, claiming that you were "right" all along.

Logical Form:

I believe X is a strong argument.

Y is also a very strong argument.

Example #1:

Reporter: Mr. Congressman, where do you stand on the clean water vs. new factory issue?

Congressman: Of course, I want our state to have the cleanest water possible. I can appreciate the petition against the new factory as I can also appreciate the new jobs introduced in our community as a result of the new factory.

Explanation: This type of "non-decision" or refusal to choose a side often eludes those looking for an answer but getting more of a non-answer in return. In our example, the congressman can later choose a side based on the outcome, looking like the guy who knew the right answer all along.

Example #2:

Scott: So do you think the earth has only been here for 6-10 thousand years?

Sam: The evidence for an old earth is very strong, but we cannot discount some of the claims made by the creationists.

Scott: So what are you saying?

Sam: I am saying that a 4.7 billion-year-old earth makes a lot of sense, but the 6000-year-old theory does, as well.

Explanation: We all know and want to shoot people like Sam. Sam is failing to assert his position. If Sam's opinion is respected in this area, no doubt people on both sides will use his statement to their advantage. This ambiguity is not helpful and is misleading.

Exception: Wishy-washy statements are sometimes acceptable to demonstrate your uncertainty on a given issue, and if these kinds of statements are followed with admissions of uncertainty or ignorance, then they are not fallacious; they are honest.

Tip: If you don't have an opinion, say that you don't have an opinion. If you don't know, say that you don't know. It's that simple.

References:

This is a logical fallacy frequently used on the Internet. No academic sources could be found.

Hedging

Description: Refining your claim simply to avoid counter evidence and then acting as if your revised claim is the same as the original.

Logical Form:

Claim X is made.

Claim X is refuted.

Claim Y is then made and is made to be the same as claim X when it is not.

Example #1:

Freddie: All women are evil, manipulative, man-haters.

Wade: Including your mother and best friend?

Freddie: Not them, but all the others.

Wade: How can you say that, when you only know maybe a hundred or so women?

Freddie: Obviously, I am talking about the ones I know.

Explanation: The claim changed quite drastically from about 3.5 billion women to about 100, yet there was no admission by Freddie of this drastic change in his argument. Freddie is guilty of committing this fallacy, and those who see Freddie's initial argument as still valid, are guilty, as well.

Example #2:

Adam: The story of Noah's ark is very probable, and almost certainly a historical and scientific fact.

Greg: So you think it is very probable that two of each animal came from around the globe, including the animals that cannot survive for very long outside their natural environments?

Adam: Well, that part did require God's help.

Greg: You think it is very probable even though virtually every geologist and natural scientist today reject the idea of a global flood?

Adam: Probability exists on many levels.

Greg: Do you really still think this story is, "very probable"?

Adam: Yes.

Explanation: Besides the multiple *ad hoc* explanations used by Adam to answer the counterclaims, each counterclaim was evidence against the initial claim, specifically the "very probable" nature of the story. Rather than concede the argument or revise the claim, Adam let his insistence to be right come before logical thought and refused to change his original claim.

Exception: If the point of argumentation is really to arrive closer to the truth, then there is no shame in revising claims. If this is done, there is no fallacy.

Fun Fact: Every time you acknowledge that you are wrong, you are one step closer to actually being right.

References:

Dowden, B. (n.d.). Fallacies | Internet Encyclopedia of Philosophy. Retrieved from http://www.iep.utm.edu/fallacy/

Historian's Fallacy

(also known as: retrospective determinism, hindsight)

Description: Judging a person's decision in the light of new information not available at the time.

Logical Form:

Claim X was made in the past.

Those who made the claim did not take into consideration Y, which was not available to them at the time.

Therefore, this was a foolish claim.

Example #1:

You should have never taken the back roads to the concert. If you had taken the main roads, you would not have been stuck in all that traffic due to the accident.

Explanation: "Thanks for that!" is the usual sarcastic response to this fallacy. Of course, had we known about the accident, the main road would have been the better choice—but nobody could have reasonably predicted that accident. It is fallacious, and somewhat pointless, to suggest that we "should have" taken the other way.

Example #2:

Judas was an idiot to turn Jesus over to the authorities. After all, he ended up committing suicide out of guilt.

Explanation: It is easy for us to blame Judas as people who know the whole story and how it played out. We have information Judas did not have at the time. Besides, if Judas never turned in Jesus, and Jesus was never killed, but died while walking on water as an old man after tripping over a wave, would Christianity exist?

Exception: Sometimes, it's funny to commit this fallacy on purpose at the expense of your friends' dignity.

Hey, nice going on that decision to buy stock in the company that was shut down a week later by the FBI for the prostitution ring. Do you have any stock tips for me?

Tip: Practice forgiveness. We all make mistakes, and most of us learn from our mistakes and become better people. Don't be so quick to crucify someone for something they did in the past, especially if you are doing so to virtue signal.

References:

Arp, R. (2013). *1001 Ideas That Changed the Way We Think*. Simon and Schuster.

Homunculus Fallacy

(also known as: homunculus argument, infinite regress)

Description: An argument that accounts for a phenomenon in terms of the very phenomenon that it is supposed to explain, which results in an infinite regress.

Logical Form:

Phenomenon X needs to be explained.

Reason Y is given.

Reason Y depends on phenomenon X.

Example #1:

Bert: How do eyes project an image to your brain?

Ernie: Think of it as a little guy in your brain watching the movie projected by your eyes.

Bert: Ok, but what is happening in the little guy in your head's brain?

Ernie: Well, think of it as a little guy in his brain watching a movie...

Explanation: This fallacy creates an endless loop that actually explains nothing. It is fallacious reasoning to accept an explanation that creates this kind of endless loop that lacks any explanatory value.

Example #2:

Dicky: So how do you think life began?

Ralphie: Simple. Aliens from another planet seeded this planet with life billions of years ago.

Dicky: OK, but how did that alien life form begin?

Ralphie: Simple. Aliens from another planet seeded that planet with life.

Explanation: This fallacy can be tricky because maybe it is true that aliens are responsible for spreading life, so the answers might be technically right, but the question implied is how life *ultimately* began, which this form of reasoning will not answer.

Exception: There might be some exceptions that rely on high-level epistemology having to do with a large enough loop and validating feedback. The important question to ask is, does the explanation have any value and is the question being answered or deflected?

Fun Fact: Several fallacies are a result of a lack of explanatory value. For example, the *homunculus fallacy* can be seen as a specific form of the *failure to elucidate*.

References:

Tulving, E. (2000). *Memory, Consciousness, and the Brain: The Tallinn Conference.* Psychology Press.

Hot Hand Fallacy

(also known as: hot hand phenomenon)

Description: The hot hand fallacy is the irrational belief that if you win or lose several chance games in a row, you are either "hot" or "cold," respectively, meaning that the streak is likely to continue and has to do with something other than pure probability. Because we are generally stupid when it comes to realizing this, and pigheaded when it comes to accepting this fact, casinos around the world make a lot of money. This is similar to the *gambler's fallacy*.

Logical Form:

Person 1 has won a probability game X times in a row.

Therefore, person 1 is "hot" and likely to win again the next game.

Example #1:

Marta: (shooting craps) Let's just cash in now. We did great, but let's quit while we're ahead.

Carlos: Forget it! We are hot! Let's see how long this streak will last!

Explanation: Statistically, Carlos and Marta are more likely to lose the next game since a) their "streak" is probability-based, not talent-based and b) the odds are against them in the game of craps. Carlos is incorrectly viewing the string of wins as a streak that is more likely to continue than not.

Example #2: There are examples based on events that are not purely probabilistic, such as shooting baskets in the game of basketball. These examples are controversial because although some of the success, some of the time can be attributed to probability alone, there is no question that talent and belief can affect the outcome.

Exception: As mentioned, a streak of favorable talent-based actions can be the result of superior physical and mental performance.

Fun Fact: The belief that you are "on fire" (i.e., performing exceptionally well) can lead to better performance, via the *self-fulfilling prophecy*. There are times when thinking too critically can negatively affect performance.

References:

The Hot Hand Fallacy: Cognitive Mistakes or Equilibrium Adjustments? Evidence from Baseball. (n.d.). Retrieved from https://www.gsb.stanford.edu/faculty-research/working-papers/hot-hand-fallacy-cognitive-mistakes-or-equilibrium-adjustments

Hypnotic Bait and Switch

Description: Stating several uncontroversially true statements in succession, followed by a claim that the arguer wants the audience to accept as true. This is a propaganda technique, but also a fallacy when the audience lends more credibility to the last claim because it was preceded by true statements. The negative can also be used in the same way.

This is a classic sales technique often referred to as, "getting the customer used to saying 'yes'!"

Logical Forms:

> *A succession of uncontroversial true claims is made.*
>
> *Therefore, claim X (which is controversial), is true.*

> *A succession of uncontroversial false claims is made.*
>
> *Therefore, claim X (which is controversial), is false.*

Example #1:

> *Do you love your country?*
>
> *Do you love your family?*
>
> *Do you care about their wellbeing?*
>
> *Then you would love Eatme ice-cream!*

Example #2:

> *Is it right that such a small percentage of Americans control the vast majority of wealth?*
>
> *Is it right that you have to work overtime just to make ends meet?*
>
> *Is it right that you can't even afford to leave the state for vacation?*
>
> *Do you really want to vote for Reggie Lipshitz?*

Explanation: As you read through the examples, you can see from where the word "hypnotic" comes. Your subconscious mind starts to take over, and it seems almost reactionary that you start chanting "yes" or "no" (as in the second example) while not really considering with what you are agreeing or disagreeing. These kinds of techniques work best in rallies where those doing the rallying count on you to act with emotion at the expense of your reason.

Exception: It's an effective persuasion technique, so if you're trying to convince your kids to stay off drugs, then manipulate away. However, if you are trying to get someone to buy a vacuum cleaner, then take your *hypnotic bait and switch* and shove it up your reusable, hypoallergenic, dust bag.

Tip: Become a human fallacy detector. Look for these kinds of techniques everywhere you go. As a result, your reasonable self will become conditioned to resist taking a back seat to emotional propaganda.

References:

This is a logical fallacy frequently used on the Internet. No academic sources could be found.

Hypothesis Contrary to Fact

(also known as: counterfactual fallacy, speculative fallacy, "what if" fallacy, wouldchuck)

Description: Offering a poorly supported claim about what might have happened in the past or future, if (the hypothetical part) circumstances or conditions were different. The fallacy also entails treating future hypothetical situations as if they are fact.

Logical Form:

If event X did happen, then event Y would have happened (based only on speculation).

Example #1:

If you took that course on CD player repair right out of high school, you would be doing well and gainfully employed right now.

Explanation: This is speculation at best, not founded on evidence, and is *unfalsifiable*. There are many people with far more useful talents who are unemployed, and many who are "gainfully" employed who are not doing well at all. Besides, perhaps those with certificates in compact disc repair are gainfully employed... at McDonald's.

Example #2:

John, if you would have taken a shower more often, you would still be dating Tina.

Explanation: Past hypotheticals that are stated as fact are most often nothing more than one possible outcome of many. One cannot ignore probabilities when making these kinds of statements. Perhaps Tina likes the smell of man sweat. Perhaps Tina would have still preferred Renaldo over John despite John's personal hygiene because of Renaldo's enormous intellect.

Exception: In either/or situations, general predictions can obviously be made without fallacy:

If you didn't flip heads on the coin, it would have been tails.

Fun Fact: Right out of college, with a degree in marketing, I worked at the Olive Garden (an Italian-like semi-fast food chain here in the States). Perhaps I should have opted for the CD repair right out of high school and saved $120,000. I am pretty sure the Olive Garden would have still hired me.

References:

Moore, W. E. (1967). *Creative and Critical Thinking*. Houghton Mifflin.

Identity Fallacy

(also known as: identity politics)

Description: When one's argument is evaluated based on their physical or social identity, i.e., their social class, generation, ethnic group, gender or sexual orientation, profession, occupation or subgroup when the strength of the argument is independent of identity.

Logical Form:

> *Person 1 makes argument X.*
>
> *Person 2 dismisses argument X because of the physical or social identity of person 1.*

Example #1:

> *S.J. Sam: Asian people in this country are systematically passed over in the tech field for non-Asians.*
>
> *Cindy: Actually, according to most research, employers are biased in favor of Asian technical workers.*
>
> *S.J. Sam: Unless you are Asian, keep your mouth shut. You can't possibly know the struggles of the Asian community!*

Explanation: S.J. Sam is making an empirical claim about a hiring preference for non-Asians. Cindy has refuted the claim that is independent of her physical or social identity (i.e., her ability to refute the argument is not dependent upon her being Asian). S.J. Sam rejects her rebuttal because she is not Asian. In addition, he pulls a *red herring* by changing the argument to "knowing the struggles" of the Asian community.

Example #2: The female staff of a large corporation holds a meeting to discuss solutions to reduce discrimination against women at the company. Men are invited but asked just to listen and not contribute to the discussion.

Explanation: The implication here is that men have nothing to add to the discussion. Ideas to reduce gender discrimination are independent of gender, that is, both men and women can have equally valid arguments.

Exception: A requirement for this fallacy is "when the strength of the argument is independent of identity." There are arguments that do rely on identity. For example, claims of feeling and perception could be unique to certain groups.

> *S.J. Sam: As a gay man, I feel that I am being discriminated against at work.*
>
> *Cindy: I don't think people at work discriminate against gays.*
>
> *S.J. Sam: You are not gay. I bet your perspective would be different if you were.*

Cindy could ask for evidence of discrimination, which would be reasonable, but she dismisses S.J. Sam's claim when she lacks the insight due to her not being part of the social group (gays).

Tip: Before you exclude any group from your discussions or ignore their arguments based on their physical or social group, make sure you have a solid reason.

References:

This is a logical fallacy frequently used on the Internet. No academic sources could be found.

If-By-Whiskey

Description: A response to a question that is contingent on the questioner's opinions and makes use of words with strong connotations. This fallacy appears to support both sides of an issue—a tactic common in politics.

Logical Form:

> *If you mean X, then (one-sided, loaded-language rant supporting side A).*
>
> *If you mean Y, then (one-sided, loaded-language rant supporting side B).*

Example #1: This example is actually the origin of the fallacy, which refers to a 1952 speech by Noah S. "Soggy" Sweat, Jr., a young lawmaker from the U.S. state of Mississippi, on the subject of whether Mississippi should continue to prohibit (which it did until 1966) or finally legalize alcoholic beverages. I think it is hilarious, so I am including it here in its entirety.

> *My friends, I had not intended to discuss this controversial subject at this particular time. However, I want you to know that I do not shun controversy. On the contrary, I will take a stand on any issue at any time, regardless of how fraught with controversy it might be. You have asked me how I feel about whiskey. All right, here is how I feel about whiskey:*

> *If when you say whiskey you mean the devil's brew, the poison scourge, the bloody monster, that defiles innocence, dethrones reason, destroys the home, creates misery and poverty, yea, literally takes the bread from the mouths of little children; if you mean the evil drink that topples the Christian man and woman from the pinnacle of righteous, gracious living into the bottomless pit of degradation, and despair, and shame and helplessness, and hopelessness, then certainly I am against it.*

> *But, if when you say whiskey you mean the oil of conversation, the philosophic wine, the ale that is consumed when good fellows get together, that puts a song in their hearts and laughter on their lips, and the warm glow of contentment in their eyes; if you mean Christmas cheer; if you mean the stimulating drink that puts the spring in the old gentleman's step on a frosty, crispy morning; if you mean the drink which enables a man to magnify his joy, and his happiness, and to forget, if only for a little while, life's great tragedies, and heartaches, and sorrows; if you mean that drink, the sale of which pours into our treasuries untold millions of dollars, which are used to provide tender care for our little crippled children, our blind, our deaf, our dumb, our pitiful aged and infirm; to build highways and hospitals and schools, then certainly I am for it.*

> *This is my stand. I will not retreat from it. I will not compromise.*

Explanation: This is an amazing insight into the human mind and the area of rhetoric. We can see how when both sides of the issue are presented through the same use of emotionally charged words and phrases, the argument is really vacuous and presents very little factual information, nor does it even take a stance on the issue.

Example #2: Having evaluated literally thousands of positions on God by people all over the belief spectrum, I thought I would create my own, "If-by-God" version of the argument, showing how carefully placed rhetoric can blur the line between the most perfect being imaginable and the most horrible being imaginable.

> *The question is if God does exist, should we love him and worship him? My position is clear, and I am not embarrassed to let the world know exactly how I feel. So here it goes.*
>
> *If by God you mean the great dictator in the sky, the almighty smiter, the God who created us with imperfections then holds us responsible for the imperfections, the God who took away paradise and eternal life from us because the first man and woman committed a "wrong" against God before they were capable of knowing right from wrong, the God who commanded his chosen people to utterly destroy every man, woman, and child in dozens of cities, the God who hardened hearts, killed first-borns, demanded blood sacrifices, commanded man to brutally kill other humans for "crimes" such as "not honoring your parents," the God who destroyed virtually all living creatures on the planet, the God who would demand that his own son be brutally murdered to pay a debt to him, the God who allows children to be born with birth defects, die young, and get cancer, the God who continues to destroy using floods, hurricanes, and other natural disasters, the God who ignores the prayers of billions of his faithful followers, the God who allows a majority of his creation to suffer through unimaginable torture for all eternity in the fiery pits of Hell, then he is certainly not deserving of our love and worship.*
>
> *But, if when you say God you mean the defender, the protector, creator of heaven and earth, the father of us all, the being of pure love, kindness, and everything good in the world, the God who led the Israelites from slavery to*

freedom, the one who looks after us all, the God who heals the sick in his son's name, the God who gave us his perfect laws for our benefit, the God who loved us so much, that he sacrificed his only son so that we can be saved, the God who allows us to spend a blissful eternity with him and our loved ones, then certainly he is deserving of our love and worship.

This is my stand. I will not retreat from it. I will not compromise.

Exception: If you are serving as a moderator and need to remain neutral, plus want to add a little "spice" in the debate, this might be a good technique.

Fun Fact: Reportedly, the example #1 speech took Sweat two and a half months to write.

References:

Brookes, T. (1979). *Guitar: an American life*. Grove Press.

Illicit Contraposition

New Terminology:

Illicit: Forbidden by the rules, or in our cases, by the laws of logic.

Contraposition: Switching the subject and predicate terms of a categorical proposition, and negating each.

Description: A formal fallacy where switching the subject and predicate terms of a categorical proposition, then negating each, results in an invalid argument form. The examples below make this more clear. This is a fallacy only for type "E" and type "I" forms, or forms using the words "no" and "some," respectively.

Logical Forms:

No S are P.

Therefore, no non-P are non-S.

Some S are P.

Therefore, some non-P are non-S.

Example #1:

No Catholics are Jews.

Therefore, no non-Jews are non-Catholics. (contraposition)

Explanation: By definition, no Catholics are Jews (using type "E" form here)—clear enough. Now let's take the contraposition of that proposition by switching the placement of "Catholics" and "Jews," and negating each, and we can see we have a false proposition. "No non-Jews are non-Catholics" clearly does not mean the same thing as "No Catholics are Jews." In this example, the premise is true but the conclusion is false (I am a non-Jew and a non-Catholic, and statistically speaking, you probably are too.)

Example #2:

Some dogs bark.

Therefore, some non-barking things are non-dogs. (contraposition)

Explanation: We now see the type "I" form in action, stating, "Some" dogs bark. This is true, but that really does not matter in determining what form of an argument is valid or not. The conclusion, "some non-barking things are non-dogs" is also a true statement (my toothbrush, which is a non-dog, does not bark), but this does not matter either. What does matter, is that it does not logically follow. Don't be misled by truth! Focus on the form of the argument. If we substitute other terms we can see the fallacy more clearly:

Some humans are mortal.

Therefore, some immortals are non-human. (contraposition)

By using the word, "some," we are not asserting that there are definitely some *that are not*. Above, just by saying that some humans are mortal, we automatically are saying that there are others who are not mortal. Therefore, our conclusion is supposing a group that does not exist, thus fallacious.

Exception: None, but remember that the following type "A" and type "O" forms are valid:

> *All P are Q.*
>
> *Therefore, all non-Q are non-P.*

> *Some P are not Q.*
>
> *Therefore, some non-Q are not non-P.*

Using the type "A" form, let's say that all humans are mortals. The contraposition: all immortals are non-human. Not only does this make sense in terms of truth, but it follows necessarily from the premise; therefore, it is valid (and not a fallacy).

Tip: Don't give up on formal fallacies! Once you get it, it actually will help you in everyday reasoning.

References:

Welton, J. (1896). *A Manual of Logic.* W. B. Clive.

Illicit Major

(also known as: illicit process of the major term)

Description: Any form of a *categorical syllogism* in which the major term is distributed in the conclusion, but not in the major premise.

Logical Form:

> *All A are B.*
>
> *No C are A.*
>
> *Therefore, no C are B.*

Example #1:

> *All hotdogs are fast food.*
>
> *No hamburgers are hotdogs.*
>
> *Therefore, no hamburgers are fast food.*

Explanation: In our example, the major term is "fast food," because it is the term that appears in the major premise (first premise) as the predicate and in the conclusion. As such, in this position, it is "undistributed."

Example #2:

> *All Jim Carrey movies are hilarious.*
>
> *No horror movies are Jim Carrey movies.*
>
> *Therefore, no horror movies are hilarious.*

Explanation: In our example, the major term is "hilarious," because it is the term that appears in the major premise (first premise) as the predicate and in the conclusion. As such, in this position, it is "undistributed."

Tip: If you are not sure if a syllogism is fallacious or not, keep substituting the items in the syllogism for other items. If a syllogism is consistent with the form but clearly doesn't make sense, you will know that it is fallacious.

References:

Neil, S. (1853). *The Art of Reasoning: A Popular Exposition of the Principles of Logic.* Walton & Maberly.

Illicit Minor

(also known as: illicit process of the minor term)

Description: Any form of a *categorical syllogism* in which the minor term is distributed in the conclusion, but not in the minor premise.

Logical Form:

All A are B.

All B are C.

Therefore, all C are A.

Example #1:

All Catholics are Christian.

All Christians are Jesus lovers.

Therefore, all Jesus lovers are Catholic.

Explanation: In our example, the minor term is "Jesus lovers" because it is the term that appears in the minor premise (second premise) as the predicate and in the conclusion. As such, in this position, it is "undistributed."

Example #2:

All Paul Newman movies are great.

All great movies are Oscar winners.

Therefore, all Oscar winners are Paul Newman movies.

Explanation: In our example, the minor term is "Oscar winners" because it is the term that appears in the minor premise (second premise) as the predicate and in the conclusion. As such, in this position, it is "undistributed."

Fun Fact: The Catholic bible has 73 books, the Protestant bible only has 66.

References:

Neil, S. (1853). *The Art of Reasoning: A Popular Exposition of the Principles of Logic*. Walton & Maberly.

Illicit Substitution of Identicals

(also known as: hooded man fallacy, masked man fallacy, intensional fallacy)

Description: A formal fallacy due to confusing the knowing of a thing (*extension*) with the knowing of it under all its various names or descriptions (*intension*).

We need to define two terms here to understand this fallacy fully: *intensional* and *extensional*. In logic and mathematics, an *intensional* definition gives the meaning of a term by specifying all the properties required to come to that definition, that is, the necessary and sufficient conditions for belonging to the set being defined. In contrast, an *extensional* definition is defined by its listing everything that falls under that definition. Confused? You should be, but relax because I am not done.

Imagine Superman, who is also Clark Kent, flew to Italy for a slice of pizza. If we said, "Clark Kent flew to Italy for pizza" we would be right, because of the *extensional context* of that statement. Conversely, if we said, "Lois Lane thinks Superman flew to Italy for pizza," we would still be making a true claim, although the context is now *intensional* as indicated by the term, "thinks." Now if we said, "Lois Lane thinks Clark Kent flew to Italy for pizza," we would be wrong and would have committed this fallacy because Lois *does not believe that*, even though *extensionally* it is the case (this is after the kiss that wiped her memory of Clark being Superman).

Logical Forms:

X is Y.

Person 1 thinks X does Z.

Therefore, person 1 thinks Y did Z.

X is Y.

Person 1 thinks Y does Z.

Therefore, person 1 thinks X did Z.

Example #1:

The lady in the pink dress is Julia Roberts.

The reporter thinks the lady in the pink dress drives a Prius.

Therefore, the reporter thinks Julia Roberts drives a Prius.

Example #2:

> *The lady in the pink dress is Julia Roberts.*
>
> *The reporter thinks Julia Roberts drives a Prius.*
>
> *Therefore, the reporter thinks the lady in the pink dress drives a Prius.*

Explanation: The examples used are just two different logical forms of the same fallacy. Because the reporter, "thinks" the statement is made in an intensional context, we cannot switch the terms. However, if we were to keep the premises in an extensional context, we could get away with switching the terms. This would be a valid logical argument form known as *Leibniz' Law*.

Exception: Technically, none, but here is the above example #1 using *Leibniz' Law*, with no fallacy:

> *The lady in the pink dress is Julia Roberts.*
>
> *The lady in the pink dress drives a Prius.*
>
> *Therefore, Julia Roberts drives a Prius.*

Fun Fact: Julia Roberts really does own a Prius (at the time of this writing).

References:

Neil, S. (1853). *The Art of Reasoning: A Popular Exposition of the Principles of Logic.* Walton & Maberly.

Imposter Fallacy

Description: When one suggests or claims, with insufficient evidence, that the group outliers who are viewed as damaging to the group are primarily made up of infiltrators of another group with the purpose of making the infiltrated group look bad.

This is similar to the *nut-picking fallacy* in that the group outliers and the "nuts" are equally as embarrassing or damaging to the group, but with the *imposter fallacy*, the outliers are claimed to be actors or imposters. This is also similar to the *no true Scotsman fallacy* in that a foundational claim is that no "true" group member would act in this way, so they must be an imposter.

Logical Form:

Group A comprises members X,Y, and Z who act in a way that damages group A's reputation.

Person 1 suggests or claims, with insufficient evidence, that members X,Y, and Z are actually part of Group B who are there to make Group A look bad.

Example #1:

Frieda Freestuff: I can't believe you support Trump. Didn't you see the Trump rally with the group of supporters holding up signs for "White Power?" Do you really want to be associated with that message?

Garry Godznguns: Those aren't Trump supporters; they are liberals pretending to be Trump supporters just to make Trump supporters look bad.

Frieda Freestuff: It's working.

Explanation: There is no question that imposters exist. It is not uncommon that political rivals will pretend to be the worst of the other group with the goal of damaging the other group's reputation. The problem here is that Garry Godznguns has no evidence to back up his claim, and there is plenty of evidence to the contrary that white supremacists and white nationalists overwhelmingly support Trump.

Example #2:

Peter Procops: I can't believe you support these protests. People are being injured and killed. Property is being destroyed. Stores are being looted. Our city looks like a war zone!

Patricia Defunddapopo: The protesters are peaceful and lawful. It was just on the news that a guy they arrested for vandalism was a white nationalist who admitted vandalizing to make the protesters look bad.

Peter Procops: It's working.

Explanation: While it is true that the guy arrested was a white nationalist who admitted vandalizing to make the protesters look bad, this was one case out of thousands. There is video documentation of known activists advocating for looting, vandalism, and even arson. The evidence strongly suggests the majority of destruction is not due to the imposters.

Exception: This is a fallacy contingent upon evidence. If enough evidence exists that the *majority* of the group outliers in question are imposters, then there is no fallacy.

Fun Fact: The *imposter fallacy* is often committed with the *deceptive sharing fallacy* when one shares a one-off story about an actual imposter.

References:

This is an original logical fallacy named by the author.

Incomplete Comparison

Description: An incomplete assertion that cannot possibly be refuted. This is popular in advertising.

Logical Form:

X is said to be superior, but to nothing specifically.

Example #1: One of my favorite candies, *Raisinets*, advertises on their package that the product contains 40% less fat. In fairness, they do have an asterisk then in much smaller writing, "than the leading candy bar."

Explanation: The question is, "40% less fat than what?" The hope is that most people won't read the fine print and make their own assumptions. "Oh, this candy bar has 40% less fat than this apple!"

Example #2:

Our widgets cost less and last longer!

Explanation: Cost less than what? Last longer than what? By not specifically saying "our competition" they cannot get in trouble when a competitor shows that their product actually costs less and last longer.

Exception: The terminology used has to be a comparison word or phrase. For example, saying "Bo Rocks!" is great. Not just because I do rock (not musically), but because "rocks" is not a comparison word. There is a complete assertion. Another exception is when the object of comparison is assumed. For example, "Johnny, you need to better in school." Clearly, the implication here is that Johnny needs to *improve*, that is, do better than he did in the past.

Tip: When possible, read the fine print.

References:

Incomplete Comparisons. (n.d.). Retrieved from http://www.mhhe.com/mayfieldpub/tsw/comp-i.htm

Inconsistency

(also known as: internal contradiction, logical inconsistency)

Description: In terms of a fallacious argument, two or more propositions are asserted that cannot both possibly be true. In a more general sense, holding two or more views/beliefs that cannot all be true together. Quotes from Yogi Berra (even if apocryphal) are great examples of fallacies, especially inconsistencies.

Logical Form:

Proposition 1 is logically inconsistent with proposition 2.

Proposition 1 and proposition 2 are both asserted or implied to be true.

Example #1:

"I never said most of the things I said." - Yogi Berra

Explanation: I know this requires no explanation, and I don't mean to insult your intelligence, but for consistency's sake, I will explain. If he had said those things, then he said them, which is a contradiction to his claim that he never said them. This is both an *internal inconsistency* and a *logical inconsistency*. It is internal because the inconsistency is contained within the statement itself; it doesn't require any other premises or arguments.

Example #2:

"Nobody goes there anymore. It's too crowded." - Yogi Berra

Explanation: Again, I apologize, but here it goes... If "nobody" went there, then it could not possibly be crowded, since "crowded" implies too many people are there. This is both an *internal inconsistency* and a *logical inconsistency*.

Exception: One needs to be able to explain how the beliefs are not inconsistent.

Tip: Think about your beliefs. Are there any inconsistent with each other? Any inconsistent with how you act and what you do?

References:

This is a logical fallacy frequently used on the Internet. No academic sources could be found.

Inflation of Conflict

Description: Reasoning that because authorities cannot agree precisely on an issue, no conclusions can be reached at all, and minimizing the credibility of the authorities, as a result. This is a form of black and white thinking—either we know the exact truth, or we know nothing at all.

Logical Form:

Authority A disagrees with authority B on issue X.

Therefore, we can say nothing meaningful about issue X.

Example #1:

My mom says that I should study for at least 2 hours each night, and my dad says just a half hour should be fine. Neither one of them knows what they are talking about, so I should just skip studying altogether.

Explanation: A disagreement among experts does not mean that both are wrong, the answer is a compromise, or that there is no answer to be known; it simply means that there is disagreement—that is all we can infer.

Example #2:

Scientists cannot agree on the age of the universe. Some say it is 13.7 billion years old, some say it is only about 13 billion years old. That's a difference of almost a billion years! It should be clear that because there is so much disagreement, then the 6000-year-old universe should be carefully considered, as well.

Explanation: Scientists who "disagree" with the estimated age of the universe do so primarily on slightly different interpretations of the same objectively valid dating methods. The difference is fairly minute in terms of percentage. Suggesting 6000 years is valid is one thing, but doing so based on the difference in interpretation from mainstream science is completely fallacious. The differences have no bearing on the truth claim of the argument (the actual age).

Exception: When the difference in professional disagreement is critical, it should be carefully examined. For example, if two doctors were debating on what medicine to give a patient, and both were claiming that the other medicine would kill the patient.

Fun Fact: When experts have very different views on scientific issues, it is very often the case that one or more of them are sharing views outside their realm of professional expertise.

References:

This is a logical fallacy frequently used on the Internet. No academic sources could be found.

Insignificant Cause

(also known as: fallacy of insignificant, genuine but insignificant cause, insufficient cause)

Description: An explanation that posits one minor factor, out of several that contributed, as its sole cause. This fallacy also occurs when an explanation is requested, and the one that is given is not sufficient to entirely explain the incident yet it is passed off as if it is sufficient.

Logical Form:

> *Factors A, B, and C caused X.*
>
> *Factor A, the least significant factor, is said to have caused X.*

Example #1:

> *Billy murdered all those people because I spanked him when he was a child.*

Explanation: Assuming that spanking did contribute to Billy's murderous behavior as an adult (which is a very weak assumption), to sell that as the cause is extremely fallacious.

Example #2:

> *The reason Donald Trump got elected was because liberals took political correctness too far.*

Explanation: Assuming liberals did take political correctness too far, and this did have some effect on voters in favor of

Donald Trump, it is unreasonable to claim that this was "the reason" for his win.

Exception: Very often causes can be "insignificant" in that they don't seem meaningful enough considering the meaning of the cause. This is one of the prime drivers of the *conspiracy theory fallacy*. For example, a lone gunman seems like an insignificant cause in the death of John F. Kennedy. This is our bias at work where we want significant causes for significant effects. "Insignificant," in the context of this fallacy, refers to "insignificant to adequately account for the cause" rather than "insignificant in meaning."

Tip: Establishing causality is very difficult. Be very weary of claims of causality in casual conversation.

References:

This is a logical fallacy frequently used on the Internet. No academic sources could be found.

Jumping to Conclusions

(also known as: hasty conclusion, hasty decision, leaping to conclusions, specificity)

Description: Drawing a conclusion without taking the needed time to evaluate the evidence or reason through the argument.

Logical Form:

> *Little or no evidence is provided or reviewed.*
>
> *Conclusion is made.*

Example #1:

> *Wife: Should we buy the house?*
>
> *Husband: The Realtor didn't say anything about any problems, so I am sure it is fine. Let's get it!*

Explanation: The husband is jumping to the conclusion that the house is without problems simply because the person who gets paid to sell the house did not mention any. This is fallacious reasoning.

Example #2:

> *It's getting late, and we still have to decide on the school budget. What do you say we just leave it as is and we can call it a night?*

Explanation: It is not reasonable to assume the conclusion that the budget should be left where it is based on the desire to go home.

Exception: There are many times when quick decisions are required, and evidence cannot be fully examined, and in such circumstances, we need to come to the best conclusion we can with the resources we have.

Tip: If anyone gives you an unreasonable timeframe for making a decision, it is almost always an attempt to discourage you from critical thought. If you cannot have what you feel is a reasonable amount of time to come to a well-reasoned conclusion—walk away.

References:

This is a logical fallacy frequently used on the Internet. No academic sources could be found.

Just Because Fallacy

(also known as: trust me, mother knows best fallacy, because I said so, you'll see)

Description: Refusing to respond to give reasons or evidence for a claim by stating yourself as the ultimate authority on the matter. This is usually indicated by the phrases, "just trust me," "because I said so," "you'll see," or "just because." The *just because fallacy* is not conducive to the goal of argumentation— that is coming to a mutually agreeable solution. Nor is it helpful in helping the other person understand why you are firm on your position. "Just because" is not a reason that speaks to the question itself; it is simply a deflection to authority (legitimate or not).

Logical Form:

X is true because I said so.

Example #1:

Trebor: Mom, can David sleepover tonight?

Mom: No.

Trebor: Why not?

Mom: Because.

Trebor: Because why?

Mom: Because I said so! End of discussion!

Explanation: "Because I said so" is not a valid reason for why a friend can't sleep over. Maybe the real reason is that sleepovers give mom a headache. Maybe mom wants Trebor to go to bed early because he is cranky the next day if he doesn't, or perhaps David is just a little brat that drives mom crazy.

Example #2:

Slick Rick: The best I can do for ya is $25,000.

Prospect: Why can't you do any better?

Slick Rick: Just because that is the lowest I can go.

Prospect: But why.

Slick Rick: Because.

Explanation: In this case, it is clear that there is some underlying reason about which Slick Rick does not want the prospect to know. This reason, almost certainly, has something to do with the fact that Slick Rick can go lower if needed.

Exceptions: There is really no exception to this rule in argumentation or serious discussion. Perhaps this is acceptable in situations where you have the authority to choose not to make an argument out of a command, like in a parent-child relationship—or perhaps your significant other has planned a surprise for you, and the "you'll see" is meant to deflect your inquiry for your own benefit.

Tip: Don't let yourself off the hook with "just because" excuses. Keep asking yourself, "what is the real reason?" The answer could uncover an issue that needs your attention.

References:

This is an original logical fallacy named by the author.

Just In Case Fallacy

(also known as: worst case scenario fallacy)

Description: Making an argument based on the worst-case scenario rather than the most probable scenario, allowing fear to prevail over reason.

Logical Form:

> It would be a good idea to accept claim X since it is possible for event Y.

Example #1:

> Maury, you should really wear a helmet when playing chess. You can easily get excited, fall off your chair, and crack your head open.

Explanation: Every decision you make has both costs and benefits. Fallacious arguments, like the one above, will attempt to get you to make a decision out of fear rather than reason, thus increasing the *perceived* cost of choosing not to wear a helmet. Of course, the cost of wearing a helmet while playing chess is peer ridicule of historic proportions.

Example #2:

> If Hell is real, then you would be wise to accept Christianity as true.

Explanation: The attempt is to get you to make a decision out of fear rather than reason, thus increasing the *perceived* cost of not accepting Christianity as true. There are many Christians who reject the idea of Hell and eternal torment by a perfectly loving God. Plus, there are over a billion people who subscribe to the religion that believes worshiping anyone besides Allah will buy you a one-way ticket into the fiery pits of Hell. Through reason, you can evaluate these choices and make a decision on reason, not on fear.

Exception: When you can come to a reasonable conclusion that preparing for the worst-case scenario is the most economically sound course of action (as in cost-benefit—not necessarily financial), then the fallacy is not committed.

Tip: Buying insurance or a warranty is not always a good idea—mitigating risk comes with costs, that are often not obvious.

References:

This is a logical fallacy frequently used on the Internet. No academic sources could be found.

Kettle Logic

Description: Making (usually) multiple, contradicting arguments, in an attempt to support a single point or idea.

Logical Form:

> *Statement 1 is made.*
>
> *Statement 2 is made and contradicts statement 1.*
>
> *Statement 3 is made and contradicts statement 1 or 2*
>
> *... etc.*

Example #1: In an example used by Sigmund Freud in *The Interpretation of Dreams*, a man accused by his neighbor of having returned a kettle in a damaged condition offered three arguments:

> *That he had returned the kettle undamaged;*

That it was already damaged when he borrowed it;

That he had never borrowed it in the first place.

Explanation: Each statement contradicts the one before. If it was already damaged, how did he return it undamaged? If he never borrowed it, how was it already damaged when he borrowed it?

Example #2:

I don't believe in God. One reason is that I think he is evil. And by the way, there is no such thing as "evil;" it is just our evaluation of what we believe is wrong.

Explanation: There are multiple statements here that all contradict, stemmed from the idea that the person does not believe in God. If he or she does not believe in God, how can he or she think God is evil? And if there is no such thing as evil, how can something be evil?

Exception: If one acknowledges that their previous argument has been defeated (explicitly or implicitly), and they make a new argument, this would be more like *moving the goalposts*.

Tip: If you are trying to be funny, kettle logic can be a great tool. In the movie "Philomena," Steve Coogan's character, Martin Sixsmith, leaves a church ceremony early. When asked why he says, "I don't believe in God, and I think he knows."

References:

Freud, S. (1913). *The Interpretation of Dreams*. Macmillan.

Least Plausible Hypothesis

Description: Choosing more unreasonable explanations for phenomena over more defensible ones. In judging the validity of hypotheses or conclusions from observation, the scientific method relies upon the *Principle of Parsimony*, also known as *Occam's Razor*, which states, *all things being equal, the simplest explanation of a phenomenon that requires the fewest* *assumptions is the preferred explanation until it can be disproved.*

This is very similar to the *far-fetched hypothesis*, but the hypotheses are generally more within reason (i.e., no leprechauns involved).

Logical Form:

Hypothesis X is used to explain Y, but hypothesis X is the least plausible.

Example #1:

Here is why I think my date never showed up: her father had a heart-attack, and she had to rush him to the hospital. In her state of panic, she forgot her cell phone and while at the hospital she was too concerned about her dad to worry about standing me up.

Explanation: While possible, it is not *probable*. It is much more probable that his date just forgot or has purposely stood him up. People tend to believe in the least probable hypotheses out of desire, emotion, or faith—not out of reason.

Example #2: Creationists have written volumes of books explaining how, given some divine intervention, a few broken natural laws, and accepting the *inconsistency* of nature, it could be possible that the universe is only 6000 years old. Accepting these theories would require the abandonment or radical reformation of virtually every science we have, as well us a new understanding of the term, "fact." So either all of that is true, or, the Biblical creation story, like hundreds of others in cultures all around the world, are simply mythology.

Explanation: Given the incomprehensible number and severity of the assumptions that would need to be made for creationism to be true, the explanation that the creation story is mythology, by far, is the most economical explanation.

Exception: This isn't about what might be possible; *Occam's Razor* is all about probabilities.

Fun Fact: "Plausibility" technically means "believability," which is highly subjective. A Flat-earther would find the flat-earth theory more plausible than the spherical earth. Clearly, who is making the claim of plausibility, matters.

References:

Wormeli, R. (2001). *Meet Me in the Middle: Becoming an Accomplished Middle-level Teacher*. Stenhouse Publishers.

Limited Depth

Description: Failing to appeal to an underlying cause, and instead simply appealing to membership in a category. In other words, simply asserting what you are trying to explain without actually explaining anything.

Logical Form:

Claim X is made about Y.

Claim X is true because Y is a member of category Z.

Example #1:

My dog goes through our garbage because he is a dog.

Explanation: We know your dog is a dog, but what about him being a dog makes him go through the garbage? By referring to your dog as a member of the category "dog," this fails to explain anything.

Example #2:

Mormons are really, really nice because they go to Mormon church.

Explanation: *Question begging* aside, simply stating that Mormons are a member of the group, "Mormon churchgoers" does not explain why they are nice. A reasonable explanation would need to include a valid causal relationship between niceness and Mormon-church-going.

Exception: At times, limited depth can be used as a shorthand when assumptions are made that no deeper explanation is needed.

I need oxygen because I am human!

Fun Fact: Mormons getting their own planet in the Mormon afterlife is actually a misconception, not official Mormon doctrine.

References:

Farha, B. (2013). *Pseudoscience and Deception: The Smoke and Mirrors of Paranormal Claims.* University Press of America.

Limited Scope

Description: The theory doesn't explain anything other than the phenomenon it explains (that one thing), and at best, is likely to be incomplete. This is often done by just redefining a term or phrase rather than explaining it.

Logical Form:

Theory X is proposed to explain Y.

Theory X explains nothing else but Y.

Example #1:

My car broke down because it is no longer working.

Explanation: "It isn't working" is just another way of saying "broke down," and fails to explain *why* it broke down.

Example #2:

People often make hasty decisions because they don't take enough time to consider their choices.

Explanation: Not taking enough time to consider choices is precisely what a hasty decision is. Again, no explanation is offered, just a definition in place of an explanation.

Exception: If "because" is replaced with a phrase like, "in other words," then it is a deliberate clarification and not a fallacy.

Fun Fact: *Limited depth* and *limited scope* fallacies are sometimes known as *fallacies of explanation.*

References:

Farha, B. (2013). *Pseudoscience and Deception: The Smoke and Mirrors of Paranormal Claims.* University Press of America.

Logic Chopping

(also known as: quibbling, nit-picking, smokescreen, splitting-hairs, trivial objections)

Description: Using the technical tools of logic in an unhelpful and pedantic manner by focusing on trivial details instead of directly addressing the main issue in dispute. Irrelevant over precision.

Pay close attention to this fallacy, because after reading this book, you may find yourself committing this fallacy more than any others, and certainly more often than you did before reading this book.

Logical Form:

A claim is made.

An objection is made regarding a trivial part of the claim, distracting from the main point.

Example #1:

John: Can you please help me push my car to the side of the road until the tow truck comes?

Paul: Why push it to the side of the road? Why not just leave it?

John: It is slowing down traffic unnecessarily where it is.

Paul: Many things slow down traffic—do you feel you need to do something about all them?

John: No, but this was my fault.

Paul: Was it really? Were you the direct cause of your car breaking down?

John: Are you going to help me move this damn car or not?!

Explanation: You can see here that Paul is avoiding the request for assistance by attempting to make a deep philosophical issue out of a simple request. While Paul may have some good points, not every situation in life calls for deep critical thought. This situation being one of them.

Example #2:

Service Tech: Your car could use some new tires.

Bart: You have a financial interest in selling me tires, why should I trust you?

Service Tech: You brought your car to me to have it checked, sir.

Bart: I brought my car to the shop where you work.

Service Tech: So should we forget about the new tires for now?

Bart: I never suggested that. Are you trying to use reverse psychology on me, so I will buy the tires?

Explanation: This kind of fallacy could easily be a result of someone with paranoid behavioral tendencies—thinking the world is out to get him or her.

Exception: Of course, there is no clear line between situations that call for critical thought and those that call for reactionary obedience, but if you cross the line, hopefully, you are with people who care about you enough to tell you.

Tip: People don't like to be made to feel inferior. You need to know when tact and restraint are more important than being right.

References:

Byerly, H. C. (1973). *A primer of logic.* Harper & Row.

Ludic Fallacy
ludus

Description: Assuming flawless statistical models apply to situations where they actually don't. This can result in the over-confidence in probability theory or simply not knowing exactly where it applies as opposed to chaotic situations or situations with external influences too subtle or numerous to predict.

Logical Form:

> Claim is made.
>
> Statistics are referenced, reason is ignored.
>
> Therefore, the statistical answer is used to support or reject the claim.

Example #1: The best example of this fallacy is presented by the person who coined this term, Nassim Nicholas Taleb in his 2007 book, *The Black Swan*. There are two people:

> Dr. John, who is regarded as a man of science and logical thinking.
>
> Fat Tony, who is regarded as a man who lives by his wits.
>
> A third party asks them, "assume a fair coin is flipped 99 times, and each time it comes up heads. What are the odds that the 100th flip would also come up heads?" Dr. John says that the odds are not affected by the previous outcomes so the odds must still be 50/50. Fat Tony says that the odds of the coin coming up heads 99 times in a row are so low (less than 1 in 6.33 × 1029) that the initial assumption that the coin had a 50/50 chance of coming up heads is most likely incorrect.

Explanation: You can imagine yourself watching a coin flip. Knowing all about the *gambler's fallacy,* you would hold out much longer than someone like Fat Tony when you get to the point where you say, "All right, something's going on here with the coin." At what point does it become fallacious reasoning to continue to insist that you are just witnessing the "inevitable result of probability"? There is no definite answer—your decision will need to be argued and supported by solid reasons.

Example #2:

> Lolita: Since about half the people in the world are female, the chances of the next person to walk out that door being female is about 50/50.

> Celina: Do you realize that is the door to Dr. Vulvastein, the gynecologist?

Explanation: Lolita is focusing on pure statistics while ignoring actual reason.

Exception: See the explanation for example #1.

Fun Fact: Chaos theory plays a huge role in our universe, and it is way beyond the scope of this book. As for this fallacy, many things that appear to be random are actually chaotic systems, or unpredictable, deterministic systems. Attempting to apply the rules of random probability in those cases will result in all kinds of errors.

References:

Taleb, N. N. (2010). *The Black Swan: Second Edition: The Impact of the Highly Improbable Fragility*. Random House Publishing Group.

Lying with Statistics

(also known as: statistical fallacy/fallacies, misunderstanding the nature of statistics [form of], fallacy of curve fitting, the fallacy of overfitting)

Description: This can be seen as an entire class of fallacies that result in presenting statistical data in a very biased way, and of course, interpreting statistics without questioning the methods behind collecting and presenting the data.

The many methods are outside the scope of this book, but if you really want to jump in here, and see how deceptive statistics can be, get the book, *How to Lie with Statistics* by Darrell Huff, a 1954 classic that is just as relevant today as it was in his time.

Logical Form:

Claim A is made.

Statistic S is manipulated to support claim A.

Example #1:

Did you see that bar graph in USA Today? It showed a HUGE spike in the moral decline of our country!

Explanation: The first question that should immediately come to mind is, how on earth can one measure morality? With such a loose definition, it is not hard to imagine one collecting and measuring the data that only supports her desired outcome for the "numbers." Furthermore, what is a "huge spike?" Visually, you can play with graphs to make numbers seem much more dramatic by not starting at zero, or by doing that little "chopped section" thing. For example, let's accept that last year 20% of all people were immoral. This year it is 22%. Not a big deal, and if shown on a graph with a vertical axis of 0% to 100%, the line connecting the 20% to the 22% would be barely inclined. However, if shown on a graph with a vertical axis of 20% to 25%, the line connecting the 20% to the 22% would appear to be a huge spike. The same data, a very different presentation.

Example #2:

Looking at that pie chart, there is a very small percentage of people who declare themselves atheist. Therefore, atheism is not that popular of a belief.

Explanation: First, atheism is better described as a lack of belief. Second, many non-believers are not even familiar with the term "atheist," and often consider themselves Christian, Jewish, or some other religion, based on their culture and family tradition, not necessarily their beliefs. Statistics don't account for this.

Exception: At times, careful and honest explanations of the data and the presentation can help one avoid statistical fallacies, but like virtually all exceptions, this can be debatable.

Variation: *Misunderstanding the nature of statistics* is related to this fallacy, but the fallacy rests on the person interpreting the statistics. For example, you might be very troubled to find out that your doctor graduated in the bottom half of her class, but that is half of all the doctors in the world, and to be expected.

Tip: There are many free, online courses on statistics. Take one. It will be worth your time (and money)!

References:

Huff, D. (1993). *How to Lie with Statistics* (Reissue edition). New York: W. W. Norton & Company.

Magical Thinking

(also known as: superstitious thinking)

Description: Making causal connections or correlations between two events not based on logic or evidence, but primarily based on superstition. Magical thinking often causes one to experience irrational fear of performing certain acts or having certain thoughts because they assume a correlation with their acts and threatening calamities.

Logical Form:

Event A occurs.

Event B occurs.

Because of superstition or magic, event A is causally connected to or correlated with event B.

Example #1:

> *Mr. Governor issues a proclamation for the people of his state to pray for rain. Several months later, it rains. Praise the gods!*

Explanation: Suggesting that appealing to the gods for rain via prayer or dance is just the kind of thing crazy enough to get you elected president of the United States, but there is absolutely no logical reason or evidence to support the claim that appealing to the gods will make it rain.

Example #2:

> *I refuse to stay on the 13th floor of any hotel because it is bad luck. However, I don't mind staying on the same floor as long as we call it the 14th floor.*

Explanation: This demonstrates the kind of *magical thinking* that so many people engage in, that, according to Dilip Rangnekar of Otis Elevators, an estimated 85% of buildings with elevators did not have a floor numbered "13." There is zero evidence that the number 13 has any property that causes bad luck—of course, it is the superstitious mind that connects that number with bad luck.

Example #3:

> *I knew I should have helped that old lady across the road. Because I didn't, I have been having bad Karma all day.*

Explanation: This describes how one who believes that they deserve bad fortune, will most likely experience it due to the *confirmation bias* and other self-fulfilling prophecy-like behavior. Yet there is no logical or rational basis behind the concept of Karma.

Exception: If you can empirically prove your magic, then you can use your magic to reason.

Tip: *Magical thinking* may be comforting at times, but reality is always what's true.

References:

Hutson, M. (2012). *The 7 Laws of Magical Thinking: How Irrational Beliefs Keep Us Happy, Healthy, and Sane.* Penguin.

McNamara Fallacy

(also known as: quantitative fallacy, Skittles fallacy)

Description: When a decision is based solely on quantitative observations (i.e., metrics, hard data, statistics) and all qualitative factors are ignored.

Logical Form:

Measure whatever can be easily measured.

Disregard that which cannot be measured easily.

Presume that which cannot be measured easily is not important.

Presume that which cannot be measured easily does not exist.

Example #1: Donald Trump Jr. Tweeted:

If I had a bowl of skittles and I told you just three would kill you. Would you take a handful? That's our Syrian refugee problem.

Explanation: Let's ignore the gross statistical inaccuracy of this quote for a moment (i.e., 1 out of every 100 or so Syrian refugees is not going to kill you). The actual quantitative data about how many Syrian refugees are likely to be terrorists is some number greater than zero. The downside of letting Syrian refugees in the U.S. can be measured quantitatively, perhaps your risk of getting killed by a terrorist will increase from 3.46 billion to one to 3.4 billion to one. The upside, for the most part, is qualitative, that is, cannot be measured easily. What is a human life worth? How do we measure the suffering of others? Since these cannot easily be measured, we ignore them and conclude that taking in Syrian refugees is a bad decision.

Example #2:

> *The numbers on gun violence speak for themselves. We should ban guns in the country!*

Explanation: While the numbers on gun violence are alarming, we can't ignore the qualitative benefits of gun ownership. When making a decision, all factors need to be considered, even if they cannot be measured quantitatively.

Exception: It is possible that certain decisions do not have any qualitative components, or the qualitative components are irrelevant. For example, very often salespeople or high-end stores will attempt to sell us overpriced products or services that we can get elsewhere for 1/2 the price. They might justify their higher prices with "service," where nobody needs "service" when buying toilet paper.

Tip: Qualitative factors are often measured with a degree of subjectivity, meaning that one might give different moral weight to an idea based on one's core values. Consider this before being too harsh in your judgment of others' political or religious views.

References:

Fischer, D. H. (1970). *Historian's Fallacies*. Harper Collins.

Meaningless Question

Description: Asking a question that cannot be answered with any sort of rational meaning. This is the textual equivalent of dividing by zero.

Logical Form:

> *Question asked.*
>
> *Question is meaningless.*

Example #1:

> *What's north of the North Pole?*

Explanation: The North Pole is the most northern point of the space in which we measure direction using the north, south, east, and west coordinates. "North" of the North Pole is meaningless.

Example #2:

What happened before time?

Explanation: "Before" is a term related to a place in time. Without time, this concept is meaningless.

Example #3:

How many angels can you fit on a head of a pin?

Explanation: Angels are said to be ghost-like in that they don't take up space. "Fit" is a word that refers to space. The question is meaningless.

Fun Fact: The answers to our three meaningless questions are 1) Northness, 2) space and energy had sex, and 3) the answer depends on if Heaven has Krispy Kreme doughnut shops or not.

References:

Yngve, V., & Wasik, Z. (2006). *Hard-Science Linguistics*. A&C Black.

Misleading Vividness

Description: A small number of dramatic and vivid events are taken to outweigh a significant amount of statistical evidence.

Logical Form:

Dramatic or vivid event X occurs (does not jibe with the majority of the statistical evidence).

Therefore, events of type X are likely to occur.

Example #1:

In Detroit, there is a 10-year-old living on the street selling drugs to stay alive. In Los Angeles, a 19-year-old prostitute works the streets. America's youth is certainly in serious trouble.

Explanation: While the stories of the 10-year-old illegal pharmacist and the 19-year-old village bicycle are certainly disturbing, they are just two specific cases out of tens of millions—a vast majority of youth live pretty regular lives and far from being considered in any "serious trouble." This is a form of *appeal to emotion* that causes us to hold irrational beliefs about a population due to a few select cases. The example could have featured two other youths:

In Detroit, there is a 10-year-old who plays the piano as beautifully as Beethoven. In Los Angeles, a 19-year-old genius is getting her PhD in nuclear physics. America's youth is certainly something of which we can be proud.

Example #2:

It was freezing today as it was yesterday. My plants are now dead, and my birdbath turned to solid ice...and it is only October! This global warming thing is a load of crap.

Explanation: Whether global warming is a "load of crap" or not, concluding that, by a couple of unusually cold days, is fallacious reasoning at its finest.

Exception: If the cases featured are typical of the population in general, then no fallacy is committed.

Tip: Don't let your pessimism or optimism cloud your judgments on reality.

References:

Nisbett, R. E., & Ross, L. (1980). *Human inference: strategies and shortcomings of social judgment*. Prentice-Hall.

Missing Data Fallacy

(also known as: missing information fallacy)

Description: Refusing to admit ignorance to the hypothesis and/or the conclusion, but insisting that your ignorance has to do with missing data that validate both the hypothesis and conclusion.

Logical Form:

> *Hypothesis H is put forward.*
>
> *Fatal Flaw F is pointed out.*
>
> *Rather than change the hypothesis to match the data, it is simply assumed that there must be data missing that will eliminate flaw F.*

Example #1:

> *Jeremy: Drinking Diet Cosie Cola will result in the reversal of male-pattern baldness.*
>
> *Rick: This has never been established scientifically.*
>
> *Jeremy: That is because it must be mixed with another ingredient.*
>
> *Rick: Which is...?*
>
> *Jeremy: They haven't found it yet.*

Explanation: Jeremy is assuming the theory is correct based on some unknown missing data (the secret ingredient), rather than admitting that the whole theory is invalid.

Example #2:

> *Gil: Scientists have no idea what the appendix is for because they refuse to accept that its function is the source of psychic powers in humans that we have forgotten how to use.*
>
> *John: Scientists actually now know that the appendix serves an important role in the fetus and in young adults. This is well documented and empirically tested.*

> *Gil: This does not mean that it still is not the source of psychic powers—this just has not been tested yet.*

Explanation: In order to protect the hypothesis from error, it is assumed, without evidence that the answer does exist, but is beyond current scientific understanding.

Exception: When the data does exist, especially when it is empirically verified, but you just don't know what it is, it is acceptable to stick with your hypothesis and admit you don't know the missing data off hand, but you can get it. For example:

> *John: The Shroud of Turin was found many years back. This is physical proof that Jesus existed.*
>
> *Gil: You know, John, there is plenty of evidence against the authenticity of this.*
>
> *John: Yeah? What specifically?*
>
> *Gil: I honestly don't know the details off the top of my head, but I can e-mail you when I get home.*

Tip: Think of the *missing data fallacy* like having four cards of a royal flush and a seven of another suit. You don't have a royal flush; in fact, you have an essentially worthless hand. The difference is, with a full deck of cards, we know that the card to complete the royal flush exists.

References:

This is an original logical fallacy named by the author.

Modal (Scope) Fallacy

(also known as: fallacy of modal logic, misconditionalization, fallacy of necessity)

Description: *Modal logic* studies ways in which propositions can be true or false, the most common being *necessity* and *possibility*. Some propositions are necessarily true/false, and others are possibly true/false. In short, a modal fallacy involves making a formal argument invalid by confusing the *scope* of what is actually necessary or possible.

Logical Form:

A conditional claim is made using a necessary truth.

Therefore, conclusion is reached that a possible truth is necessary with no conditional statement.

Example #1:

If Debbie and TJ have two sons and two daughters, then they must have at least one son.

Debbie and TJ have two sons and two daughters.

Therefore, Debbie and TJ must have at least one son.

Explanation: We are told that Debbie and TJ have two sons and two daughters, so logically, by necessity, they must *have at* least one son. However, to say that Debbie and TJ *must* have at least one son, is to *confuse the scope of the modal*, or in this case, to take the *contingent fact* that applies to the specific case that is conditional upon Debbie and TJ having the two sons and two daughters, to the general hypothetical case where they don't have to have any children. Therefore, if they don't *have to* have any children, then they certainly don't *have to* (*necessary fact*) have at least one son.

Example #2:

If Barak is President, then he must be at least 35-years old.

Explanation: Technically this is fallacious. There is no condition in which someone *necessarily* is a certain age. More accurately, we would say:

It must be the case that if Barak is President, then he is 35 or older.

The "must" in this second statement covers the whole condition, not just the age of the president.

Exception: This is one of those fallacies that would make you look foolish for calling someone out on, unless you are among all academic philosophers. In casual argumentation many people do mean "possibility" and not "necessity." Remember to offer others a charitable interpretation of their argument.

Fun Fact: According to Article II of the U.S. Constitution, the president of the United States must be a natural-born citizen of the United States; be at least 35 years old; have been a resident of the United States for 14 years; and be able to identify a snake, an elephant, and an alligator.

References:

Curtis, G. N. (1993). *The Concept of Logical Form*. Indiana University.

Moralistic Fallacy

(also known as: moral fallacy)

Description: When the conclusion expresses what is, based only on what one believes ought to be, or what isn't is based on what one believes ought not to be.

This is the opposite of the *naturalistic fallacy*.

In his 1957 paper, Edward C. Moore defined the *moralistic fallacy* as the assertion that moral judgments are of a different order from factual judgements. Over the years, this concept has been simplified to deriving an "is" from an "ought."

Logical Forms:

> *X ought to be.*
>
> *Therefore, X is.*

> *X ought not to be.*
>
> *Therefore, X is not.*

Example #1:

> *Adultery, as well as philandering, is wrong.*

Therefore, we have no biological tendency for multiple sex partners.

Explanation: While, morally speaking, adultery and philandering may be wrong, this has no bearing on the biological aspect of the desire or need. In other words, what we *shouldn't do* (according to moral norms), is not necessarily the same as what we are *biologically influenced* to do. Also note that moral judgments are more commonly stated as facts (e.g., "philandering *is* wrong") than expressed as "oughts" (e.g., "philandering *ought to be* wrong"). This causes people to confuse the *naturalistic* and *moralistic* fallacies.

Example #2:

Being mean to others is wrong.

Therefore, it cannot possibly be part of our nature.

Explanation: While, morally speaking, being mean to others may be wrong, this has no bearing on the biological aspect of the desire or need. Again, what we *shouldn't do* (according to moral norms), is not necessarily the same as what we are *biologically influenced* to do.

Exception: An argument can certainly be made that an ought is the same as an is, but it just cannot be assumed.

Fun Fact: The *naturalistic* and the *moralistic* fallacies are often confused with the *appeal to nature* fallacy. One reason, perhaps, is because what is "natural" is another way of saying what is, is. But with the *naturalistic* and the *moralistic* fallacies, the conclusion does not have to be based on what is "natural;" it just has to be based on what is. For example,

Men and women ought to be equal. Therefore, women are just as strong as men and men are just as empathetic as women.

This is another example of the *moralistic fallacy* but not an *appeal to nature*.

References:

Moore, E. C. (1957). The Moralistic Fallacy. *The Journal of Philosophy*, 54(2), 29–42. https://doi.org/10.2307/2022356

Pinker, S. (2003). *The Blank Slate: The Modern Denial of Human Nature*. Penguin.

Moving the Goalposts

(also known as: gravity game, raising the bar, argument by demanding impossible perfection)

Description: Demanding from an interlocutor that he or she address more and more points after the initial counter-argument has been satisfied refusing to concede or accept the interlocutor's argument.

Logical Form:

> *Issue A has been raised, and adequately answered.*
>
> *Issue B is then raised, and adequately answered.*
>
> *.....*
>
> *Issue Z is then raised, and adequately answered.*
>
> *(despite all issues adequately answered, the interlocutor refuses to conceded or accept the argument.*

Example #1:

> *Ken: There has to be an objective morality because otherwise terms like "right" and "wrong" would be meaningless since they have no foundation for comparison.*
>
> *Rob: The terms "right" and "wrong" are based on cultural norms, which do have a subjective foundation—one that changes as the moral sphere of the culture changes. The term "heavy" does not have an objective standard, yet we have no problem using that term in a meaningful way. In fact, very few relational terms have any kind of objective foundation.*

Ken: But without an objective morality, we would all be lost morally as a race.

Rob: Many would say that we are.

Ken: But how can you say that torturing children for fun is morally acceptable in any situation?

Rob: Personally, I wouldn't, but you are implying that anything that is not objective must necessarily be seen in all possible ways. A feather may not be seen as "heavy" to anyone, but that doesn't mean its "lightness" is still not relative to other objects.

Ken: But God is the standard of objective morality. Prove that wrong!

Rob: That I cannot do.

Explanation: Ken starts with a statement explaining why he thinks there *has to be* an objective morality—a statement based on a reasonable argument that can be pursued with reason and logic. Rob adequately answers that objection, as indicated by Ken's move away from that objection to a new objection. This pattern continues until we arrive at an impossible request. Despite all the objections being adequately answered, at no time does Ken concede any points or abandon the argument.

Example #2: Perhaps the most classic example of this fallacy is the argument for the existence of God. Due to the understanding of nature through science, many of the arguments that used to be used for God (or gods) were abandoned, only to be replaced with new ones, usually involving questions to which science has not definitively answered yet. The move from creationism to *intelligent design* is a prime example. Currently the origin of life is a popular argument for God (although a classic *argument from ignorance*), and an area where we very well may have a scientific answer in the next decade, at which time, the "origin of life" argument will fade away and be replaced by another, thus moving the figurative goalposts farther back as our understanding of the natural world increases.

Exception: This fallacy should not be confused with an argument or set of arguments, with multiple propositions inherent in the argument. The reason for the difference between this kind of argument and the *moving the goalposts fallacy*, is a subtle one, but indicated by a strong initial claim (" has to be," "must," "required for," etc.) that gets answered and/ or what appears to be *ad hoc* objections that follow eventually leading to an impossible request for proof.

Fun Fact: The name "moving the goalposts" comes from the analogy of kicking a perfect field goal in American football, only to have the goalposts be moved on you. This would be very unfair.

References:

This is a logical fallacy frequently used on the Internet. No academic sources could be found.

Multiple Comparisons Fallacy

(also known as: multiple comparisons, multiplicity, multiple testing problem, the look-elsewhere effect)

Description: Claiming that unexpected trends that occur through random chance alone in a data set with a large number of variables are meaningful.

In inductive arguments, there is always a chance that the conclusion might be false, despite the truth of the premises. This is often referred to as "confidence level." In any given study or poll, there is a confidence level of less than 100%. If a confidence level is 95%, then one out of 20 similar studies will have a false conclusion. If you make multiple comparisons (either in the same study or compare multiple studies), say 20 or more where there is a 95% confidence level, you are likely to get a false conclusion. This becomes a fallacy when that false conclusion is seen as significant rather than a statistical probability.

This fallacy can be overcome by proper testing techniques and procedures that are outside the scope of this book.

Logical Forms:

Out of N studies, A produced result X and B produced result Y. Tomorrow's headlines read, "Studies show Y."

The study's significance level was X.

The study compared multiple variables until some significant result was found.

Example #1:

100 independent studies were conducted comparing brain tumor rates of those who use cell phones to those who don't.

90 of the tests showed no significant difference in the rates.

5 of the tests showed that cell phone users were more than twice as likely to develop tumors than those who don't use cell phones.

5 of the tests showed that cell phone users were half as likely to develop tumors than those who don't use cell phones.

FunTel Mobile's new ad, "Studies show: Cell phone users are half as likely to develop brain tumors!"

Explanation: Because we did multiple tests, i.e., compared multiple groups, statistically we are likely to get results that fall within the acceptable margin of error. These must be disregarded as anomalies or tested further, but not taken to be meaningful while ignoring the other results.

Example #2:

In our study, we looked at 100 individuals who sang right before going to bed, and 100 individuals who did not sing. Here is what we found: Over 90% of the individuals who sang slept on their backs, and just 10% slept on their stomachs or sides. This is compared to 50% of those who did not sing, sleeping on their backs and 50% sleeping on their stomachs or sides. Therefore, singing has something to do with sleeping position.

Explanation: What this study did not report, is that over 500 comparisons were done between the two groups, on everything from quality of sleep to what they ate for breakfast the next day. Out of all the comparisons, most were meaningless, thus were discarded—but as expected via the law statistics and probability, there were some anomalies, the sleeping position being the most dramatic.

Exception: Only proper testing and accurate representation of the results would lead to non-fallacious conclusions.

Fun Fact: In a group of 23 random people, it is more likely than not that at least two of the people in the group have the same birthday. This is referred to a the *birthday paradox* and it is a classic example of the *multiple comparisons fallacy*.

References:

Walsh, J. (1996). *True Odds: How Risk Affects Your Everyday Life.* Silver Lake Publishing.

Naturalistic Fallacy

(also known as: is-ought fallacy, arguing from is to ought, is-should fallacy)

Description: When the conclusion expresses what ought to be, based only on what is, or what ought not to be, based on what is not. This is very common, and most people never see the problem with these kinds of assertions due to accepted social and moral norms. This bypasses reason and we fail to ask why something that *is, ought* to be that way.

This is the opposite of the *moralistic fallacy*.

A more traditional use of the *naturalistic fallacy* is committed when one attempts to define "good" as anything other than itself. The philosopher G. E. Moore (1873-1958) argued that it is a mistake to try to define the concept "good" in terms of some natural property (thus, the name "naturalistic"). Defining the concept "good," Moore argued, is impossible since it is a simple concept; a concept that cannot be defined in terms of any other concept. Not all philosophers agree that this is a fallacy. Some have argued that ethical terms, such as "good" can be defined in nonethical natural terms. They believe that ethical judgments directly follow from facts, i.e., it is possible to argue from a fact to a value.

Logical Forms:

X is.

Therefore, X ought to be.

X is not.

Therefore, X ought not to be.

Example #1:

Homosexuality is / ought to be morally wrong (moral property) because it is not normal (natural property).

or

Homosexuality is not normal (natural property); therefore, it is / ought to be morally wrong (moral property).

Explanation: If we break this down, we can say the claim is that homosexuality (X) is not normal (X is not). We are arguing that homosexuality is morally wrong (X ought not to be) because it is not normal (X is not). The claim that homosexuality is not normal is based on defining normality as "commonly occurring." We can see the flaw in this argumentation through a simple analogy: lying, cheating, and stealing are normal (in that most people do it at some time in their lives), but this doesn't make those actions morally good.

Example #2:

Nature gives people diseases and sickness; therefore, it is morally wrong to interfere with nature and treat sick people with medicine.

Explanation: If we break this down, we can say that the claim that nature gives people diseases and sickness is a declaration of what is (i.e., a natural property of the world). From this, we are deriving an ought (i.e., we ought not interfere...). The wording and order of these arguments can be confusing, but remember that the underlying fallacy here is the deduction of an ought from an is.

We go against nature (or what is) all the time. We cannot sometimes use nature as a moral baseline and at other times condemn her for her careless attitude and indifference toward the human race.

Exception: At times, our morality will be in line with what is— but if we are justifying a moral action, we need to use something besides simply what is.

Fun Fact: The *naturalistic* and the *moralistic* fallacies are often confused with the *appeal to nature* fallacy. One reason, perhaps, is because what is "natural" is another way of saying what is, is. But with the *naturalistic* and the *moralistic* fallacies, the conclusion does not have to be based on what is "natural;" it just has to be based on what is. For example,

> *Since wars have taken place since the beginning of recorded history, then they can't be morally wrong.*

This is another example of the *naturalistic fallacy* but not an *appeal to nature*.

References:

Pinker, S. (2003). *The Blank Slate: The Modern Denial of Human Nature*. Penguin.

Tanner, J. (2006). The naturalistic fallacy. *The Richmond Journal of Philosophy*, 13, 1–6.

Negating Antecedent and Consequent

(also known as: improper transposition)

New Terminology:

> **Transposition (contraposition):** In a syllogism, taking the antecedent and consequent in the first premise, then "transposing" them in the second premise, and negating each term.

Description: A formal fallacy where in the valid transpositional form of an argument, we fail to switch the antecedent and consequent. The valid form of this argument is as follows:

If P then Q.

Therefore, if not-Q then not-P.

Notice we switch (transpose) the P and the Q, then negate them both. We commit the fallacy when we fail to transpose (switch) them.

Logical Forms:

If P then Q.

Therefore, if not-P then not-Q.

If not-P then not-Q.

Therefore, if P then Q.

Example #1:

If Barry Manilow sings love songs, then he is gay.

Therefore, if Barry Manilow does not sing love songs, then he is not gay.

Explanation: Besides the wildly incorrect premise that if Barry sings love songs he is gay, the conclusion fails to switch the antecedent (Barry Manilow sings love songs) with the consequent (he is gay); therefore, it is fallacious. However, if we did transpose the antecedent and the consequent in the conclusion, it would be a perfectly valid formal argument, even though the premise might not be a reasonable assumption. Remember, a valid, non-fallacious formal argument does not have to have a true conclusion, it just needs to be truth-preserving—in the case that the premises are all true.

If Barry Manilow sings love songs, then he is gay.

Therefore, if Barry Manilow is not gay, then he does not sing love songs.

Example #2:

> *If Tom thinks that all people who sing love songs are gay, then he is an idiot.*
>
> *Therefore, if Tom doesn't think that all people who sing love songs are gay, then he is not an idiot.*

Explanation: We have the same problem with the failure to transpose the antecedent (Tom thinks that all people who sing love songs are gay) with the consequent (he is an idiot) in the conclusion, although we did negate them both. I hope you can see that just because Tom does not think all people who sing love songs are gay, does not mean that Tom is not an idiot for some other reason. This argument is invalid, thus fallacious.

Fun Fact: Barry Manilow was born "Barry Alan Pincus."

References:

Carlsen-Jones, M. T. (1983). *Introduction to Logic.* McGraw-Hill.

Negative Conclusion from Affirmative Premises

(also known as: illicit affirmative)

Description: The conclusion of a standard form categorical syllogism is negative, but both of the premises are positive. Any valid forms of categorical syllogisms that assert a negative conclusion must have at least one negative premise.

Logical Form:

> *If A is a subset of B, and B is a subset of C, then A is not a subset of C.*

Example #1:

> *All cats are animals.*
>
> *Some pets are cats.*

Therefore, some pets are not animals.

Explanation: The conclusion might be true—I had a pet rock growing up, but the argument still does not logically support that. Think of sets and subsets. All cats are animals: we have a set of animals and a subset of cats. "Some" pets are cats: so all we know is that there is a part of our set, "pets" that intersects with the subset, "cats," but we don't have the information we need to conclude logically that some pets are not animals. This argument is invalid, thus as a formal argument, it is fallacious.

Example #2:

> *All boys are sports fans.*
>
> *Some bakers are boys.*
>
> *Therefore, some bakers are not sports fans.*

Explanation: The conclusion might be true—but the argument still does not logically support that for the same reasons in the first example. This argument is invalid, thus as a formal argument, it is fallacious.

Fun Fact: I taught my pet rock how to play dead. It was its only trick.

References:

Goodman, M. F. (1993). *First Logic.* University Press of America.

Nirvana Fallacy

(also known as: perfect solution fallacy, perfectionist fallacy)

Description: Comparing a realistic solution with an idealized one, and discounting or even dismissing the realistic solution as a result of comparing to a "perfect world" or impossible standard, ignoring the fact that improvements are often good enough reason.

Logical Form:

> *X is what we have.*

Y is the perfect situation.

Therefore, X is not good enough.

Example #1:

What's the point of making drinking illegal under the age of 21? Kids still manage to get alcohol.

Explanation: The goal in setting a minimum age for drinking is to deter underage drinking, not abolish it completely. Suggesting the law is fruitless based on its failure to abolish underage drinking completely, is fallacious.

Example #2:

What's the point of living? We're all going to die anyway.

Explanation: There is an implication that the goal of life is not dying. While that is certainly a worthwhile goal, many would argue that it is a bit empty on its own, creating this fallacy where one does not really exist.

Exception: Striving for perfection is not the same as the *nirvana fallacy*. Having a goal of perfection or near perfection, and working towards that goal, is admirable. However, giving up on the goal because perfection is not attained, despite major improvements being attained, is fallacious.

Tip: Sometimes good enough is really good enough.

References:

George Mason University law review. (1991).

No True Scotsman

(also known as: appeal to purity [form of], no true Christian, no true crossover fallacy [form of])

Description: When a universal ("all," "every," etc.) claim is refuted, rather than conceding the point or meaningfully revising the claim, the claim is altered by going from universal to specific, and failing to give any objective criteria for the specificity.

Logical Form:

All X are Y.

(the claim that all X are Y is clearly refuted)

Then all true X are Y.

Example #1: In 2011, Christian broadcaster, Harold Camping, (once again) predicted the end of the world via Jesus, and managed to get many Christians to join his alarmist campaign. During this time, and especially after the Armageddon date had passed, many Christian groups publicly declared that Camping is not a "true Christian." On a personal note, I think Camping was and is as much of a Christian as any other self-proclaimed Christian and religious/political/ethical beliefs aside, I give him credit for having the cojones to make a falsifiable claim about his religious beliefs.

Example #2:

John: Members of the UbaTuba White Men's Club are upstanding citizens of the community.

Marvin: Then why are there so many of these members in jail?

John: They were never true UbaTuba White Men's Club members.

Marvin: What's a true UbaTuba White Men's Club member?

John: Those who don't go to jail.

Explanation: This is a very common form of this fallacy that has many variations. Every time one group member denounces another group member for doing or saying something that they don't approve of, usually by the phrase, "he is not really a *true* [insert membership here]," this fallacy is committed.

The universal claim here is that no UbaTuba White Men's Club member will ever (universal) go to jail. Marvin points out how clearly this is counterfactual as there are many UbaTuba White Men's Club members in jail. Instead of conceding or meaningfully revising the claim, the implication that no "UbaTuba White Men's Club members" is changed to "no true UbaTuba White Men's Club members," which is not meaningful because John's definition of a "true UbaTuba White Men's Club member" apparently can only be demonstrated in the negative if an UbaTuba White Men's Club member goes to jail. This results in the *questionable cause fallacy* as it is also an *unfalsifiable* claim, and of course, it commits the *no true Scotsman* fallacy.

Exception: A revised claim going from universal to specific that does give an objective standard would not be fallacious. If this were the case, a false claim would still have been made, but no fallacy would follow.

Variations: The more generic *appeal to purity* can be seen when the claim is that someone "does not have enough of" something, which is why they are not meeting the condition. For example, "If you have the desire for success, you will succeed!" Billy has the desire but is not succeeding. Therefore, Billy's desire is not strong (or pure) enough. The difference between the *appeal to purity* and the *no true Scotsman* is one of degree versus authenticity.

Another variation is what I call the *no true crossover fallacy*. This fallacy is committed when one denies, for the purpose of protecting one of the groups, that an individual can be a part of two or more non-exclusionary groups. During the protests in the spring of 2020, many businesses have been vandalized, looted, and even burned down. When people blamed this on the protesters, the defense was that "protesters protest and looters loot." The implication is that the moment a protester loots, they become a "looter," and no longer are part of the group "protesters." This is a way of absolving every "true" member of the group "protesters" from any wrongdoing. It is likely that there are a group of looters who are opportunists and have no ideological position and would not qualify in any reasonable way as "protesters." It is clear, however, that there are protesters who believe looting is an effective tool for protesting. Similarly, attempting to absolve police officers from wrongdoing because "police officers police and criminals commit crimes" is equally as fallacious for all the same reasons.

Tip: People will sometimes claim outright that if any person who claims to be a member of group X and has Y characteristic, is not a member of group X. Ask them if those who claim to be a member of group X and has Y characteristic would agree.

References:

Flew, A. (1984). *A Dictionary of Philosophy: Revised Second Edition.* Macmillan.

Non Sequitur

(also known as: derailment, "that does not follow," irrelevant reason, invalid inference, non-support, argument by scenario [form of], false premise [form of], questionable premise [form of])

Description: When the conclusion does not follow from the premises. In more informal reasoning, it can be when what is presented as evidence or reason is irrelevant or adds very little support to the conclusion.

Logical Form:

> Claim A is made.
>
> Evidence is presented for claim A.
>
> Therefore, claim C is true.

Example #1:

> People generally like to walk on the beach. Beaches have sand. Therefore, having sand floors in homes would be a great idea!

Explanation: As cool as the idea of sand floors might sound, the conclusion does not follow from the premises. The fact that people generally like to walk on sand does not mean that they want sand in their homes, just like because people generally like to swim, they shouldn't flood their houses.

Example #2:

Buddy Burger has the greatest food in town. Buddy Burger was voted #1 by the local paper. Therefore, Phil, the owner of Buddy Burger, should run for president of the United States.

Explanation: I bet Phil makes one heck of a burger, but it does not follow that he should be president.

Exception: There really are no exceptions to this rule. Any good argument must have a conclusion that follows from the premises.

Variations: There are many forms of non sequiturs including a*rgument by scenario*, where an irrelevant scenario is given in an attempt to support the conclusion. Other forms use different rhetorical devices that are irrelevant to the conclusion.

False or *questionable premises* could be seen as errors in facts, but they can also lead to the conclusion not following, so just keep that in mind, as well.

Tip: One of the best ways to expose *non sequiturs* is by constructing a valid analogy that exposes the absurdity in the argument.

References:

Hyslop, J. H. (1892). *The Elements of Logic, Theoretical and Practical*. C. Scribner's Sons.

Notable Effort

(also known as: "E" is for effort)

Description: Accepting good effort as a valid reason to accept the truth of the conclusion, even though the effort is unrelated to the truth.

Logical Form:

Person 1 made a notable effort to prove Y.

Therefore, Y is true.

Example #1:

Judge: In all my years as a federal judge I have never seen a defendant make such a good effort to prove his innocence. As a result, I rule for the defendant.

Explanation: The fact that the defendant made a good effort to prove his innocence means nothing to the fact that he is actually innocent or not—unless he *succeeded* in his efforts. The judge's ruling would be based on emotion and not reason.

Example #2:

How can you possibly deny his claim? William wrote an entire book trying to explain why he thinks his claim is true. Therefore, it must be true.

Explanation: The fact that William made a *notable effort* to prove his claim does not mean that he did.

Exception: As long as the effort is unrelated to the truth of the claim, there are no exceptions.

Tip: Enough with the "everyone's a winner" mentality. As long as we keep rewarding *all* effort, we devalue the effort that leads to *successful results*. The world needs losers as well—just don't be one of them.

References:

This is a logical fallacy frequently used on the Internet. No academic sources could be found.

Nutpicking Fallacy

Description: When someone presents an atypical or weak member of a group as if they are a typical or strong representative.

Logical Form:

Person X is presented as a typical or strong representative of group Y.

Person X is actually an atypical or weak member of group Y.

Therefore, Person X is seen as a typical or strong representative of group Y.

Example #1: Politically ideological individuals on social media consistently post quotes, articles, and stories about the heroes on their side of the political spectrum and villains on the other side in an attempt to influence public perception of their political adversaries. The implied message is, "See, this is what the liberals, are like and this is what the conservatives are like."

Example #2: After the killing of George Floyd, the police officer responsible has been presented by those calling to defund the police as a strong representative of the police in the United States. This representation triggers people's *availability bias* resulting in an inaccurate view of police in general. At the same time, FOX News will report on hero cops who save babies, get killed in the line of duty, and replace broken refrigerators for senior citizens[6]. Neither of these portrayals is typical or a strong representation of police in general.

Exception: As Stephen Woodford points out in his video in the reference, sometimes "nuts" permeate the group to the extent that the "nut" is typical of the group. An example is flat-earthers. I say that unapologetically.

Variation: A variation of this fallacy is *overextended outrage*. Essentially, this is like picking the nuts for the purpose of expressing or inciting outrage toward an entire group.

Fun Fact: I have heard a couple of people refer to the *cherry picking fallacy* as the *nutpicking fallacy*. Review the *cherry picking fallacy* and you will see that there are notable differences.

---

[6] https://www.foxnews.com/lifestyle/florida-woman-911-refrigerator-broke-cops-new-one

References:

Rationality Rules: https://www.youtube.com/watch?v=CVHvdjUZAzI

Overextended Outrage

(also known as: overextended moral outrage, overextended political outrage)

Description: This is a form of poor statistical thinking where one or more statistically rare cases are implied to be the norm or the trend (without evidence) for the purpose of expressing or inciting outrage toward an entire group. It is a form of extreme *stereotyping*, based on the cognitive bias known as the *group attribution error*.

Logical Form:

Person 1 does something bad.

Person 1 is a member of group X.

Outrage is expressed towards group X.

Example #1: *FAUX News* runs a story about an illegal immigrant who committed a horrible crime. The commentators talk about this case for weeks, expressing outrage about the serious danger illegal immigrants pose to the good people of the United States.

Explanation: Violent crime by illegal immigrants is rarer than violent crime committed by U.S. citizens[7]. However, if the narrative a media outlet is trying to sell is that illegal immigrants are dangerous, then they can influence public opinion by inferring that one example of such violence is characteristic of the group. Expressing outrage is a way to make the influence even more effective.

---

[7] Adelman, R., Reid, L. W., Markle, G., Weiss, S., & Jaret, C. (2017). Urban crime rates and the changing face of immigration: Evidence across four decades. Journal of Ethnicity in Criminal Justice, 15(1), 52–77. https://doi.org/10.1080/15377938.2016.1261057

Example #2: *The Huffaluf Post* runs a story about a Republican who assaulted a Muslim woman and told her to "go back where she came from." The story is shared millions of times and picked up by other liberal media outlets. Liberals are discussing this story on social media saying how outraged they are at Republicans for their hatred of Muslims.

Explanation: People and the media (biased media) tend to associate a physical or social identity to the perpetrator of a crime for the purpose of damaging the group's public perception. Why a "Republican" man? How many Republicans are assaulting Muslim women? How many Democrats are? The data are ignored for the benefit of the narrative being sold.

Exception: There is no exception. If it is "overextended," then the problem is being exaggerated, and a group of people is unfairly demonized.

Tip: Next time you read about a story that makes you feel outraged, direct your outrage to the individuals directly involved in the story. Don't demonize an entire physical or social identity.

References:

This is an original logical fallacy named by the author.

Oversimplified Cause Fallacy

Description: When a contributing factor is assumed to be the cause, or when a complex array of causal factors is reduced to a single cause. It is a form of simplistic thinking that implies something is either a cause, or it is not. It overlooks the important fact that, especially when referring to human behavior, causes are very complex and multi-dimensional.

Logical Form:

X is a contributing factor to Y.

X and Y are present.

Therefore, to remove Y, remove X.

Example #1:

Lead poisoning can contribute to violent behavior.

Many inner city children have dangerous levels of lead in their blood.

*Therefore, violent crime in the inner city **can be solved** by curing the lead problem.*

Explanation: We already established that lead poisoning *can contribute* to violent behavior (note the probabilistic language). This means that there is some unspecified chance. We are taking an unreasonable leap in suggesting that violent crime can be *solved* (binary language) by curing the lead problem. And, in case you missed it, there is *question begging* here in assuming that violent *behavior* leads to violent *crime*.

Example #2:

A sedentary lifestyle contributes to obesity.

People have become more sedentary in the last few decades.

*Therefore, the rise in obesity **can be fixed** by people getting more exercise.*

Explanation: We made the leap from "contributes" to "can be fixed." At best, we can conclude that the problem of obesity can be *mitigated* by people getting more exercise.

Example #3:

Smoking has been empirically proven to cause lung cancer.

Therefore, if we eradicate smoking, we will eradicate lung cancer.

Explanation: Even though it is reasonable to consider smoking a "cause" of lung cancer versus a "contributing factor" to lung cancer, assuming it is the **only** cause is fallacious.

Tip: Establishing causality is extremely tricky. Unless you are stating an established fact, start using more probabilistic language such as "contributes to," "leads to," "has been known to reduce the effects of," or similar language.

References:

Hurley, P. J. (2011). *A Concise Introduction to Logic*. Cengage Learning.

Overwhelming Exception

Description: A generalization that is technically accurate, but has one or more qualifications which eliminate so many cases that the resulting argument is significantly weaker than the arguer implies. In many cases, the listed exceptions are given in place of evidence or support for the claim, not in addition to evidence or support for the claim.

Logical Form:

Claim A is made.

Numerous exceptions to claim A are made.

Therefore, claim A is true.

Example #1:

Besides charities, comfort, community cohesion, rehabilitation, and helping children learn values, religion poisons everything.

Explanation: Besides being a *self-refuting statement*, the listing of the ways religion does not poison everything, is a clear indicator that the claim is false, or at best, very weak.

Example #2:

Our country is certainly in terrible shape. Sure, we still have all kinds of freedoms, cultural diversity, emergency rooms and trauma care, agencies like the FDA out to protect us, the entertainment industry, a free market, national parks, we are considered the most powerful nation in the world, have amazing opportunities, and free public education, but still...

Explanation: We have many reasons supporting the opposite claim—that this country is in great shape still, or at least that it is not in *terrible* shape. By the time all the reasons are listed, the original claim of our country being in terrible shape is a lot less agreeable.

Exception: The fewer exceptions, the less overwhelming, the less likely the fallacy.

Fun Fact: This fallacy is usually made by people who are well on their way to seeing the reasonable conclusion in the argument, but can't quite let go of their unreasonable belief or claim.

References:

Lindgren, J. (1983). More Blackmail Ink: A Critique of Blackmail, Inc., Epstein's Theory of Blackmail. *Connecticut Law Review*, 16, 909.

Package-Deal Fallacy

(also known as: false conjunction)

Description: Assuming things that are often grouped together must always be grouped together, or the assumption that the ungrouping will have significantly more severe effects than anticipated.

Logical Form:

> *X and Y usually go together.*
>
> *Therefore, X or Y cannot be separated.*

Example #1:

> *Michael is part of the Jackson Five. Without Tito and company, he will never make it.*

Explanation: Michael Jackson was sure great in the *Jackson Five*, but as history proves, he was legendary on his own. Assuming he would not make it on his own is a judgment call not founded on evidence or reason.

Example #2:

> *If indoor smoking laws are passed for bars, the bars will go out of business since people who drink, smoke while they drink.*

Explanation: This was a common argument against the banning of indoor smoking for bars and other drinking establishments. The fear of separating smoking and drinking arose from the fear of going out of business, not from statistical data or any other evidence that would normally be deemed reasonable. Many years later, it appears that the smoking ban had no significant impact on these kinds of establishments[8].

Exception: An exception can be made for personal tastes.

> *I can't even imagine eating just a peanut-butter sandwich without jelly (or Fluff).*

Tip: Never underestimate the human ability to adapt and prosper.

References:

This is a logical fallacy frequently used on the Internet. No academic sources could be found.

Poisoning the Well

(also known as: discrediting, smear tactics, appeal to ethos [form of])

Description: To commit a preemptive *ad hominem* attack against an interlocutor. That is, to prime the audience with adverse information about the interlocutor from the start, in an attempt to make your claim more acceptable or discount the credibility of your interlocutor's claim.

---

[8] Mark Engelen, Matthew Farrelly & Andrew Hyland: The Health and Economic Impact of New York's Clean Indoor Air Act. July 2006, p. 21

Logical Form:

Adverse information (be it true or false) about person 1 is presented.

Therefore, the claim(s) of person 1 will be false.

Example #1:

Tim: Boss, you heard my side of the story why I think Bill should be fired and not me. Now, I am sure Bill is going to come to you with some pathetic attempt to weasel out of this lie that he has created.

Explanation: Tim is *poisoning the well* by priming his boss by attacking Bill's character, and setting up any defense Bill might present as "pathetic." Tim is using this fallacious tactic here, but if the boss were to accept Tim's advice about Bill, she would be committing the fallacy.

Example #2:

I hope I presented my argument clearly. Now, my interlocutor will attempt to refute my argument by his own fallacious, incoherent, illogical version of history.

Explanation: Not a very nice setup for the interlocutor. As an audience member, if you allow any of this "poison" to affect how you evaluate the interlocutor's argument, you are guilty of fallacious reasoning.

Exception: Remember that if a person states facts relevant to the argument, it is not an *ad hominem* attack. In the first example, if the other "poison" were left out, no fallacy would be committed.

Tim: Boss, you heard my side of the story why I think Bill should be fired and not me. Now, I am sure Bill is going to come to you with his side of the story, but please keep in mind that we have two witnesses to the event who both agree that Bill was the one who told the client that she had ugly children.

Variation: The *appeal to ethos* involves rejection of an argument based on a character attack of the person making the argument.

Gertie: Tony says that the movie starts at 8:00 tonight.

Jane: Well, Tony is misogynist pig!

Gertie: Hmm, we better double check that time then.

Fun Fact: To understand how powerful priming the audience with adverse information can be, consider the Rosenhan experiment[9] where eight mentally healthy students and researchers briefly feigned auditory hallucinations in order to get admitted to psychiatric hospitals. After admission, they said they were no longer having hallucinations and acted normally. One of the patients, who was also a student, was taking notes for the experiment which was interpreted as pathological "writing behavior" by one of the hospital staff.

References:

Walton, D. (1998). *Ad Hominem Arguments*. University of Alabama Press.

Political Correctness Fallacy

(also known as: PC fallacy)

Description: This is a common one in recent history. It is the assumption or admission that two or more groups, individuals, or ideas of groups or individuals, are equal, of equal value, or both true, based on the recent phenomenon of political correctness, which is defined as, a term which denotes language, ideas, policies, and behavior seen as seeking to minimize social and institutional offense in occupational, gender, racial, cultural, sexual orientation, certain other religions, beliefs or ideologies, disability, and age-related contexts, and, as purported by the term, doing so to an excessive extent.

---

[9] https://en.wikipedia.org/wiki/Rosenhan_experiment

This can be seen as an over-correction of *stereotyping*.

Logical Form:

> *Claim A is politically incorrect.*
>
> *Therefore, claim A is false.*

Example #1:

> *Racial/cultural profiling at airports is wrong. An adult, middle-eastern male is just as likely to be a terrorist as a four-year-old American girl.*

Explanation: While many things are possible, including a four-year-old American girl being a terrorist, profiling works on probabilities. Inserting political correctness here goes against reason in asserting that every person is just as likely to be a terrorist.

Example #2:

> *The masked individual who committed the crime was about 6'2," and took down four male security guards by hand. It is just as likely that the criminal was a woman.*

Explanation: While it is certainly possible that a 6'2" female martial-arts master is the criminal, it is highly unlikely, and it would be a waste of resources to question an even number of men and women based on the desire not to discriminate.

Example #3:

> *Everyone is entitled to his or her own religious beliefs. So if dancing in the streets naked is part of their ritual, we must extend them that right.*

Explanation: Are any and all religiously-based behaviors acceptable? Must we allow all expression of religion? Where do we draw the line and why?

Example #4:

Sacrificing virgins is part of that tribe's culture and heritage. Therefore, it is just as acceptable as our culture's tradition of eating a hot dog at a baseball game.

Explanation: Here we enter the realm of morality and choose to protect a "cultural belief" over saving the life of a young girl.

These examples—and this fallacy—are very controversial. Like all fallacies, arguments need to be made. I am making an argument that PC can be a fallacy in many cases. You might agree, you might disagree. In either case, be prepared to argue for your position with valid reasons.

Exception: See above.

Tip: At its core, being "PC" is the belief that minimizing social and institutional offense is a kind and compassionate thing to do. Don't confuse this with the fallacy of determining the truth of a claim based on its perceived political correctness. Reality doesn't care about social and institutional offense.

References:

This is an original logical fallacy named by the author.

Post-Designation

(also known as: fishing for data)

Description: Drawing a conclusion from correlations observed in a given sample, but only after the sample has already been drawn, and without declaring in advance what correlations the experimenter was expecting to find.

Logical Form:

A sample from a dataset is drawn.

A correlation is found that was not looked at nor is it statistically surprising.

The correlation is seen as being meaningful.

Example #1:

In looking at the records of my students, I have found that 9 out of 10 are an only child. Therefore, society is moving towards one-child families.

Explanation: When you start looking at data with no expectations, anything goes, and any data due to random, statistical anomalies will stand out as "odd." In this case, the fact that 9 out of 10 kids don't have siblings is outside of the norm, but that is the nature of probability. If you were hypothesizing that most kids don't have siblings, and you found this data, then it would provide more of a reason to do further research in making a more justified conclusion.

Example #2:

In looking at the difference between 100 Christians and 100 atheists, we found that Christians were significantly more likely to eat tuna fish.

Explanation: When you fish for data, you are bound to catch something—in this case, tuna. Notice that because we were looking for anything, we are bound to find it.

Exception: At times, truth is revealed in data whether we look for it or not, but we need to realize that meaningless statistical anomalies are to be expected when looking at data.

Fun Fact: *Post-designation* appears to be just a different name for the *multiple comparisons fallacy*. I have kept both entries because I have expanded the *multiple comparisons fallacy* to include multiple comparisons between studies, which doesn't seem to fit the *post-designation* fallacy's definition.

References:

This is a logical fallacy frequently used on the Internet. No academic sources could be found.

Post Hoc
post hoc ergo propter hoc

(also known as: after this, therefore because of this, post hoc rationalization)

Description: Claiming that because event Y followed event X, event Y must have been caused by event X, without properly establishing causality.

Logical Form:

> *Y occurred, then X occurred.*
>
> *Therefore, Y caused X.*

Example #1: Doug is convinced he has lucky underwear. One time when he forgot to put on his lucky underwear, he got a parking ticket. Doug concludes that because he forgot to wear his lucky underwear, he got the ticket. Doug doesn't wash his lucky underwear often. This part isn't relevant to the example, but it is disturbing nonetheless.

Explanation: Doug is not making any attempts to determine the most probabilistic causal factors for getting the parking ticket. Instead, largely because of the *confirmation bias*, he is making a claim of causality based on the order of events (first he forgot his lucky underwear, then he got the ticket.)

Example #2:

> *Tony: I bought a book on the law of attraction and two days later I won $30k in a lottery. I wasn't a believer of the law of attraction before, but now I am!*

Explanation: Although Tony bought the lottery ticket prior to buying the book, he believes that the act of wanting to win badly enough *caused* him to win the lottery, because first came the desire, then the win. The fact is, there is no evidence that his desire had any effect on the win whatsoever. To suggest this is the case, in addition to *ad hoc reasoning*, would be *magical thinking* since there is no naturalistic mechanism that could account for his desire resulting in his win.

Exception: If one claims that Y caused X by adding additional details that properly establish causality, this fallacy would not apply.

Fun Fact: There is some non-mystical truth to the law of attraction. That which you obsess over you are more likely to adjust your behaviors in a way that will help make your obsession a reality. For example, if you want to graduate college more than anything, you will most likely study harder, ask for extra help, and blow off fewer classes. No magic required.

References:

Post Hoc, Ergo Propter Hoc on JSTOR. (n.d.). Retrieved from https://www.jstor.org/stable/20126985?seq=1

Pragmatic Fallacy

Description: Claiming that something is true because the person making the claim has experienced, or is referring to someone who has experienced, some practical benefit from *believing* the thing to be true. The practical benefit is often summarized as "it works." The person is confusing the truth-value of the claim with the results from believing the claim to be true.

Logical Form:

I believe X is true.

Believing in X results in practical benefit Y.

Therefore, X is true.

Example #1:

Starbeam: Of course, astrology is true!

Nate: How do you know this?

Starbeam: Because on the days I forget to consult my horoscope, things always go wrong.

Explanation: Astrology is a pseudoscience that claims divine information about human affairs and terrestrial events by studying the movements and relative positions of celestial objects. Starbeam is almost certainly experiencing a host of cognitive biases, including the *confirmation bias*, where she notices the things that go wrong and ignores all that goes right on the days she forgets to read her horoscope. There is also likely some *self-fulfilling prophecy* going on where she interprets things that happen to her in a negative light, allowing her to maintain the belief in the power of horoscopes. Starbeam is committing the *pragmatic fallacy* because she is claiming astrology is true due to her "evidence" that horoscopes work for her.

Example #2: People all over the world under different religions that believe in all kinds of gods claim that their particular religion is true because of how believing in their religion makes them feel, the practical benefits they get from being a member of that religion (e.g., community support, social programs, etc.), their belief that they are loved, and more.

Explanation: All of these reasons as to why religion "works" might be sufficient for why believing in a religion can be good but these reasons do not address the truth-claims the religion makes about the existence of gods, angels, an afterlife, a soul, and similar claims of existence.

Exception: This is not a fallacy when what is claimed to be true is the fact that something "works," and works is defined subjectively (i.e., works for the person and not for everyone). For example, it is fair to say that prayer "works" when "works" is defined as giving (some) people a sense of peace and comfort.

> *Seth: Prayer works!*
>
> *Tina: What do you mean by "works" and how do you know this?*
>
> *Seth: I mean that it gives me a sense of peace and comfort.*
>
> *Tina: Will it work for me?*
>
> *Seth: I don't know.*

Tip: Don't underestimate the power of the placebo, especially when it comes to pain management. The mind is very powerful, and if it can trick you into thinking a cheap and harmless placebo improves your overall well-being, let it.

References:

http://skepdic.com/pragmatic.html

Prejudicial Language

(also known as: variant imagization)

Description: Loaded or emotive terms used to attach value or moral goodness to believing the proposition.

Logical Form:

Claim A is made using loaded or emotive terms.

Therefore, claim A is true.

Example #1:

All good Catholics know that impure thoughts are the work of the devil, and should be resisted at all costs.

Explanation: The phrase "all good Catholics" is the loaded or *prejudicial language* being used. The implication is that Catholics who *don't* resist impure thoughts are "bad Catholics," which is not fair—they may just not be as strong willed, or perhaps they don't agree with the Church's views on sex.

Example #2:

Students who want to succeed in life will do their homework each and every night.

Explanation: The assertion is that students who *don't* do their homework every night *don't* want to succeed in life, which is bad reasoning. Perhaps the student is sick one night, tired, doesn't understand the work, or was busy making out with his father's secretary in the office supply closet next to the memo pads. The point is, dad, you cannot assume that just because I skipped homework a few nights that it means I didn't want to succeed in life!

Exception: This is often used for motivation, but even if the intent is honorable, it is still fallacious.

Tip: *Prejudicial language* can be a powerful and effective persuasion tool. Use it in addition to a well-reasoned argument, not in place of one.

References:

Damer, T. E. (2008). *Attacking Faulty Reasoning: A Practical Guide to Fallacy-Free Arguments*. Cengage Learning.

Proof by Intimidation
argumentum verbosium

(also known as: proof by verbosity, fallacy of intimidation)

Description: Making an argument purposely difficult to understand in an attempt to intimidate your audience into accepting it, or accepting an argument without evidence or being intimidated to question the authority or *a priori* assumptions of the one making the argument.

Logical Form:

Claim A is made by person 1.

Person 1 is very intimidating.

Therefore, claim A is true.

Example #1:

Professor Xavier says that the egg certainly came before the chicken. He won the Nobel prize last year for his work in astronomy, and the MMA world championship—so I don't dare question his claim.

Explanation: Professor X sure sounds like a brilliant and tough guy, but that is not evidence for his claim.

Example #2:

> *Dr. Professor Pete said, with the utmost eloquence, masterful stage presence, and unshakable confidence, that 1+1=3. Therefore, 1+1=3.*

Explanation: Despite the intellectually intimidating presence of Dr. Professor Pete, 1+1 still equals 2.

Exception: If you live in a state where you can be killed for asking questions, then this is not a fallacy, but a survival technique.

Tip: If you live in a state where you can be killed for asking questions, move.

References:

Terrell, D. B. (1967). *Logic: A Modern Introduction to Deductive Reasoning*. Holt, Rinehart and Winston.

Proof Surrogate

Description: A claim masquerading as proof or evidence, when no such proof or evidence is actually being offered.

Logical Form:

> *Claim X is made.*
>
> *Claim X is expressed in such a way where no evidence is forthcoming, or no requests for evidence are welcome.*
>
> *Therefore, X is true.*

Example #1:

> *Jose writes that "people are mostly good at heart." The author is simply wrong.*

Explanation: The arguer states that the author is "simply wrong" yet offers no reasons. Words and phrases such as "simply," "obviously," "without question," etc., are indicators that no such evidence will be presented.

Example #2:

Politician X is crooked—this is an indisputable fact known by everyone except politician X's supporters.

Explanation: The language "this in an indisputable fact" is a surrogate for the evidence showing that politician X is crooked.

Exception: Claims that are universally accepted as self-evident truths don't apply.

If you put your penis in a wood chipper, it's going to hurt.

Tip: If you have a penis, don't put it in a wood chipper.

References:

Dowden. (1993). *Logical Reasoning Im*. Thomson Learning EMEA, Limited.

Proving Non-Existence

Description: Demanding that one proves the non-existence of something in place of providing adequate evidence for the existence of that something. Although it may be possible to prove non-existence in special situations, such as showing that a container does not contain certain items, one cannot prove universal or absolute non-existence.

Logical Form:

I cannot prove that X exists, so you prove that it doesn't.

If you can't, X exists.

Example #1:

God exists. Until you can prove otherwise, I will continue to believe that he does.

Explanation: There may be decent reasons to believe in the existence of God, but, "because the existence of God cannot be disproven," is not one of them.

Example #2:

> *Sheila: I know Elvis' ghost is visiting me in my dreams.*
>
> *Ron: Yeah, I don't think that really is his ghost.*
>
> *Sheila: Prove that it's not!*

Explanation: Once again we are dealing with confusion of probability and possibility. The inability to, "prove," in any sense of the word, that the ghost of Elvis is not visiting Sheila in her dreams is an impossible request because there is no test that proves the existence and presence of a ghost, so no way to prove the negative or the non-existence. It is up to Sheila to provide proof of this claim, or at least acknowledge that actually being visited by Elvis' ghost is just a *possibility*, no matter how slim that possibility is.

Exception: If Ron were to say, "That is impossible," "there is no way you are being visited," or make some other claim that rules out any possibility no matter how remote (or crazy), then Sheila would be in the right to ask him for proof—as long as she is making a point that he cannot know that for certain, and not actually expecting him to produce proof.

Tip: If you think you are being visited by aliens, gods, spirits, ghosts, or any other magical beings, just ask them for information that you can verify, specifically with a neutral third-party that would prove their existence. This would be simple for any advanced alien race, any god or heavenly being. Some ideas of things to ask for:

- future lottery numbers (of course you will give all your winnings to charity)
- answers to scientific problems that do have scientific answers, but aren't yet known
- exact details of major future events

But if these beings just tell you things such as:

- passages/ideas from the Bible
- whether you should take that new job or not

- where you left your car keys

- that they really exist, and others will continue to doubt you

- that you should never question their existence

...or anything else which is just as likely to come from your imagination that is untestable and *unfalsifiable*, then you might want to reconsider the fact that your being of choice is really paying you visits.

References:

You Can Prove a Negative. (n.d.). Retrieved from http://www.psychologytoday.com/blog/believing-bull/201109/you-can-prove-negative

Psychogenetic Fallacy

Description: Inferring some psychological reason why an argument is made then assuming it is invalid, as a result.

Logical Form:

Person 1 makes argument X.

Person 1 made argument X because of the psychological reason Y.

Therefore, X is not true.

Example #1:

George: Man, those girls are smokin' hot!

Derek: No, they're not. You're a victim of the cheerleader effect. When girls are together in a group, each girl looks a lot better than if you were to see her without the other girls.

Explanation: Besides the fact that "smokin' hot" is a subjective evaluation, meaning that the girls could be hot to George but not Derek, Derek is assuming George's evaluation is wrong because of the psychological effect known as the *cheerleader effect*.

Example #2:

> Lucas: I remember when I was about three years old my mother saved me from almost being eaten by a shark.
>
> Katie: I doubt that. What you are experiencing is what cognitive psychologists refer to as a "false memory."

Explanation: There are two problems here that make Katie guilty of fallacious reasoning. First, she is assuming Lucas' story is not true because of a false memory. Second, she is phrasing this objection with unwarranted confidence.

Exception: The more extraordinary the argument or claim, the more reasonable it is to assume a psychological effect is involved. However, even in the most extraordinary of claims, the effect should only be proposed, not assumed.

> Marge: Last night in bed, aliens visited me. They paralyzed me for about 30 seconds while they stood over me, then they disappeared right in front of my eyes while I regained the ability to move and speak.
>
> Kristine: That sounds like a classic case of what is called a hypnogogic hallucination with sleep paralysis. It is a dream-like state where you are not quite sleeping or awake. Your brain shuts down your ability to move and talk while you are unconscious during a normal sleep cycle, but in the case of sleep paralysis, you retain consciousness—but only for a brief time. So the odds are, you weren't really visited by aliens.

Fun Fact: As video recorders on cell phones became more ubiquitous, reports of alien encounters have dropped considerably.

References:

Segal, R. A. (1980). The social sciences and the truth of religious belief. *Journal of the American Academy of Religion*, 403–413.

Quantifier-Shift Fallacy

(also known as: illicit quantifier shift)

Description: A fallacy of reversing the order of two quantifiers.

Logical Form:

> *Every X has a related Y.*
>
> *Therefore, there is some Y related to every X.*

Example #1:

> *Everybody has a mother.*
>
> *Therefore, there is some woman out there who is the mother of us all.*

Explanation: While it is true that everyone has (or had) a mother, the term "mother" is not a singular term that is shared —it is implied that it is a category in which many mothers reside. The conclusion is asserting the opposite of the meaning —that there is actually just one mother shared by everyone. This form of reasoning is invalid; therefore, fallacious.

Example #2:

> *Everybody has a brain.*
>
> *Therefore, there is a single brain we all share.*

Explanation: Everybody has *his or her own* brain, not one we all share. Although I have met many people who seem not to have their own brain. This form of reasoning is invalid; therefore, fallacious.

Tip: Remember that a quantifier is an expression (e.g. all, some) that indicates the scope of a term to which it is attached.

References:

Cook, R. T. (2009). *A Dictionary of Philosophical Logic.* Edinburgh University Press.

Quantum Physics Fallacy

(also known as: appeal to quantum physics)

Description: Using quantum physics in an attempt to support your claim, when in no way is your claim related to quantum physics. One can also use the weirdness of the principles of quantum physics to cast doubt on the well-established laws of the macro world.

Perhaps the greatest mind in quantum physics, Richard Feynman, once said, "I think I can safely say that nobody understands quantum mechanics," and he is probably right. People recognize that this is perhaps the most bizarre, paradoxical, and incomprehensible area of study, that is also a respectable science. So, if you can manage to connect the truth of your argument to quantum physics, it would be unlikely that there would be many people who know enough about quantum physics to assert that your connection is invalid. Thus your argument gains credibility out of ignorance.

The mysterious nature of quantum physics is a breeding ground for superstition, religious claims, "proof" of God, universal consciousness, and many other *unfalsifiable* claims.

Logical Form:

> *Quantum physics supports the idea that X is Y.*
>
> *Therefore, X is Y.*
>
> *(although quantum physics supports no such thing)*

Example #1:

> *Depook: Quantum physics provides evidence that a cosmic consciousness exists.*
>
> *Sam: ???*

Explanation: Sam knows nothing about quantum physics, so really cannot respond, yet Depook did not establish an argument as to how it provides evidence, he just made the assertion.

Example #2:

Depook: Quantum physics is the language of God. It has been shown that quantum particles contain information that can instantly communicate information over any distance, anywhere in or outside the universe.

Sam: ???

Explanation: Sam knows nothing about quantum physics, so really cannot respond. Depook did expand on his assertion here, relied on the *argument by gibberish* in order to make what sounded like scientific claims which, in fact, were not. According to everything we know about quantum physics, information cannot travel faster than light—otherwise, it could create a *time travel paradox*.

Exception: Making a scientific claim about quantum physics, using the scientific method, is not fallacious.

Tip: Pick up an introductory book on quantum physics, it is not only a fascinating subject, but you will be well prepared to ask the right questions and expose this fallacy when used.

References:

This is an original logical fallacy named by the author.

Questionable Cause
cum hoc ergo propter hoc

(also known as: butterfly logic, ignoring a common cause, neglecting a common cause, confusing correlation and causation, confusing cause and effect, false cause, non causa pro causa, third cause, third-cause fallacy, juxtaposition [form of], reversing causality/wrong direction [form of])

Description: Concluding that one thing caused another, simply because they are regularly associated.

Logical Form:

A is regularly associated with B; therefore, A causes B.

Example #1:

Every time I go to sleep, the sun goes down. Therefore, my going to sleep causes the sun to set.

Explanation: I hope the fallacious reasoning here is very clear and needs no explanation.

Example #2:

Many homosexuals have AIDS. Therefore, homosexuality causes AIDS.

Explanation: While AIDS is found in a much larger percentage of the homosexual population than in the heterosexual population, we cannot conclude that homosexuality is the cause of AIDS, any more than we can conclude that heterosexuality is the cause of pregnancy.

Exception: When strong evidence is provided for causation, it is not a fallacy.

Variation: The *juxtaposition fallacy* is putting two items/ideas together, implying a causal connection, but never actually stating that one exists.

It's funny how whenever you are around, the room smells bad.

Reversing causality or *wrong direction* is just what is sounds like—it is still a false cause, but the specific case where one claims something like the sun sets because night time is coming.

Fun Fact: To establish causality you need to show three things: 1) that X came before Y, 2) that the observed relationship between X and Y didn't happen by chance alone, and 3) that there is nothing else that accounts for the X then Y relationship.

References:

Johnson, R. H., & Blair, J. A. (2006). *Logical Self-defense*. IDEA.

Rationalization

(also known as: making excuses)

Description: Offering false or inauthentic excuses for our claim because we know the real reasons are much less persuasive or more embarrassing to share, or harsher than the manufactured ones given.

Logical Form:

> Reason A is given for claim B, although reason A is not the real reason.

Example #1:

> I can't go with you to that opera because I have a deadline at work coming up, plus I need to wash my hair that night.

Explanation: The real reason is, "I don't want to go," but that might hurt some feelings, so manufactured reasons (excuses) are given in place of the authentic and honest reason.

Example #2:

> I believe in winged horses because the Koran is historically accurate and it would never get such an important fact wrong.

Explanation: The person actually believes in winged horses out of *faith*, but recognizes that is not a persuasive argument—especially to the non-believer of Islam. Out of the desire to hold on to his faith, he adopts a common defense (historical accuracy) and gives that as the reason.

Exception: Is it acceptable to rationalize to protect someone's feelings? I will leave that to you to answer, realizing that all situations are unique.

Tip: Whenever possible, give honest reasons stated in diplomatic ways.

References:

Fallacies | Internet Encyclopedia of Philosophy. (n.d.). Retrieved from http://www.iep.utm.edu/fallacy/#Rationalization

Red Herring
ignoratio elenchi

(also known as: beside the point, misdirection [form of], changing the subject, false emphasis, the Chewbacca defense, irrelevant conclusion, irrelevant thesis, clouding the issue, ignorance of refutation)

Description: Attempting to redirect the argument to another issue to which the person doing the redirecting can better respond. While it is similar to the *avoiding the issue fallacy*, the *red herring* is a deliberate diversion of attention with the intention of trying to abandon the original argument.

Logical Form:

Argument A is presented by person 1.

Person 2 introduces argument B.

Argument A is abandoned.

Example #1:

Mike: It is morally wrong to cheat on your spouse, why on earth would you have done that?

Ken: But what is morality exactly?

Mike: It's a code of conduct shared by cultures.

Ken: But who creates this code?...

Explanation: Ken has successfully derailed this conversation off of his sexual digressions to the deep, existential, discussion on morality.

Example #2:

Billy: How could the universe be 6000 years old when we know the speed of light, the distance of astronomical objects (13+ billion light years away), and the fact that the light has reached us[10]?

Marty: 6000 years is not a firm number. The universe can be as old as about 10,000 years.

Billy: How do you figure that?...

Explanation: Marty has succeeded in avoiding the devastating question by introducing a new topic for debate... shifting the young-earth creation timeline where it does not necessarily coincide with the Bible.

Exception: Using a *red herring* to divert attention away from your interlocutor's *red herring*, might work, but do two wrongs make a right?

Variation: *Misdirection* is a more generic term for diverting attention away from something. This could be for the purpose of entertainment, avoiding embarrassment, or any other purpose including argumentation.

Tip: Impress your friends by telling them that there is no such fish species as a "red herring;" rather it refers to a particularly pungent fish—typically a herring but not always—that has been strongly cured in brine and/or heavily smoked.

References:

Hurley, P. J. (2011). *A Concise Introduction to Logic.* Cengage Learning.

---

[10] The most distant object yet confirmed in the universe is a self-destructing star that exploded 13.1 billion light years from Earth. The object is a gamma-ray burst (GRB) – the brightest type of stellar explosion. The burst is dubbed GRB 090423 for the date of its discovery.

Reductio ad Hitlerum
reductio ad hitlerum

(also known as: argumentum ad Hitlerum, playing the Nazi card, Hitler card)

Description: The attempt to make an argument analogous with Hitler or the Nazi party (when it really isn't). Hitler is probably the most universally despised figure in history, so any connection to Hitler, or his beliefs, can (erroneously) cause others to view the argument in a similar light. However, this fallacy is becoming more well known as is the fact that it is most often a desperate attempt to render the truth claim of the argument invalid out of lack of a good counter argument.

Logical Forms:

> *Person 1 suggests that Y is true.*
>
> *Hitler liked Y.*
>
> *Therefore, Y is false.*

> *Person 1 suggests that Y is true.*
>
> *Person 1's rhetoric sounds a bit like Hitler's.*
>
> *Therefore, Y is false.*

Example #1:

> *Peter Gibbons: It's NOT wrong. INITECH is wrong. INITECH is an evil corporation, all right? Chochkies is wrong. Doesn't it bother you that you have to get up in the morning and you have to put on a bunch of pieces of flair?*
>
> *Joanna: Yeah, but I'm not about to go in and start taking money from the register.*
>
> *Peter Gibbons: Well, maybe you should. You know, the Nazis had pieces of flair that they made the Jews wear.*
>
> *Joanna: What?*

Explanation: The above was from the classic masterpiece film, *Office Space*. Out of desperation, Peter plays the "Nazi card" in order to make the idea of being made to wear flair more appalling. This somewhat jarring statement misdirects the argument, and the focus is taken off Joanna's last response, which was quite good.

Example #2:

> *My professor is making me redo this assignment. Do you know who else forced people to do things they didn't want to do? Hitler.*

Explanation: Yes, Hitler forced people to do things they didn't want to do. Of course, the extent of "force" used by the professor is quite different than the extent of the force used by Hitler, so the professor is really nothing like Hitler in any meaningful way, thus the argument is fallacious.

Exception: Sometimes it might be worth risking the fallacy to prevent disaster.

> *Mr. President, I can appreciate your desire to make some changes in the White House, but that new hand gesture you are proposing we use to show our allegiance to you is way too much like the one Hitler used. On a similar note, that Charlie Chaplin mustache doesn't work on you.*

Fun Fact: The Hitler mustache style is known as the *toothbrush mustache*. It was made famous by such comedians as Charlie Chaplin and Oliver Hardy. Hitler later became the person most associated with the mustache style and ended that fashion trend. I wish Hitler was also known for wearing mom jeans.

References:

Strauss, L. (1953). *Natural Right and History*. University of Chicago Press.

Regression Fallacy

(also known as: regressive fallacy)

Description: Ascribing a cause where none exists in situations where natural fluctuations exist while failing to account for these natural fluctuations.

Logical Form:

> B occurred after A (although B naturally fluctuates).
>
> Therefore, A caused B.

Example #1:

> I had a real bad headache, then saw my doctor. Just by talking with him, my headache started to subside, and I was all better the next day. It was well worth the $200 visit fee.

Explanation: Headaches are a part of life, and naturally come and go on their own with varying degrees of pain. They *regress to the mean* on their own, the "mean" being a normal state of no pain, with or without medical or chemical intervention. Had the person seen a gynecologist instead, the headache would have still subsided, and it would have been a much more interesting visit—especially if he were a man.

Example #2:

> After surgery, my wife was not doing too well—she was in a lot of pain. I bought these magnetic wristbands that align with the body's natural vibrations to reduce the pain, and sure enough, a few days later the pain subsided! Thank you magic wristbands!

Explanation: It is normal to be in pain after any significant surgery. It is also normal for the pain to subside as the body heals—this is the body *regressing to the mean*. Assuming the magic wristbands caused the pain relief and ignoring the regression back to the mean, is fallacious.

Exception: Of course, if the "cause" is explained as the natural regression to the mean, then in a way it is not fallacious.

My headache went away because that's what headaches eventually do—they are a temporary disruption in the normal function of a brain.

Fun Fact: Seeing a doctor can have a real effect on pain relief, even if the doctor does nothing but provide a sympathetic ear. This is known as the *psychosocial context of the therapeutic intervention* and is often considered part of the *placebo effect*.

References:

Poulton, E. C. (1994). *Behavioral Decision Theory: A New Approach.* Cambridge University Press.

Reification

(also known as: abstraction, concretism, fallacy of misplaced concreteness, hypostatisation, pathetic fallacy [form of])

Description: When an abstraction (abstract belief or hypothetical construct) is treated as if it were a concrete, real event or physical entity—when an idea is treated as if had a real existence.

Logical Form:

Abstraction X is treated as if it were concrete, a real event, or a physical entity.

Because the abstraction is seen as if it were concrete, a real event, or a physical entity, the conclusion is true.

Example #1:

Dr. Simmons: I am working on a way to lengthen the human lifespan to about 200 years.

Misty: You are declaring war on Mother Nature, and Mother Nature always wins!

Explanation: Here, "Mother Nature" is being portrayed as an autonomous being capable of going to war with humanity. If this were the case, it would seem that messing with Mother

Nature is futile. In reality, we are part of nature and can and always have changed nature, sometimes for the worse, but often for the better.

Example #2:

If you are open to it, love will find you.

Explanation: Love is an abstraction, not a little fat flying baby with a bow and arrow that searches for victims. Cute sayings such as this one are implicit arguments and can serve as bad advice for people who would otherwise make an effort to find a romantic partner, but choose not to, believing that this "love entity" is busy searching for his or her ideal mate.

Exception: In most cases, these are used as rhetorical devices. When the reification is deliberate and harmless, and not used as evidence to support a claim or conclusion, then it is not fallacious.

It's time to grab my future by the balls.

The future is an abstraction. It does not have testicles. If it did, you probably wouldn't want to grab them because your future might sue you for sexual misconduct.

Variation: The *pathetic fallacy* is the treatment of inanimate objects as if they had human feelings, thought, or sensations. Think of cursing at your computer when it does not give you the results you expect.

Fun Fact: *Reification* is similar to *anthropomorphism,* except that *reification* does not have to deal with human qualities.

References:

reification | literature | Britannica.com. (n.d.). Retrieved from https://www.britannica.com/topic/reification

Relative Privation

(also known as: it could be worse, it could be better)

Description: Trying to make a scenario appear better or worse by comparing it to the best or worst case scenario.

Logical Forms:

Scenario S is presented.

Scenario B is presented as a best-case.

Therefore, Scenario S is not that good.

Scenario S is presented.

Scenario B is presented as a worst-case.

Therefore, Scenario S is very good.

Example #1:

Be happy with the 1972 Chevy Nova you drive. There are many people in this country who don't even have a car.

Explanation: This person does have a very crappy car by any reasonable standard. Only comparing his situation with people who have no cars, does his Chevy Nova look like a Rolls Royce. It is fallacious to make a reasonable judgment based on these extreme cases.

Example #2:

Son: I am so excited! I got an "A" on my physics exam!

Dad: Why not an "A+"? This means that you answered something incorrectly. That is not acceptable!

Explanation: The poor kid is viewing his success from a very reasonable perspective based on norms. However, the father is using a best case scenario as a comparison, or a very unreasonable perspective. The conclusion "it is not acceptable," is unreasonable and, therefore, fallacious.

Exception: When used intentionally to manipulate emotions (especially with good intentions), not to make an argument on reason, then this might be acceptable.

I know that you just lost your job, but at least you still have a great education and plenty of experience, which will help you get another job.

Fun Fact: My first car was a crappy, 1972 Chevy Nova that I bought for $50 in my sophomore year in high school. This was when I first learned about correlation. Me driving that car was strongly correlated with my lack of female companions.

References:

This is a logical fallacy frequently used on the Internet. No academic sources could be found.

Retrogressive Causation

Description: Invoking the cause to eliminate the effect, or calling on the source to relieve the effect of the source.

Logical Form:

X causes/is the source of Y.

In order to eliminate or relieve Y, do more of X.

Example #1:

Jen: Don't you realize that all this drinking you are doing is making your family miserable?

Bridget: Yes, I do.

Jen: Then what are you doing about it?

Bridget: Drinking to forget.

Explanation: Bridget has a drinking problem that she is dealing with by drinking some more—because the effects of drinking make her (temporarily) forget/not worry about the greater scale effects of her drinking. Her reasoning that this is a good idea is fallacious.

Example #2:

David: We have way too much police presence in this city.

Pete: What are you going to do about it?

David: Vandalize, loot, and perhaps a little arson.

Explanation: The primary role of the police is to enforce laws. David is suggesting that breaking the laws will facilitate his goal of having the police force reduced.

Exception: In some cases, one may not be trying to eliminate the effect, but rather continue the cycle for some higher purpose. For example, if one learns to feel constant guilt by going to church and is relieved of that guilt by going to confession, they might find meaning in the constant "spiritual cleansing" ritual. While this might seem like irrational thinking to some, it would not fit under this fallacy.

Fun Fact: People are easily persuaded to act against their self-interests. If acting against their self-interest is for some higher purpose, the behavior would not be considered irrational.

References:

This is a logical fallacy frequently used on the Internet. No academic sources could be found.

Righteousness Fallacy

Description: Assuming that just because a person's intentions are good, they have the truth or facts on their side. Also see *self-righteousness fallacy*.

Logical Form:

Person 1 made claim X.

Person 1 has good intentions.

Therefore, X is true.

Example #1:

Ricki: Do you think aborted fetuses have feelings?

Jenni: I follow the lead of my grandmother who is the most honorable and kind person I know. She says they do have feelings.

Explanation: Jenni's grandmother might be the queen of honor with kindness oozing from her orthopedic shoes, but these qualities are independent of one's ability to know facts or come to an accurate conclusion based on available data.

Example #2:

The president wants to bomb that country because he thinks they are preparing to launch a nuclear attack against us. I know the president wants to do the right thing for the good of the American people, so if he says there have nukes, they have nukes!

Explanation: The good intentions of the president are separate from the president's ability to get solid intelligence on foreign affairs. If we are convinced of the president's good intentions, the best we can do is claim that we believe that the president believes he is doing the right thing.

Exception: This relates to facts, not subjective truth. We can use the idea of righteousness to conclude how we feel about a person.

Fun Fact: This is related to the cognitive bias, the *halo effect*.

References:

This is an original logical fallacy named by the author.

Rights To Ought Fallacy

(also known as: constitutional rights fallacy)

Description: When one conflates a reason for one's rights (constitutional or other) with what one *should* do. This is common among staunch defenders of "rights" who fail to see that rights are not the same as optimal courses of action. It can be a way of attempting to hide the fact that the "should" is based on one's subjective moral values (or at least values that are not shared by the interlocutor) rather than a more objective law to which virtually everyone acknowledges.

Logical Form:

Person A should not have done X.

Person A had every right to do X; therefore, person A should have done X.

Example #1:

Carl: Hi Billy, it is great to meet you! I think you will be happy here at Friendly Manufacturing, Inc.

Billy: Hey, you're Irish! Irish people make great factory workers—that is where they are happiest. I am surprised to see you in management.

Carl: Excuse me??

Billy: Don't mind me. I am just expressing my constitutional right to freedom of speech. Do you have a problem with our Constitution? Do you hate America?

Explanation: Billy is clearly ignorant when it comes to the realities of cultural differences, and he seriously lacks social skills. He is correct that he has every right to express his opinions, but he does not seem to mind offending and hurting others by making his opinions known. Constitutional rights do not exist in a vacuum—they are part of the larger system that includes social conventions such as tact, appropriate behavior, and kindness.

Example #2:

A top reality TV superstar from the hit show "Goose Galaxy" recently did an interview with GM magazine (Geese Monthly). In this interview, he told the interviewer that, according to his beliefs, the Galactic Emperor has decreed that all MAC users are "sinful" and MAC use leads to having sex with computers. When many MAC users and non-MAC users alike expressed their outrage at what they felt was an offensive and demonstrably false proposition, defenders of

"Goose Galaxy" screamed that the TV superstar had every right to say those things as his speech is protected by the First Amendment.

Explanation: The claim made was that the comments were offensive and demonstrably false (as no research has been able to demonstrate that MAC use leads to having sex with computers), and the reality TV star *should not* have said those things, yet the "Goose Galaxy" supporters countered with the fact that the reality TV star had the right to say those things; therefore, he *should have*. Notice that no claim was made about rights—this is a *strawman*. The fallacy extends beyond the *strawman* because the defenders of "Goose Galaxy" are conflating the reality TV star's constitutional rights with the claim that he *should* have said those things.

Exception: When one's values are in line with the rights, then claiming one "should" exercise his or her rights is not fallacious —as long as the reason given does not have to do with rights:

I feel that it is morally wrong to use a MAC; therefore, I should speak out against MAC users; and yes, it is my constitutional right to do so.

Tip: Just because you have the right to be a galactic jackass, doesn't mean you should.

References:

This is an original logical fallacy named by the author.

Scapegoating

Description: Unfairly blaming an unpopular person or group of people for a problem or a person or group that is an easy target for such blame.

Logical Form:

Nobody likes or cares about X.

Therefore, X is to blame for Y.

Example #1:

> *I know I got drunk, slapped the waitress on the behind, then urinated in the parking lot... from inside the restaurant, but that was Satan who had a hold of me.*

Explanation: The person is avoiding personal responsibility and blaming "Satan" for his actions. Satan is an easy target—he does not show up to defend himself, and a surprising number of people believe he exists and actually does cause immoral behavior.

Example #2:

> *The reason New Orleans was hit so hard with the hurricane was because of all the immoral people who live there.*

Explanation: This was an actual argument seen in the months that followed hurricane Katrina. Ignoring the validity of the claims being made, the arguer is blaming a natural disaster on a group of people.

Exception: There is no exception when people are being unfairly blamed.

Fun Fact: *Scapegoating* meets a deep psychological need for justice, or more accurately, the *belief* that justice has been served.

References:

Douglas, T. (2002). *Scapegoats: Transferring Blame*. Routledge.

Self-righteousness Fallacy

Description: Assuming that just because your intentions are good, you have the truth or facts on your side. Also see *righteousness fallacy*.

Logical Form:

> *You make claim X.*

You have good intentions.

Therefore, X is true.

Example #1:

Ricki: Do you think aborted fetuses have feelings?

Jenni: Any honorable and kind person would have to say they do have feelings. So yes.

Explanation: Jenni might be the queen of honor with kindness oozing from her puppy-dog eyes, but these qualities are independent of one's ability to know facts or come to an accurate conclusion based on available data.

Example #2:

Jenni: Is a fetus a human being?

Ricki: No, because I am not a monster and would never suggest killing an unwanted human being is okay.

Explanation: Ricki is making a claim about a fetus and using the fact that she is "not a monster" to support the claim, which is independent of her intentions.

Exception: This relates to facts, not subjective truth. We can use the idea of righteousness to conclude how we feel about something or someone. For example,

Jenni: Do you consider a fetus to be as valuable as a human being?

Ricki: No, because I am not a monster and would never suggest killing an unwanted human being is okay.

Fun Fact: *Self-righteous* is defined as having or characterized by a certainty, especially an unfounded one, that one is totally correct or morally superior. The *self-righteousness fallacy* follows a more generic definition of being correct because of "good intentions."

References:

This is a logical fallacy frequently used on the Internet. No academic sources could be found.

Selective Attention

Description: Focusing your attention on certain aspects of the argument while completely ignoring or missing other parts. This usually results in irrelevant rebuttals, *strawman fallacies*, and unnecessarily drawn-out arguments.

Logical Form:

Information is presented.

Response addresses only some of the information, completely ignoring the rest.

Example #1:

News Anchor on TV: The Dow Jones was up 200 points today, NASDAQ closed up 120 points, unemployment is and has been declining steadily, but foreclosures have not budged.

Jimbo: Did you hear that? Our economy is in the crapper!

Explanation: While there are many problems with the reasoning of Jimbo, due to his *selective attention*, and possible pessimism when it comes to the economy, he did not let the good news register and/or did not take that information into consideration before concluding that our economy is still in the "crapper," based on that one piece of news on foreclosures.

Example #2: Most of us are guilty of *selective attention* when the information is about us. We tend to embrace the information that makes us feel good and ignore the information that does not.

Exception: Ignoring irrelevant information is a good thing when evaluating arguments. The key is to know what is irrelevant.

Fun Fact: *Selective attention* is mostly a cognitive bias in that it happens subconsciously. It becomes a fallacy when it shows up in argumentation.

References:

This is a logical fallacy frequently used on the Internet. No academic sources could be found.

Self-Sealing Argument

(also known as: vacuous argument)

Description: An argument or position is self-sealing if and only if no evidence can be brought against it no matter what.

Logical Form:

> *Claim X is made.*
>
> *Reason Y is given for claim X.*
>
> *Reason Y can not possibly be refuted.*

Example #1:

> *Wherever you go, there you are.*

Explanation: You can't argue against that position, and as a result, it is *vacuous*, or meaningless.

Example #2:

> *Tina: My life is guided by destiny.*
>
> *Mary: How do you know that?*
>
> *Tina: Whatever comes my way is what was meant to be.*

Explanation: We have the same vacuity problem here, except this one is less obvious and protected by a philosophical belief system. There is no possible way we can know what "destiny may have in store for us," thus no way to argue against it. As a result, it is meaningless—it is the equivalent of saying everything happens because it happens.

Exception: Holding beliefs that are unfalsifiable is not fallacious, especially when stated as beliefs or opinions. This becomes fallacious when an unfalsifiable claim is presented as evidence in argumentation.

Tip: Realize that most superstitious beliefs are centered around self-sealing or vacuous arguments, that is why so many people refuse to let go of superstitious beliefs—because they cannot be proven false.

References:

Blair, J. A. (2011). *Groundwork in the Theory of Argumentation: Selected Papers of J. Anthony Blair.* Springer Science & Business Media.

Shifting of the Burden of Proof
onus probandi

(also known as: burden of proof [general concept], burden of proof fallacy, misplaced burden of proof, shifting the burden of proof)

Description: Making a claim that needs justification, then demanding that the interlocutor justifies the opposite of the claim. The burden of proof is a legal and philosophical concept with differences in each domain. In everyday debate, the burden of proof typically lies with the person making the claim, but it can also lie with the person denying a well-established fact or theory. Like other non-black and white issues, there are instances where this is clearly fallacious, and those which are not as clear.

Logical Form:

Person 1 is claiming Y, which requires justification.

Person 1 demands that person 2 justify the opposite of Y.

Person 2 refuses or is unable to comply.

Therefore, Y is true.

Example #1:

> Jack: I have tiny, invisible unicorns living in my anus.
>
> Nick: How do you figure?
>
> Jack: Can you prove that I don't?
>
> Nick: No.
>
> Jack: Then I do.

Explanation: Jack made a claim that requires justification. Nick asked for the evidence, but Jack shifted the burden of proof to Nick. When Nick was unable to refute Jack's (*unfalsifiable*) claim, Jack claimed victory.

Example #2:

> Audrey: I am a human being. I am not a cyborg from the future here to destroy humanity.
>
> Fred: Prove that you are human! Cyborgs don't pass out when they lose a lot of blood. Here's a knife.
>
> Audrey: Get to bed, Freddie. And no more SYFY channel before bed!

Explanation: Audrey is making a claim of common knowledge, perhaps sparked by Fred's suspicions. Fred is asking Audrey to prove the claim when he is the one that should be justifying his objection to the claim of common knowledge.

Exception: Again, the question of who has the burden of proof is not always as simple as demonstrated in these examples. Often, this is an argument itself.

Tip: If possible, justify your argument with evidence even if you might not have the burden of proof. The only time you might not want to do this is when it gives credibility to an outrageous accusation or claim.

References:

Bunnin, N., & Yu, J. (2008). *The Blackwell Dictionary of Western Philosophy*. John Wiley & Sons.

Shoehorning

Description: The process of force-fitting some current affair into one's personal, political, or religious agenda. Many people aren't aware of how easy it is to make something look like confirmation of a claim after the fact, especially if the source of the confirmation is something in which they already believe, like Biblical prophecies, psychic predictions, astrological horoscopes, fortune cookies, and more.

Logical Form:

> *Current event X is said to relate to agenda Y.*
>
> *Agenda Y has no rational connection to current event X.*

Example #1: This example is taken from the *Skeptic's Dictionary* (http://www.skepdic.com/shoehorning.html).

> *After the terrorist attacks on the World Trade Center and the Pentagon on September 11, 2001, fundamentalist Christian evangelists Jerry Falwell and Pat Robertson shoehorned the events to their agenda. They claimed, "liberal civil liberties groups, feminists, homosexuals and abortion rights supporters bear partial responsibility...because their actions have turned God's anger against America." According to Falwell, God allowed "the enemies of America...to give us probably what we deserve." Robertson agreed. The American Civil Liberties Union has "got to take a lot of blame for this," said Falwell and Robertson agreed. Federal courts bear part of the blame, too, said Falwell, because they've been "throwing God out of the public square." Also, "abortionists have got to bear some burden for this because God will not be mocked," said Falwell and Robertson agreed.*

Explanation: It should be very clear how these religious leaders attempted to profit from the September 11 attacks by *shoehorning*.

Example #2: For thousands of years people have been rushing to scripture to try to make sense out of a current situation. Without a doubt, the same verses have been used over and over again for centuries as a prophecy of a current event. This is *shoehorning*. A great example of this is the BP oil spill in April of 2010. It has been suggested that the verses from Revelation 8:8–11 predicted this environmental disaster:

> *"The second angel blew his trumpet, and something like a great mountain, burning with fire, was thrown into the sea. A third of the sea became blood, a third of the living creatures in the sea died, and a third of the ships were destroyed ... A third of the waters became wormwood, and many died from the water, because it was made bitter."*

With over 31,000 verses, the probability of NOT finding a verse in the Bible that can be made to fit virtually any modern-day situation is next to zero, but what if you had 2,000 years of history to play with? It's not difficult to see how quickly these "fulfilled prophecies" can add up.

Exception: Explaining events is legitimate when reason is being used—and sometimes it may actually fit into your ideological agenda.

Fun Fact: Did you every notice website with crazy conspiracy theories tend to be horribly designed? *Haig's Law* states: "The awfulness of a website's design is directly proportional to the insanity of its contents and creator."

References:

shoehorning - The Skeptic's Dictionary - Skepdic.com. (n.d.). Retrieved from http://www.skepdic.com/shoehorning.html

Slippery Slope

(also known as absurd extrapolation, thin edge of the wedge, camel's nose, domino fallacy)

Description: When a relatively insignificant first event is suggested to lead to a more significant event, which in turn leads to a more significant event, and so on, until some ultimate, significant event is reached, where the connection of each event is not only unwarranted but with each step it becomes more and more improbable. Many events are usually present in this fallacy, but only two are actually required—usually connected by "the next thing you know..."

Logical Form:

If A, then B, then C, ... then ultimately Z!

Example #1:

We cannot unlock our child from the closet because if we do, she will want to roam the house. If we let her roam the house, she will want to roam the neighborhood. If she roams the neighborhood, she will get picked up by a stranger in a van, who will sell her in a sex slavery ring in some other country. Therefore, we should keep her locked up in the closet.

Explanation: In this example, it starts out with reasonable effects to the causes. For example, yes, if the child is allowed to go free in her room, she would most likely want to roam the house—95% probability estimate[11]. Sure, if she roams the house, she will probably want the freedom of going outside, but not necessarily "roaming the neighborhood," but let's give that a probability of say 10%. Now we start to get very improbable. The chances of her getting picked up by a stranger (.05%) in a van (35%) to sell her into sex slavery (.07%) in another country (40%) is next to nothing when you do all the math:

.95 x .10 x .0005 x .35 x .0007 x .4 = about 1 in 25,000,000.

Morality and legality aside, is it really worth it to keep a child locked in a closet based on those odds?

Example #2:

If you accept that the story of Adam and Eve was figurative, then you will do the same for most of the Old Testament stories of similar literary styles. Once you are there, the New Testament and the story of Jesus does not make sense, which

---

[11] I am basing these estimates on my best guess... this is not meant to be an accurate study on child abduction, just an illustration of how odds work in the fallacy.

will lead you to believe that the resurrection of Jesus was a "spiritual" one. Once you accept that, you won't be a Christian anymore; you will be a dirty atheist, then you will have no morals and start having sex with animals of a barnyard nature. So you better take the story of Adam and Eve literally, before the phrase, "that chicken looks delicious," takes on a whole new meaning.

Explanation: Accepting the story of Adam and Eve as figurative rarely (it is sad that I cannot confidently say "never") leads to bestiality.

Exception: When a chain of events has an inevitable cause and effect relationship, as in a mathematical, logical, or physical certainty, it is not a fallacy.

Tip: The concept of a "bad day" is part of this fallacy. You wake up in the morning, and you discover that you are out of coffee. From there, you fallaciously reason that this means you will be grumpy, late for work, then behind all day in work, then have to stay late, then miss dinner with the family, then cause more friction at home, etc. This is only true if you act it out as if it is true. Of course, with an already bad attitude, you look back on the day, block out the good and wallow in the bad, just so you can tell yourself, that you were right all along about having a "bad day."

Don't let that happen.

References:

Walton, D. N. (1992). *Slippery Slope Arguments*. Clarendon Press.

Special Pleading

Description: Applying standards, principles, and/or rules to other people or circumstances, while making oneself or certain circumstances exempt from the same critical criteria, without providing adequate justification. Special pleading is often a result of strong emotional beliefs that interfere with reason.

Logical Form:

If X then Y, but not when it hurts my position.

Example #1:

Yes, I do think that all drunk drivers should go to prison, but your honor, he is my son! He is a good boy who just made a mistake!

Explanation: The mother in this example has applied the rule that all drunk drivers should go to prison. However, due to her emotional attachment to her son, she is fallaciously reasoning that he should be exempt from this rule, because, "he is a good boy who just made a mistake," which would hardly be considered adequate justification for exclusion from the rule.

Example #2:

Superstition is a belief or practice resulting from ignorance, fear of the unknown, trust in magic or chance, or a false conception of causation—unless it's astrology.

Explanation: It has been said that one's superstition is another's faith. The standard of superstition has been defined by the person and violated by astrology. However, while the person in the example rejects all other sources of superstition using certain criteria, the superstitious belief of their preference is exempt from these criteria.

Exception: "Adequate justification" is subjective, and can be argued.

Tip: If you are accused of special pleading, take the time to consider honestly if the accusation is warranted. This is a fallacy that is easy to spot when others make it yet difficult to spot when we make it.

References:

Walton, D. (1999). *One-Sided Arguments: A Dialectical Analysis of Bias.* SUNY Press.

Spiritual Fallacy

(also known as: spiritual excuse)

Description: Insisting that something meant to be literal is actually "spiritual" as an explanation or justification for something that otherwise would not fit in an explanation.

Logical Form:

X makes no sense; therefore, X was meant in a "spiritual" sense.

Example #1:

Of course, the Koran is not a history or science book, but each and every story in it does contain a spiritual truth.

Explanation: Because we cannot define or prove a "spiritual truth," anything can be a spiritual truth.

Example #2:

Harold Camping, the preacher who predicted the rapture in 2011, said that the rapture actually did come, but it was a "spiritual" rapture. Of course, there is no way to demonstrate this.

Explanation: We can't use "spiritual" as a get-out-of-jail-free card to cover up an apparent contradiction.

Exception: It is not a fallacy when it is specifically referred to as "spiritual."

"and drank the same spiritual drink; for they drank from the spiritual rock that accompanied them, and that rock was Christ." (1 Cor 10:4)

Tip: Next time you get pulled over for speeding, tell the cop you were only "spiritually" speeding. See if that works.

References:

This is an original logical fallacy named by the author.

Spin Doctoring

(also known as: spinning)

Description: Presenting information in a deceptive way that results in others interpreting the information in such a way that does not reflect reality but is how you want the information to be interpreted.

Logical Form:

X represents reality.

Information is presented in such a way that Y appears to represent reality.

Example #1: Senator Elizabeth Warren was recently under attack because it was discovered that the men on her staff were paid, on average, considerably more than the women on her staff—an issue that Warren has campaigned on many times. While the facts are true (men are paid more on her staff), in many analyses, relevant data was excluded such as the criteria necessary to prove the claim that women on Senator Warren's staff were paid less than their male counterparts for equivalent work[12]. In fairness to some conservative outlets that reported this story, some used this as an example to show that there is more to the story than just raw numbers.

Example #2:

Simon: It is pretty darn clear that God is against homosexuality. According to Leviticus 20:13, "If a man lies with a male as with a woman, both of them shall be put to death for their abominable deed; they have forfeited their lives."

Bret: You don't understand. This was before Jesus. After Jesus, God was okay with it. Besides, these were specific

---

[12] Elizabeth Warren Pays Female Staffers Less Than Their Male Counterparts? (2017, April 6). Retrieved April 13, 2017, from http://www.snopes.com/elizabeth-warren-staff-pay/

instructions to a specific people during a specific historical period.

Explanation: Very often, people's ideas of God are a result of their values, not the other way around. This is made clear by the cultural shifts on moral issues that correlate with people's interpretation of the Bible (one example being Christian's views on homosexuality[13]). Bret may genuinely believe his narrative, but it was most likely a result of the *spin doctoring* of another person or organization.

Exception: They are situations where there is no objective truth to a view and data can be looked at in multiple ways, such as the classic "is the glass half-full or half-empty" question.

Tip: Consider the source's biases. This will help with detecting *spin doctoring*.

References:

This is a logical fallacy frequently used on the Internet. No academic sources could be found.

Spotlight Fallacy

Description: Assuming that the media's coverage of a certain class or category is representative of the class or category in whole.

Logical Form:

The media have been covering X quite a bit by describing it as Y.

Therefore, X can be described as Y.

---

13 http://www.pewresearch.org/fact-tank/2015/12/18/most-u-s-christian-groups-grow-more-accepting-of-homosexuality/

Example #1:

It seems like we are constantly hearing about crimes committed on our streets. America is a very dangerous place.

Explanation: The media reports on stories of interest, which include crimes. It does not report on all the non-crimes. Assuming from this, "American is a very dangerous place" is fallacious reasoning.

Example #2:

I am seeing more and more miracles being reported on respectable news programs. The other day there was a story about a guy who had trouble walking, prayed to the recently deceased Pope, now walks just fine! Miracles are all around us!

Explanation: People love stories of hope and miracles. You won't find stories about how someone prayed to be healed then died. These are not the kind of stories that attract viewers and sell papers. As a result, the *spotlight fallacy* makes us think the rare cases, almost certainly due to normal and necessary statistical fluctuations, seem like the norm. Believing that they are, is fallacious reasoning.

Exception: Complete coverage of a small, manageable class, by an unbiased media outlet, may accurately be representative of the entire class.

Tip: Be very selective of the types of "news" programs you watch.

References:

Tanner, K. (2013). Common Nonsense Based on Faulty Appeals. In *Common Sense* (pp. 31–43). Apress. https://doi.org/10.1007/978-1-4302-4153-9_3

Statement of Conversion

Description: Accepting the truth of a claim based on a conversion story without considering any evidence for the truth of the claim.

Logical Form:

I used to believe in X.

Therefore, X is wrong.

Example #1:

I used to be a Christian, now I know better.

Explanation: All this tells us is that the arguer changed his mind. We don't know why. Accepting this as evidence against Christianity would be fallacious reasoning.

Example #2:

There used to be a time when I didn't believe, now I see the light and have accepted Jesus as my savior!

Explanation: All this tells us is that the arguer changed his mind. We don't know why. Accepting this as evidence for Christianity would be fallacious reasoning.

Exception: It might be the case where the person with the conversion story has some expertise or direct experience related to the claim, so their conversion story is reasonable evidence for the truth of the claim.

I used to think that the earth was flat, then Elon Musk took me to the space station in one of his ships. I am no longer a flat-earther, and I can't believe what an idiot I was listening to YouTube videos of 40-year-old guys living in their parent's basement over NASA.

Tip: Remember not to confuse people's *interpretations* of their experiences as actual experiences. People who were unbelievers in aliens visiting earth and changed their mind based on "aliens visiting them in their dreams" are almost certainly misinterpreting their experiences.

References:

This is a logical fallacy frequently used on the Internet. No academic sources could be found.

Stereotyping (the fallacy)

Description: The general beliefs that we use to categorize people, objects, and events while assuming those beliefs are accurate generalizations of the whole group.

Logical Form:

All X's have the property Y (this being a characterization, not a fact).

Z is an X.

Therefore, Z has the property Y.

Example #1:

French people are great at kissing. Julie is French. Get me a date!

Explanation: "French people are great at kissing" is a stereotype, and believing this to be so is a fallacy. While it may be the case that *some* or even *most* are great at kissing, we cannot assume this without valid reasons.

Example #2:

Atheists are morally bankrupt.

Explanation: This isn't an argument, but just an assertion, one not even based on any kind of facts. Stereotypes such as these usually arise from prejudice, ignorance, jealousy, or even hatred.

Exception: Statistical data can reveal properties of a group that are more common than in other groups, which can affect the probability of any individual member of the group having that property, but we can never assume that all members of the group have that property.

Tip: Remember that people are individuals above being members of groups or categories.

References:

MAC, M. J. T., PhD, CSAC. (2006). *Critical Thinking for Addiction Professionals*. Springer Publishing Company.

Stolen Concept Fallacy

Description: Requiring the truth of the something that you are simultaneously trying to disprove.

Logical Form:

Person 1 is attempting to disprove X.

X is required to disprove X.

Example #1:

Reason and logic are not always reliable, so we should not count on it to help us find truth.

Explanation: Here we are using reason to disprove the validity of reason, which is unreasonable—reasonably speaking.

Example #2:

Science cannot be trusted. It is a big conspiracy to cover up the truth of the Bible and the creation story. I saw fossils in the creation museum with humans and dinosaurs together, which proves science is wrong!

Explanation: Geology is a branch of science. Using science (examining fossils through the science of geology) to disprove science is absurd, a contradiction and, therefore, a fallacy in reasoning.

Exception: Intentional irony.

Fun Fact: The *nofallacies fallacy* is the belief that fallacies do not exist (not really).

References:

Peikoff, L. (1993). *Objectivism: The Philosophy of Ayn Rand.* Penguin.

Strawman Fallacy

Description: Substituting a person's actual position or argument with a distorted, exaggerated, or misrepresented version of the position of the argument.

Logical Form:

Person 1 makes claim Y.

Person 2 restates person 1's claim (in a distorted way).

Person 2 attacks the distorted version of the claim.

Therefore, claim Y is false.

Example #1:

Ted: Biological evolution is both a theory and a fact.

Edwin: That is ridiculous! How can you possibly be absolutely certain that we evolved from pond scum!

Ted: Actually, that is a gross misrepresentation of my assertion. I never claimed we evolved from pond scum. Unlike math and logic, science is based on empirical evidence and, therefore, a scientific fact is something that is confirmed to such a degree that it would be perverse to withhold provisional consent. The empirical evidence for the fact that biological evolution does occur falls into this category.

Explanation: Edwin has ignorantly mischaracterized the argument by a) assuming we evolved from pond scum (whatever that is exactly), and b) assuming "fact" means "certainty."

Example #2:

Zebedee: What is your view on the Christian God?

Mike: I don't believe in any gods, including the Christian one.

Zebedee: So you think that we are here by accident, and all this design in nature is pure chance, and the universe just created itself?

Mike: You got all that from me stating that I just don't believe in any gods?

Explanation: Mike made one claim: that he does not believe in any gods. From that, we can deduce a few things, like he is not a theist, he is not a practicing Christian, Catholic, Jew, or a member of any other religion that requires the belief in a god, but we cannot deduce that he believes we are all here by accident, nature is chance, and the universe created itself. Mike might have no beliefs about these things whatsoever. Perhaps he distinguishes between "accident" and natural selection, perhaps he thinks the concept of design is something we model after the universe, perhaps he has some detailed explanation based on known physics as to how the universe might have first appeared, or perhaps he believes in some other supernatural explanation. Regardless, this was a gross mischaracterization of Mike's argument.

Exception: At times, an interlocutor might not want to expand on the implications of his or her position, so making assumptions might be the only way to get the interlocutor to point out that your interpretation is not accurate, then they will be forced to clarify.

Tip: Get in the habit of *steelmanning* the argument. The opposite of the *strawman* is referred to as the *steelman*, which is a productive technique in argumentation where the one evaluating the argument makes the strongest case for the argument, assuming the best intentions of the interlocutor. This technique prevents pointless, time-wasting bickering and demonstrates respect for both the interlocutor and the process of critical argumentation. Consider the following dialog:

Johan: The progressive left is making it more difficult for me to vote blue this coming election.

Sebastian: Why is that?

Johan: It primarily has to do with the endorsement of the riots.

Sebastian: So if I understand you correctly, you are saying that the democratic establishment appears to be supporting riots rather than condemning them?

Johan: Yes, that is exactly it.

At this point, Sebastian can present a case for why Johan's argument fails—*his actual argument*. Sebastian will also likely be taken more seriously by Johan since he demonstrated goodwill in his attempt to accurately portray Johan's argument.

References:

Hurley, P. J. (2011). *A Concise Introduction to Logic*. Cengage Learning.

Style Over Substance

(also known as: argument by slogan [form of], cliché thinking - or thought-terminating cliché, argument by rhyme [form of], argument by poetic language [form of])

Description: When the arguer embellishes the argument with compelling language or rhetoric, and/or visual aesthetics. This comes in many forms as described below. "If it sounds good or looks good, it must be right!"

Logical Form:

Person 1 makes claim Y.

Claim Y sounds catchy.

Therefore, claim Y is true.

Example #1:

A chain is only as strong as its weakest link.

Explanation: Most applications of language, like the example above, are not taken literally, but figuratively. However, even figurative language is a way to make an argument. In this case, it might be used to imply that a team is no better than the least productive member of that team which is just not true. Very often the "weakest links" fade away into the background and the strong players lead the team.

Example #2:

> It's not a religion; it is a relationship.

Explanation: "Yeah... wow, I can see that!" is the common response to a cliché that diverts critical thought by substitution of poetry, rhyme, or other rhetoric. In fact, these are not arguments, but assertions absent of any evidence or reasons that rely on one's confusion of their emotional connection to language with the truth of the assertion. Tell me *why* it's not a religion. Tell me what a relationship is exactly.

Do not accept information as truth because it sounds nice.

Exception: Compelling language or rhetoric can be useful when used in addition to evidence or strong claims.

Tip: Keep in mind that for every poetic saying there is another one with an opposite meaning. They rarely ever make good arguments.

Variations: The *argument by slogan* fallacy is when a slogan (catchy phrase) is taken as truth because it sounds good and we might be used to hearing it, e.g. "Coke is the real thing!" Bumper stickers are great examples of *argument by slogan*: "Born Again? Excuse me for getting it right the first time."

Cliché thinking is the fallacy when sayings like, "leave no stone unturned," are accepted as truth, regardless of the situation—especially if taken literally.

When poetic language is used in an argument as reason or evidence for the truth of the conclusion, the *argument by poetic language* fallacy is committed.

The *argument by rhyme* uses words that rhyme to make the proposition more attractive. It works... don't ask me how, but it does ("if it doesn't fit, you must acquit"). Rhymes tend to have quite a bit of persuasive power, no matter how false they might be. The best defense against this kind of fallacious rhetoric is a good counter attack using the same fallacy.

Whoever smelled it, dealt it!

Whoever denied it, supplied it!

References:

This is a logical fallacy frequently used on the Internet. No academic sources could be found.

Subjectivist Fallacy

(also known as: relativist fallacy)

Description: Claiming something is true for one person, but not for someone else when, in fact, it is true for everyone (objective) as demonstrated by empirical evidence.

Logical Form:

Person 1 claims that Y is true.

Person 2 claims that Y is true for some people, but not for everyone (even though empirical evidence demonstrates otherwise).

Example #1:

Jane: You know, smoking might not be the most healthy habit to start.

Terry: Smoking is unhealthy for most people, but not for me.

Explanation: Sorry Terry, smoking is unhealthy for everyone —you are no different.

Example #2:

Jack: Sorry, your argument is full of contradictions.

Ted: Contradictions only apply to the carnal mind, not the spiritual one.

Explanation: Besides being a case of the *subjectivist fallacy*, Ted is also moving outside the realm of reason and logic.

Exception: Many things are actually true or false, depending on the person to which the rule may or may not apply.

While Twinkies may be horrible to you, I find them delicious— baked, spongy sunshine with a white, creamy, cloud-like center, with the power to make any problem go away—even if just for a brief, magical moment.

Tip: Stay away from Twinkies.

References:

Peacocke, C. (2005). *The Realm of Reason*. Clarendon Press.

Subverted Support

Description: The attempt to explain some phenomenon that does not actually occur or there is no evidence that it does. It is a form of *begging the question*.

Logical Form:

X happens because of Y (when X doesn't really even happen)

Example #1:

The reason billions of children starve to death each year is because we live in a world that does not care.

Explanation: Billions of children don't starve to death each year—not even close. If it were close, it might be better categorized as an exaggeration, but this would be more of an attempt to get the audience to accept the assertion as a fact while focusing more on the reason rather than the assertion itself.

Example #2:

The reason the firmament, a tent-like structure that kept the "waters above" from flooding the earth as described in the Bible, is no longer there today, is because it was destroyed during Noah's flood.

Explanation: The reason the firmament isn't there today is because it never existed. To attempt to explain it is to get the audience to assume it existed.

Exception: If the argument is preceded with a declaration that the phenomenon does occur, then what would be the *subverted support* is simply a reason given.

The firmament, a tent-like structure that kept the "waters above" from flooding the earth as described in the Bible, once covered the earth. It is no longer there today because it was destroyed during Noah's flood.

Tip: Exaggeration is a risky technique you want to avoid. On the one hand, it can make your argument more compelling (technically, by misrepresenting the truth). On the other hand, if you are called out for your exaggeration, it will damage the credibility of your argument as well as your own credibility.

References:

This is a logical fallacy frequently used on the Internet. No academic sources could be found.

Sunk-Cost Fallacy

(also known as: argument from inertia, concorde fallacy, finish the job fallacy)

Description: Reasoning that further investment is warranted on the fact that the resources already invested will be lost otherwise, not taking into consideration the overall losses involved in the further investment.

Logical Form:

X has already been invested in project Y.

Z more investment would be needed to complete project Y, otherwise X will be lost.

Therefore, Z is justified.

Example #1:

I have already paid a consultant $1000 to look into the pros and cons of starting that new business division. He advised that I shouldn't move forward with it because it is a declining market. However, if I don't move forward, that $1000 would have been wasted, so I better move forward anyway.

Explanation: What this person does not realize is that moving forward will most likely result in the loss of much more time and money. This person is thinking short-term, not long-term, and is simply trying to avoid the loss of the $1000, which is fallacious thinking.

Example #2: There are ministers, priests, pastors, and other clergy all around the world who have invested a significant portion of their lives in theology, who can no longer manage to hold supernatural beliefs—who have moved beyond faith. Hundreds of them recognize those sunk costs and are searching for the best way to move on (see http://www.clergyproject.org) whereas many others cannot accept the loss of their religious investment, and continue to practice a profession inconsistent with their beliefs.

Explanation: Of course, the clergy who have not moved beyond faith and are living consistently with their beliefs have not committed this fallacy.

Exception: If a careful evaluation of the hypothetical outcomes of continued investment versus accepting current losses and ceasing all further investment have been made, then choosing the former would not be fallacious.

Tip: Is there any part of your life where you continue to make bad investments because you fear to lose what was already invested? Do something about it.

References:

Besanko, D., & Braeutigam, R. (2010). *Microeconomics*. John Wiley & Sons.

Suppressed Correlative

(also known as: fallacy of lost contrast, fallacy of the suppressed relative)

Description: The attempt to redefine a *correlative* (one of two mutually exclusive options) so that one alternative encompasses the other, i.e. making one alternative impossible. The redefinition, therefore, makes the word it is redefining essentially meaningless.

Logical Form:

> *Person 1 claims that all things are either X or not X (the correlatives: X–not X).*

> *Person 2 defines X such that all things that you claim are not X are included in X (the suppressed correlative: not X).*

Example #1:

> *Rick: I need to know if we should stop for lunch or not. You are either hungry or not hungry, which is it?*

> *Tina: If being hungry is being able to eat, I am always hungry.*

Explanation: If we redefine hungry as, "being able to eat" then for the few occasions where people are medically incapable, everyone is always hungry, and it has lost all meaning.

Example #2:

> *Kent: My new car is really fast.*

> *Cal: I doubt that it is as fast as a jet fighter so, therefore, it is not fast.*

Explanation: In Kent's statement, there is an implied correlative, that is, his car is either fast or not fast. Now if what Cal says is true, then no cars would ever be considered "fast," and speed would lose all meaning for cars.

Exception: Refusing to give into a *false dichotomy* is not the same as committing the *suppressed correlative* fallacy. In example #1, while one cannot be both hungry and not hungry, one can be a little bit hungry.

> Rick: I need to know if we should stop for lunch or not. You are either hungry or not hungry, which is it?
>
> Tina: I am a little bit hungry, so go ahead and stop if you are hungry otherwise I can wait.

Note that this fallacy is not committed because Tina did not attempt to redefine "hungry" so "not hungry" is essentially impossible.

Tip: Whenever presented with just two options, take a moment to consider if those are actually your only two options.

References:

Shafer-Landau, R. (2007). *Ethical Theory: An Anthology*. John Wiley & Sons.

Survivorship Fallacy

(also known as: survivorship bias)

Description: This is best summed up as "dead men don't tell tales." In its general form, the survivorship fallacy is basing a conclusion on a limited number of "winner" testimonies due to the fact we cannot or do not hear the testimonies of the losers. This is based on the cognitive bias called the *survivorship bias*.

Logical Form:

> There are X winners and Y losers.
>
> We only hear the testimonies of the winners.

Therefore, our conclusion is based on X winners.

Example #1: Let's use the example of automobile accidents since we have relatively good data on these. According to the National Highway Traffic Safety Administration[14], roughly 32,000 people die each year on the roads in the United States. The number of people involved in fatal accidents is roughly double that amount, meaning that about half of the people survive, and half die. Let's say that 80% of people involved in a fatal accident reach out for supernatural help. Given an even distribution among survivors and non-survivors, this would mean that 25,600 people who reach out for supernatural help die and 25,600 who reach out for supernatural help live to tell about it. Now we need to add in the 20% of survivors who did not reach out for supernatural help that lived: 6,400. So what we end up with is a group of 32,000 survivors, 80% of whom appear to have been saved by supernatural intervention. Of course, dead men don't tell tales, so we forget about the 80% of those who died and reached out for supernatural help and didn't get it. Because of the *survivorship bias*, we have a radically biased sample that leads to a fallacious conclusion.

Example #2: The survivorship bias is used by scammers and con artists who take advantage of the "statistically ignorant" public. One common scam is something I call the "prophetic investor." The scammer will send an e-mail to a very large group of people (say 10 million) with a claim that they have a perfect track record for picking winning investments. But they tell you not to take their word for it, let them prove it you by picking a stock a day for 7 days in a row that increases in value. Then, they say when you are convinced, call them and invest with them. Here's how the scam works:

> *Day 1: Five different stocks are chosen, and each stock is sent to 2 million people as the winning pick. Let's say three of those stocks make money, and two don't. The 4 million people who received the stock pick that lost money are removed from the list (kind of like dying).*

> *Day 2: Another 5 stocks are chosen. This time, each stock is only sent to the "survivors," about 1.2 million people each get*

---

[14] https://www.nhtsa.gov/

a new pick. Out of that group, perhaps just two stocks are winners. That means that 2.4 million people got the winning stock: two days in a row! You can see where this is headed...

...

Day 7: After the final day of sending, about 100,000 "survivors" remain on the list. These are people who have been sent the winning picks 7 days in a row and are convinced that the "investor" must be legitimate. After all, what are the chances that anyone would pick 7 winning stocks in a row with that much confidence?

Tip: Whether someone is selling you investment services or a religion, think about the survivorship bias and how you might be jumping to an inaccurate conclusion.

References:

Swedroe, L. E. (2005). *The Only Guide to a Winning Investment Strategy You'll Ever Need: The Way Smart Money Preserves Wealth Today.* St. Martin's Press.

Texas Sharpshooter Fallacy

(also known as: clustering illusion)

Description: Ignoring the difference while focusing on the similarities, thus coming to an inaccurate conclusion. Similar to the *gambler's fallacy*, this is an example of inserting meaning into randomness. This is also similar to the *post-designation fallacy,* but with the *Texas sharpshooter fallacy* the focus is generally a result of deliberate misleading.

Logical Form:

X and Y are compared by several criteria.

A conclusion is made based on only the criteria that produce the desired outcome.

Example #1:

The "prophet" Nostradamus wrote about 500 years ago:

Beasts wild with hunger will cross the rivers,

The greater part of the battle will be against Hister.

He will cause great men to be dragged in a cage of iron,

When the son of Germany obeys no law.

Surely he must have had some vision of Hitler!

Explanation: When you focus on just that prediction, then it might seem that way, but realize that Nostradamus made over 1000 "predictions," most (all?) of which are vague nonsense. Given that many predictions, it is statistically impossible NOT to match at least one with an actual event. Again, if you ignore the noise (the predictions that do not make any sense), it looks amazing. By the way, "Hister" is the Latin name for the Danube River.

Example #2:

SuperCyberDate.con determined that Sally and Billy are a great match because they both like pizza, movies, junk food, Janet Jackson, and vote republican.

Explanation: What SuperCyberDate.con did not take into consideration were the 245 other likes and dislikes that were very different for both Sally and Billy—such as the fact that Billy likes men.

Exception: It's never a good idea to ignore the differences in the data while only focusing on the similarities.

Fun Fact: The name *"Texas sharpshooter fallacy"* comes from the idea that someone could shoot randomly at a barn, then draw a bullseye around the largest cluster, making it appear as if they were a sharpshooter.

References:

Forshaw, M. (2012). *Critical Thinking For Psychology: A Student Guide.* John Wiley & Sons.

Tokenism

Description: Interpreting a token gesture as an adequate substitute for the real thing.

Logical Form:

> Problem X exists.
>
> Solution Y is offered.
>
> Solution Y is inadequate to solve problem X but accepted as adequate.

Example #1:

> The presidential nominee has been accused of being racist. But he recently stated that he really liked the movie, "Roots," so I guess he isn't racist.

Explanation: Liking one movie that exposes racism and encourages equality, is far from the same as not being a racist.

Example #2:

> Mr. McBoss' company consists of 50 executives who are all men, and 50 secretaries who are all women. To show he is all about equal opportunity, he has agreed to hire a woman executive.

Explanation: This "token" gesture does not come close to making up for the disproportionate hiring practices of Mr. McBoss' company.

Example #3: In the summer of 2020 when racial tensions were high, many media sources did their part to solve racism by capitalizing the "B" when referring to black people while keeping the "w" lowercase when referring to white people. Some sources that picked up this story saw this as a token gesture to help shield them from public claims of racism.

Exception: If a token gesture is seen as a token, and not as an adequate substitute, it is not a fallacy.

I know I have a weight problem, and I am trying. So far, I have replaced my usual breakfast of doughnuts with a single grapefruit.

Fun Fact: Some attempts to solve racism are Stupid with a capital "S."

References:

Cogan, R. (1998). *Critical Thinking: Step by Step*. University Press of America.

Traitorous Critic Fallacy
ergo decedo

Description: Responding to criticism by attacking a person's perceived favorability to an out-group or dislike to the in-group as the underlying reason for the criticism rather than addressing the criticism itself, and suggesting that they stay away from the issue and/or leave the in-group. This is usually done by saying something such as, "Well, if you don't like it, then get out!"

Logical Form:

> *Person 1 offers criticism against group 1.*
>
> *Person 2 responds to the criticism by disingenuously asking them why they don't leave group 1.*

Example #1:

> *Gertrude: I am tired of having to fill out these forms all day. Can't we find a more efficient system?*
>
> *Cindy-Lou: If you're not happy with the way we do things, we can find someone who is!*

Explanation: Cindy-Lou did not address the concern, but essentially threatened Gertrude to shut up or lose her job. This example might also be seen as *appeal to force*.

Example #2:

> *Steve: In Sweden, college is free for citizens. How come we can't do that here?*
>
> *Ed: If you like Sweden so much, move there. The USA would be glad to be rid of your liberal ass!*

Explanation: Besides *begging the question* (Steve did not say he liked Sweden), Ed refused to address the question asked and deflected with a disingenuous question on why Steve does not move to Sweden.

Exception: Repeated expressions of favoritism for the out-group and dislike of the in-group could justify a why-don't-you-join-the-out-group type of response.

Tip: Remember the old saying about the grass being greener on the other side.

References:

This is a logical fallacy frequently used on the Internet. No academic sources could be found.

Two Wrongs Make a Right

Description: When a person attempts to justify an action against another person because the other person did take or would take the same action against him or her.

Logical Forms:

> *Person 1 did X to person 2.*
>
> *Therefore, person 2 is justified to do X to person 1.*

> *Person 1 believes that person 2 would do X to person 1.*
>
> *Therefore, person 1 is justified to do X to person 2.*

Example #1:

Jimmy stole Tommy's lunch in the past.

Therefore, it is acceptable for Tommy to steal Jimmy's lunch today.

Explanation: It was wrong for Jimmy to steal Tommy's lunch, but it is not good reasoning to claim that Tommy stealing Jimmy's lunch would make the situation right. What we are left with, are two kids who steal, with no better understanding of why they shouldn't steal.

Example #2:

It looks like the waiter forgot to charge us for the expensive bottle of champagne. Let's just leave—after all, if he overcharged us, I doubt he would chase us down to give us our money back that we overpaid.

Explanation: Here the reasoning is a bit more fallacious because we are making an assumption of what the waiter might do. Even if that were true, two ripoffs don't make the situation right.

Exception: There can be much debate on what exactly is "justified retribution" or "justified preventative measures."

Fun Fact: Three lefts make a right.

References:

This is a logical fallacy frequently used on the Internet. No academic sources could be found.

Type-Token Fallacy

Description: The type-token fallacy is committed when a word can refer to either a type (representing an abstract descriptive concept) or a token (representing an object that instantiates a concept) and is used in a way that makes it unclear which it refers to. This is a more specific form of the *ambiguity fallacy*.

Logical Forms:

Reference to type is made.

Response refers to token.

Reference to token is made.

Response refers to type.

Example #1:

Salesperson: Toyota manufactures like four dozens of cars, so if you don't like this one you can see others.

Prospect: I would have guessed they made closer to millions of cars.

Explanation: The salesperson was referring to the different types of cars (models) Toyota makes, not how many instances (or tokens) of each car were manufactured. By not specifically stating "types of cars" or "models," the statement was ambiguous and unnecessarily confusing.

Example #2:

Greg: I have the same suit as George Clooney.

Tim: Do you guys take turns wearing it?

Explanation: Greg means that he had the same type of suit as George Clooney. Tim was probably being a smart-ass with his response, but in case he wasn't, he confused the type with the token (that unique suit).

Tip: As always, be as clear in your communication as possible and avoid any unnecessary confusion.

References:

Wetzel, L. (2014). Types and tokens. In E. N. Zalta (Ed.), *The Stanford Encyclopedia of Philosophy* (Spring 2014). Metaphysics Research Lab, Stanford University. Retrieved from https://plato.stanford.edu/archives/spr2014/entriesypes-tokens/

Unfalsifiability

(also known as: untestability)

Description: Confidently asserting that a theory or hypothesis is true or false even though the theory or hypothesis cannot possibly be contradicted by an observation or the outcome of any physical experiment, usually without strong evidence or good reasons.

Making unfalsifiable claims is a way to leave the realm of rational discourse, since unfalsifiable claims are often faith-based, and not founded on evidence and reason.

Logical Form:

X is true (when X is cannot possibly be demonstrated to be false)

Example #1:

I have tiny, invisible unicorns living in my anus. Unfortunately, these cannot be detected by any kind of scientific equipment.

Explanation: While it may actually be a fact that tiny, invisible, mythological creatures are occupying this person's opening at the lower end of the alimentary canal, it is a theory that is constructed so it cannot be falsified in any way; therefore, should not be seriously considered without significant evidence.

Example #2:

Priests can literally turn wine into the blood of Jesus.

Explanation: Surely, we can examine the liquid and see if it at least changes chemically, can we not? No. Because transubstantiation is not about a physical or chemical change, but a change in "substance"—which, of course, is not a material change and, therefore, impossible to falsify. Furthermore, the claim is not that it "might be" happening, but it certainly is happening, adding to the fallaciousness of the claim. The only evidence for this is some ambiguous verses in the Bible—so ambiguous that over a billion Christians don't subscribe to the belief that transubstantiation occurs. So we have *unfalsifiability*, belief of certainty, and very weak evidence.

Exception: All unfalsifiable claims are not fallacious; they are just unfalsifiable. As long as proper skepticism is retained and proper evidence is given, it could be a legitimate form of reasoning.

Tip: Never assume you must be right simply because you can't be proven wrong.

References:

Flanagan, O. J. (1991). *The Science of the Mind*. MIT Press.

Unreasonable Inclusion Fallacy

Description: Attempting to broaden the criteria for inclusion in an ill-famed group or associated with a negative label to the point where the term's definition is changed substantially to condemn or criminalize a far less malicious or deleterious behavior.

Logical Form:

Person A is accused of bad behavior X.

Group Y traditionally does not include individuals with bad behavior X.

Person A is said to be a part of group Y for bad behavior X.

Person A is accused of bad behavior X.

Label Y traditionally does not include bad behavior X.

Person A is given label Y for bad behavior X.

Example #1: Tony does not agree that every black person in America should be compensated financially for the history of slavery. Therefore, Tony is a racist.

Explanation: The term "racist" is an extremely pejorative term that has traditionally been associated with those holding beliefs of racial supremacy—the belief that one's race is superior to other races. By expanding the definition to include "those who don't agree with policies that benefit another race," we fallaciously equate the behavior with the label's or group's far more malicious roots. Not only does this unreasonably characterize the person who is against the policy, but it also waters down the meaning of "racist" to the point where traditional racists are unreasonably seen more favorably because the term "racism" has been expanded to include a spectrum of far less malicious behaviors.

Example #2: Suzie and Patty went on a date. Patty told herself and her friends that she was not going to have sex on the first date, but she did anyway because she was caught up in the moment. The next day, Patty said that Suzie was very seductive, and Patty couldn't resist her advances. Patty's friends convince her that she was raped.

Explanation: Patty's friends' goal was to show sympathy to Patty. They did this by giving her victim status and criminalizing Suzie's behavior by unreasonably viewing Suzie as a "rapist." Universally, if Suzie's behavior is accepted as "rape," the definition has radically changed, which not only demeans victims of "traditional" rape by associating them with those who were seduced by their date but conflates actual rapists with those who are just seductive.

Example #3: Ricardo had a hamburger for lunch. Antonio, Ricardo's vegan friend, argues that he is a murderer.

Explanation: "Murder" is traditionally defined as the unlawful killing of another human being. A cow isn't a human being, killing a cow isn't unlawful, and Ricardo didn't kill the cow he ate. It is unreasonable to put Ricardo, a guy who at a hamburger, in the same category as Jeffrey Dahmer, a guy who ate his human victims he killed. Antonio is using the term "murderer" in a fallacious attempt to associate a similar level of malice with Ricardo's behavior.

Exception: See the *appeal to definition*. Terms change and evolve as do criteria. What makes this a fallacy is a) the definition is changed substantially and b) for the purpose of condemning or criminalizing a far less malicious or deleterious behavior.

Fun Fact: This is not unlike the "everyone gets a trophy" phenomenon where the (implied) definition of "winner" is changed substantially to include all those who lost as well ("you're all winners," says the coach). This may be good for lifting spirits, but it is antithetical to reason.

Reference:

This is an original logical fallacy named by the author.

Unwarranted Contrast

(also known as: some are/some are not)

Description: Assuming that *implicature* means *implication*, when it logically does not. *Implicature* is a relation between the fact that someone makes a statement and a proposition. *Implication* is a relation between propositions, that is, the meanings of statements.

Logical Forms:

> *Some S are P.*
>
> *Therefore, some S are not P.*

> *Some S are not P.*
>
> *Therefore, some S are P.*

Example #1:

> *Some atheists are human.*
>
> *Therefore, some atheists are not human.*

Explanation: This might be the case, but we cannot logically *imply* that this is the case because the use of "some" does not logically imply that it does not mean "all." In everyday use, "some" does *implicate* "not all," that is why this is fallacious and could be used to deceive without technically lying.

Example #2:

Some Christians are not Jews.

Therefore, some Christians are Jews.

Explanation: Just because we stated that some Christians are not Jews, does not mean we can logically conclude that some Christians are Jews. While we may *implicate* it, the statement does not *imply* it.

Fun Fact: This is another of those odd fallacies that are included for completeness sake. People don't typically use "some" in place of "all" or "none."

References:

Hansen, H. V., & Pinto, R. C. (1995). *Fallacies: Classical and Contemporary Readings.* Penn State Press.

Use-Mention Error

(also known as: UME)

Description: Confusing the word used to describe a thing, with the thing itself. To avoid this error, it is customary to put the word used to describe the thing in quotes.

This fallacy is most common when used as an *equivocation*.

Logical Form:

"X" is the same as X.

Example #1:

My son is made up of five letters.

Explanation: The words (mention), "my son," are made up of five letters. My son (use) is made up of molecules.

Example #2:

Tyrone: I am a sophisticated word genius.

Suzie: Prove it. Define some.

Tyrone: An unspecified amount or number of. Proven!

Explanation: Suzie meant to "define some words" but Tyrone defined the word "some." Tyrone thinks he won the exchange but he did not really define any sophisticated words.

Example #3: Many podcast hosts, journalists, and other public figures who discuss issues of race have got themselves in serious trouble by reporting on people who use the "N-word," by actually using the word themselves (I won't use it here because I don't want to be one of those casualties). This is because a small, but vocal, group view the mention of the word as nefarious as the use of the word, when the two are substantially different.

Exception: When this "fallacy" is used in humor and riddles.

Fun Fact: What part of London is in France? The letter "n."

References:

Azzouni, J. (2010). *Talking About Nothing: Numbers, Hallucinations and Fictions*. Oxford University Press.

Weak Analogy

(also known as: bad analogy, false analogy, faulty analogy, questionable analogy, argument from spurious similarity, false metaphor)

Description: When an analogy is used to prove or disprove an argument, but the analogy is too dissimilar to be effective, that is, it is unlike the argument more than it is like the argument.

Logical Form:

X is like Y.

Y has property P.

Therefore, X has property P.

(but X really is not too much like Y)

Example #1:

Not believing in the literal resurrection of Jesus because the Bible has errors and contradictions, is like denying that the Titanic sank because eye-witnesses did not agree if the ship broke in half before or after it sank.

Explanation: This is an actual analogy used by a Christian debater (one who usually seems to value reason and logic). There are several problems with this analogy, including:

- The Titanic sank in recent history

- We know for a fact that the testimonies we have are of eye-witnesses

- We have physical evidence of the sunken Titanic

Example #2:

Believing in the literal resurrection of Jesus is like believing in the literal existence of zombies.

Explanation: This is a common analogy used by some atheists who argue against Christianity. It is a *weak analogy* because:

- Jesus was said to be alive not just undead

- If God is assumed, then God had a reason to bring Jesus (himself) back—no such reason exists for zombies

- Zombies eat brains, Jesus did not (as far as we know)

Exception: It is important to note that analogies cannot be "faulty" or "correct," and even calling them "good" or "bad" is not as accurate as referring to them as either "weak" or "strong." The use of an analogy is an argument in itself, the strength of which is very subjective. What is weak to one person, is strong to another.

Tip: Analogies are very useful, powerful, and persuasive ways to communicate ideas. Use them—just make them strong.

References:

Luckhardt, C. G., & Bechtel, W. (1994). *How to Do Things with Logic*. Psychology Press.

Willed Ignorance

Description: Refusing to change one's mind or consider conflicting information based on a desire to maintain one's existing beliefs.

Logical Form:

> *I believe X.*
>
> *You have evidence for Y.*
>
> *I don't want to see it because I don't want to stop believing in X, so X is still true.*

Example #1:

> *I don't want anything coming in the way of me and my beliefs; therefore, I will only socialize with people who share my beliefs.*

Explanation: This is a common form of the fallacy—excluding oneself from society as a whole to smaller subgroups where the same general opinions are shared. There is an implied claim here that the beliefs are true.

Example #2:

> *Carl: Exercise causes cancer.*
>
> *Janet: That is not true. I have mountains of evidence I can show you that demonstrates the opposite.*
>
> *Carl: You keep your exercise propaganda to yourself. I know what I know. Now if you will excuse me, I have to binge watch Baywatch.*

Explanation: Carl is blissfully ignorant in his belief that allows him to avoid the wonderful pain of exercise. Perhaps Carl does suspect that he is wrong, but feels he does not have to change his belief until he is proven wrong. Thus, he will not allow Janet the opportunity to prove him wrong.

Exception: There may be circumstances where ignorance is truly bliss, and it is better to maintain a positive illusion than to be exposed to a hard truth that one is not psychologically prepared to accept.

Fun Fact: This fallacy is similar to the *confirmation bias*, but as a fallacy, it is used in argumentation.

References:

This is a logical fallacy frequently used on the Internet. No academic sources could be found.

Wishful Thinking

Description: When the desire for something to be true is used in place of/or as evidence for the truthfulness of the claim. Wishful thinking, more as a cognitive bias than a logical fallacy, can also cause one to evaluate evidence very differently based on the desired outcome.

Logical Form:

I wish X were true.

Therefore, X is true.

Example #1:

I know in my heart of hearts that our home team will win the World Series.

Explanation: No, you don't know that, and what the heck is your "heart of hearts" anyway? This is classic *wishful thinking* —wanting the home team to win so pretending that it is/has to be true.

Example #2:

I believe that when we die, we are all given new, young, perfect bodies, and we spend eternity with those whom we love. I can't imagine the point of life if it all just ends when we die!

Explanation: The fact that one doesn't like the idea of simply not existing is not evidence for the belief. Besides, nobody seemed to mind the eternity they didn't exist before they were born.

Exception: When *wishful thinking* is expressed as a hope, wish, or prayer and no belief is formed as a result, then it is not a fallacy because no direct or indirect argument is being made.

I really hope that I don't have to spend my eternity with my Aunt Edna, who really loved me, but she drove me nuts with her constant jabbering.

Tip: Wishing for something to be true is a powerful technique when and only when, a) you have influence on what it is you want to be true and b) you take action to make it come true—not just wish for it to be true.

References:

Andolina, M. (2002). *Practical Guide to Critical Thinking*. Cengage Learning.

Pseudo-Logical Fallacies

Recall my test for what qualifies as a logical fallacy:

1. **It must be an error in reasoning, not a factual error.**

2. **It must be commonly applied to an argument** either in the form of the argument or the interpretation of the argument.

3. **It must be deceptive** in that it often fools the average adult.

There are many so-called logical fallacies that can be found on the Internet that don't meet one or more of these criteria, yet people will still refer to them as logical fallacies. Since there are no objective criteria for most logical fallacies, people can call anything a logical fallacy if they want. But we are better than "people;" we are logical fallacy elitists. So those that aren't worth of the name "logical fallacy" we will call *pseudo-logical fallacies*. If these pseudo-logical fallacies were celebrities, none of them would be invited to the Oscars, but they might be invited on the *Hollywood Squares*. Just like *Hollywood Squares* can sometimes be entertaining to watch (as long as that lady with the stupid sock puppet is not on), this list can be well worth the read. For each item in the following list, I have added my comments as to why the pseudo-logical fallacy did not make the prime-time list.

Abductive Fallacy: The fallacy of applying an inadequate simulation methodology to a given simulation task. This appears in one academic paper and mentioned just a couple of times on the Internet. It is unclear if this can be applied to an argument. In addition, the failure to apply adequate simulation methodology sounds more like a lack of specialized knowledge rather than a deficiency in reasoning.

Absence of Evidence: This is the idea that based on an absence of evidence, we can form a reasonable conclusion. Sometimes we can if we expect to see evidence and we don't. This is a complex topic in epistemology and too nuanced to call simply label a fallacy. See *argument from ignorance* for a more fallacious version of this.

Alternative Fact/Alternative Truth: Another word for "fiction" or "lie." This is more about lying than errors in reasoning. Perhaps it might qualify as fallacious reasoning if a person believes that alternative facts are the same things as facts.

Appeal to Biased Authority: This has been identified some sources as a fallacy when the expertise of an authority is not discounted because they are likely to be biased. This is not an error in reasoning. In fact, the opposite is a fallacy (see *ad hominem circumstantial*). The argument should be evaluated on its own merits. While it is true that biased sources are more likely to present information that benefits them in some way, we must not dismiss the argument being made for that reason.

Another definition of this fallacy is referring to a biased source. This is either the *confirmation bias* or simply poor methodology for determining truth.

Appeal to Envy (Argumentum ad invidiam): Attempting to persuade by making one envious, rather than by evidence. Rarely is this used to conclude that a claim is true. It is more of a persuasion technique.

Appeal to Privacy: Refusing to open a topic for discussion because it is deemed "private." This is sometimes referred to as the *mind your own business fallacy*. I don't see an error in reasoning here. If a topic is personal or private, then it is to that person. If the claim is that because it private then it must be true, that would be fallacious, but I would think this is quite rare.

Appeal to Snobbery: An attempt to make one feel part of the elite if they accept the claim. This is more of a marketing/ persuasion technique than a fallacy. It is rarely used in argument form, but more to get someone to want something.

Appeal to the Stone (argumentum ad lapidem): This is dismissing a claim as absurd without demonstrating proof for its absurdity. This is a classic example of simply not giving a clear reason for rejecting an argument or proposition. It is not an error in reasoning; it is the refusal to use it. We can also say an argument is "crazy," "stupid," "non-sensical," "idiotic," "f'ed up," etc. Each possible adjective does not require its own fallacy.

Appeal to Values: A rhetorical strategy use to connect one's values to the argument. This can be fallacious if there is no real connection.

Appeal to Virtue: A rhetorical strategy use to connect that which one holds virtuous to the argument. This can be fallacious if there is no real connection.

Argument by Dismissal: An argument is rejected without saying why. The person who is rejecting the argument may have a good reason; they just refuse to share it. So we cannot assume that this is an error in reasoning. It could better be described as a conscious choice not to participate in the argument.

Argument by Laziness: Making an argument without bothering collecting support for the claims being made. This is simply a refusal to engage or make the required effort to engage.

Argument by Rhetorical Question: Setting up questions in such a way to get the answers you want. This is more rhetoric than a fallacy.

Argument by Uninformed Opinion: *(see argument by laziness)*

Argument from Design: Assuming because something looks designed, it probably was. This is more of a specific argument than a fallacy.

Argument from Final Consequences: Confusing cause and effect, starting with an effect and then assuming a cause. This is rarely used and is covered by the *questionable cause* fallacy (cum hoc ergo propter hoc).

Argument to the Future: Arguing that someday, evidence will be discovered to justify your conclusion. This could be fallacious or not, depending on the reasons that one has to think that evidence will one day be discovered to justify the conclusion. If one has no reasons, then it would fit under other fallacies such as the *appeal to faith* or *wishful thinking*.

Argumentum ad Captandum: Any specious or unsound argument that is likely to win popular acceptance. This is a general style of rhetoric rather than a specific fallacy.

Argumentum ad Exemplum (Argument to the Example): Arguing against a particular example cited rather than the question itself. This is rarely used, and when it is, it is used in different ways that match other fallacies.

Bad Seed: Attempting to undermine someone's reasoning or argument by pointing our their "bad" family history, when it is an irrelevant point. This is a very specific form of the *genetic fallacy*. It is rarely used.

Barking Cat: Demanding that a problem should not be solved before other, more important problems are solved. As long as one has good reasons for this, there is no fallacy.

Blood is Thicker than Water (Favoritism): Assuming truth because of a close connection with the one making the statement. This is not quite an error in reasoning. If anything, it is a natural bias where we tend to give those we like the benefit of the doubt.

Bribery (Material Persuasion, Material Incentive, Financial Incentive): Paying someone to agree with your position, or accepting payment to agree. This is not an error in reasoning.

Canceling Hypotheses: The argument defends one hypothesis by proposing a second hypothesis to explain the lack of evidence in support of the first hypothesis. That is, the second hypothesis cancels or undermines the predictions made by the first hypothesis. This is mostly covered under the fallacy *conspiracy theory*.

Chronological Snobbery: Thinking, art, or science of an earlier time is inherently inferior when compared to that of the present. This is more of bias, and when used in argument form, is covered by the *appeal to novelty* or *argument from age*.

Confesses Under Torture: Assuming what one confesses under torture must be true. It is difficult to determine how much the torture affected the truth of the confession. This is not an error in reasoning.

Damning with Faint Praise: To attack a person by formally praising him, but for an achievement that shouldn't be praised. This is more of a rhetorical device than a fallacy.

Digression: A temporary departure from the main subject in speech or writing. This is not fallacious in itself.

Disregarding Known Science: Ignoring scientific facts that are inconvenient to a position. This is better characterized as a cognitive bias or perhaps even a form of lying.

Dogmatism: The tendency to lay down principles as incontrovertibly true, without consideration of evidence or the opinions of others. This is a broad pattern of thinking, rather than a more specific error in reasoning. There are many already mentioned fallacies that cover this category.

Double Bind: Setting up a situation in which no matter what the person does or answers, he or she is wrong. This is more of a dilemma in communication than a fallacy.

Double Counting: Counting events or occurrences in probability or in other areas where a solution counts events two or more times, resulting in an erroneous number of events or occurrences which is higher than the true result. This is a specific statistical fallacy.

Essentializing Fallacy: Suggesting that something is what it is and it will always be that way when in fact, that is not the case. This is simply factually incorrect.

Exception That Proves the Rule: Exceptions to rules are evidence against rule, never for the rules. This is a strange relic from old law that means little in argumentation today.

Failure to State: Never actually stating a position on the topic, rather constantly being on the attack or asking questions. This protects the person from attack. This is not really an error in reasoning. One can argue against a bad argument without having to hold a position on the argument.

Fallacy of Multiplication: The assumption that if work Y can be accomplished with N resources, that if N*X resources were available, then work Y*X could be accomplished. This is a statistical error.

Fallacy of the Crucial Experiment: Claiming some idea has been proved by a pivotal discovery. This is too subjective. What is "pivotal" to one person might not be to another. Also, something could be "pivotal" in one of many ways.

Faulty Sign: Incorrectly assumes that one event or phenomenon is a reliable indicator or predictor of another event or phenomenon. This is very similar to many of the fallacies related to causality. This name is rarely used.

Furtive Fallacy: When outcomes are asserted to have been caused by the malfeasance of decision makers. This is more of a psychological phenomenon similar to paranoia than a fallacy.

God Wildcard Fallacy: Excuses a contradiction in logic or reason by "divine mystery." The God wildcard comes in many forms and is played when honest questioning leads to absurd or illogical conclusions. This is a very specific form of the *appeal to mystery*.

Golden Hammer Fallacy: Proposing the same type of solution to different types of problems. This is more of an error in creativity or knowledge than reasoning.

Hifalutin' Denunciations: Denouncing an argument or interlocutor with vague, pretentious, and grand-sounding generalized accusations. This is more of a type of rhetoric than a fallacy.

Historical Fallacy: A logical fallacy originally described by philosopher John Dewey in *The Psychological Review* in 1896. The fallacy occurs when a person reads into a process the results that occur only because of that process. This is rarely used.

Hoyle's Fallacy (the Junkyard Tornado): An argument used to derive the probability of both abiogenesis and the evolution of higher life forms as comparable to "the chance that a tornado sweeping through a junkyard might assemble a

Boeing 747." The "fallacy" is an argument against this idea. This is a specific instance of fallacious reasoning rather than a common fallacy.

I Wish I Had a Magic Wand: Erroneously proclaiming oneself powerless to change a bad or objectionable situation, thinking there is no alternative. Not an error in reasoning.

In a Certain Respect and Simply (secundum quid et simpliciter): Take an attribute that is bound to a certain area and assume that it can be applied to a wider domain than was originally intended. Rarely used.

Insignificance: Making a minor cause seem major. Not really a fallacy.

Intentional Fallacy: A term used in 20th-century literary criticism to describe the problem inherent in trying to judge a work of art by assuming the intent or purpose of the artist who created it. This is a very specific fallacy and not common.

Knights and Knaves: Treating information coming from other persons as if it were always right or always wrong, based on the person. This is very similar to the *genetic fallacy*.

Lack of Proportion: Exaggerating or downplaying evidence important in the argument. Extreme cases could actually be a form of suppressed evidence. This is more of a form of deception where a lack of reasoning cannot be blamed.

Latino Fallacy: Finding an argument, fallacy, or claim that has a Latin translation more credible than it would be without the translation. This is a specific form of the *argument from age*.

Lip Service: Pretending to agree when it's clear that you don't really agree. This is more of a form of deception where a lack of reasoning cannot be blamed.

Lump of Labor Fallacy (Lump of Jobs Fallacy): The contention that the amount of work available to laborers is fixed. This can be debatable, depending on the economist asked. This is not a problem with reasoning.

Mind Projection Fallacy: Coined by physicist and Bayesian philosopher E.T. Jaynes, the mind projection fallacy occurs when one believes with certainty that the way he sees the world reflects the way the world really is. This is more of a cognitive bias than a fallacy.

Monopolizing the Question: Asking a question and then immediately giving the answer, in a way "forcing" your answer on the audience. This is more of a rhetorical device than a fallacy.

Motte-and-bailey Fallacy: When an arguer advances a controversial position, but when challenged, they insist that they are only advancing a more modest position. This is a more specific version of *equivocation*.

Needling: Attempting to make the other person angry, especially by continual criticism or questioning. In previous editions, I had this listed as a form of the *ad hominem* fallacy. However, it is more of a tactic and not an error in reasoning.

Norm of Reciprocity: A technique used to exploit people's natural tendency to want to repay debts. In an argument, one may concede a point causing an unwarranted concession from the other side, out of the desire to repay the favor. This is more of a technique than an error in reasoning. When used in argumentation, it can be an effective counter to the cognitive bias *the backfire effect*.

Not Invented Here: Ideas and arguments are not evaluated equally if they come from outside a social sphere. This is a specific form of the *genetic fallacy*.

Outdated Information: If outdated information is used in an argument, it would technically be more of an error in the truth of the premises than in reason, but be aware of this when doing your fact checking.

Over-Fitting: When a statistical model describes random error or noise instead of the underlying relationship. This is specific to statistics.

Packing the House: Filling the audience with friends, shills, or others who will cheer incessantly after you speak or make an argument, badger your interlocutor, and otherwise make for an unfair environment that will make your arguments appear much stronger and your interlocutor's much weaker. Related to *pomp and circumstance.* This is more of a strategy than having to do with reasoning or directly with an argument.

Paralogism: Can generally refer to any fallacious or illogical argument. Not a fallacy in itself.

Paralysis of Analysis (Procrastination): Reasoning that since all data is never in, no legitimate decision can ever be made and any action should always be delayed until forced by circumstances. Not necessarily fallacious.

Pigeonholing: A term used to describe processes that attempt to classify disparate entities into a small number of categories. This usually covers a wide variety of more specific fallacies.

Pious Fraud: A fraud done for a what is believed to be a good end, on the theory that the end justifies the means. Not necessarily fallacious.

Probabilistic Fallacy: When inferences from the premises to the conclusion violate the laws of probability. This is rarely seen in everyday usage.

Psychologist's Fallacy: A fallacy that occurs when an observer presupposes the universality of his or her own perspective when analyzing a behavioral event. This is rarely seen in everyday usage. Also, since the time of William James (the psychologist who first described this fallacy), it is well understood that this is problematic in research, thus not deceptive.

Reductionism: This is more of a philosophy than a fallacy, although those who don't subscribe to the philosophy will often refer to it as a fallacy. It is reducing things to the interaction of their parts. For example, if one claims we are just biochemistry, then those who believe we are also a "soul" will consider this claim a fallacy.

Referential Fallacy: A theory of language that claims that the meaning of a word or expression lies in what it points to out in the world. This is rarely seen in everyday usage.

Retrospective Determinism: Assuming that because something happened, it necessarily had to happen, i.e. that it was the only possible outcome. Irrespective of a deterministic worldview, this fallacy explains nothing.

Sanctioning the Devil: Avoiding debate with someone because debating him would give him undue credit. Really not a fallacy, but can be considered one by the flat-earther you are refusing to debate.

Scope Fallacy: There are many specific fallacies detailed in this book that fit the under the category of "scope fallacy." These have to do mostly with ambiguity.

Sealioning: A subtle form of trolling involving "bad-faith" questions. You disingenuously frame your conversation as a sincere request to be enlightened, placing the burden of educating you entirely on the other party. This is not a fallacy; it is more of a form of deception. As always, be careful in assuming you know the other person's intent. On the surface, "sealioning" looks a lot like legitimate and honest Socratic inquiry.

Self-Deception: The process or fact of misleading ourselves to accept as true or valid what is false or invalid. This is more of a cognitive process that underlies fallacies.

Self-Fulfilling Prophecy: The process of prophesying will itself produce the effect that is prophesied, but the reasoner doesn't recognize this and believes the prophecy is a significant insight. This is not commonly applied to an argument.

Sherlock Holmes Fallacy: Remember that Sherlock Homes was a fictional character, even if based on a real one. His method of deduction was often stated as "when you have eliminated the impossible, whatever remains, however improbable, must be the truth." There are many flaws with this method in real life. This is more of a bad scientific methodology than a fallacy.

Sly Suggestions: Suggesting that your ideas may be true without making solid statements that can be proven wrong. "You may be our next millionaire! Just subscribe to this service and you will find out if you are or not." This is a marketing gimmick, not commonly used in argumentation.

Sour Grapes: Denigrating something just because you can't have it. "Your new Lamborghini is okay, but the seats are too low to the ground. I prefer my Chevy." Not commonly used within argumentation.

Snow Job: There are several uses of this phrase: 1) "Proving" a claim by overwhelming an audience with mountains of irrelevant facts, numbers, documents, graphs and statistics that they cannot be expected to understand, 2) a strong effort to make someone believe something by saying things that are not true or sincere, or 3) an attempt to deceive or persuade by using flattery or exaggeration. All of these uses are closer to lying than a fallacy.

Syllogistic Fallacy: This is a general category of formal fallacies that occur in syllogisms.

Taboo: Refusing to examine critically a belief or argument because it's not acceptable to do so, for whatever reason. This is the refusal to reason.

Tautology: Using different words to say the same thing, even if the repetition does not provide clarity. Tautology can also refer to a series of self-reinforcing statements that cannot be disproved because the statements depend on the assumption that they are already correct (a form of *begging the question*). This is generally not deceptive in argument form.

Testimonials: Statements from, "authorities," in the sense that they are said to know about what they are testifying. In business, vendor-provided testimonials should not be taken too seriously as they can easily be exceptions to the norm or just made up—as in, "John G. from Ohio says..." While testimonials could be arguments, they are generally not. If they are, they fall under the *appeal to authority* fallacy.

There Is No Alternative: Discouraging critical thought by announcing that there is no realistic alternative to a given standpoint, status or action, ruling any and all other options irrelevant, or announcing that a decision has been made, and any further discussion is simply a waste of time (or even insubordination or disloyalty).

Too Broad: The definition includes items which should not be included. This is more of an error of fact than reason.

Too Narrow: The definition does not include all the items which should be included. This is more of an error of fact than reason.

Vacuous truth: In mathematics and logic, a vacuous truth is a statement that asserts that all members of the empty set have a certain property. This is beyond the scope of fallacies.

Undoability: Claiming something is not possible rather than you (or someone else) cannot do it. This is very similar to the *argument from ignorance*.

Weasel Wording: Using ambiguous words in order to mislead or conceal a truth: "Save up to 50% or more!" This is more of a marketing gimmick than a fallacy.

Whataboutism/Whataboutery: People are called out on their "whataboutery" when they point out hypocrisy in response to an argument. A "what about you" response does not address the argument, thus, is problematic akin to avoiding the issue.

Word Magic: Assuming just because there is a word for it, it must exist. This is questionable as a deceptive argument. For example, there is the word "unicorn" but most people aren't tricked into thinking they must exist because of the word.

Cognitive Biases, Effects, and Heuristics

Here is a partial list of cognitive biases, effects, and heuristics that are not specifically logical fallacies. All of these are involved in the reasoning process and can lead to accepting bad arguments.

Actor–observer Bias: A tendency to attribute one's own actions to external causes, while attributing other people's behaviors to internal causes.

Example: "I tripped because of the uneven pavement. You tripped because you are a klutz."

Ambiguity Effect: A bias in decision making where people tend to select options for which the probability of a favorable outcome is known, over an option for which the probability of a favorable outcome is unknown.

Example: "I'll go with the double cheeseburger over the house special burger. I have had the double cheeseburger before, and I know it is good."

Anchoring or Focalism: A bias in decision making where one relies too heavily on the first piece of information offered (or the "anchor").

Example: "The guy asking for donations asked me if I wanted to give $100 or even just $20. So I gave him $20 which appears to be the minimum." Actually, they will take any amount as a donation. Those proposed amounts were anchors to get higher donations—and it worked.

Attentional Bias: The tendency for a person's perception to be affected by his or her recurring thoughts at the time.

Example: (As Jimmy is watching *Shark Week* on television). "Jimmy, you want to go for a swim in the ocean?" "No! Are you freakin' nuts!?"

Authority Bias: The tendency to attribute greater accuracy to the opinion of a general authority figure (not one specific to the topic at hand) and be more influenced by that opinion.

Example: "Leonard Nimoy said on *In Search Of* that ancient aliens might have built the pyramids. Spock doesn't lie!"

Automation Bias: The tendency to favor suggestions from automated decision-making systems and to ignore contradictory information made without automation, even if it is correct.

Example: "This Facebook online quiz said that I am most like the Disney princess, Belle! Although my wife says I am more like Mulan, I agree with the Facebook quiz."

Availability Cascade: A self-reinforcing process in which a collective belief gains more and more plausibility through its increasing repetition in public discourse (or "repeat something long enough, and it will become true").

Example: Cults that repeat the same ideas over and over brainwash their members.

Availability Heuristic: A mental shortcut that relies on immediate examples that come to mind when evaluating a specific topic, concept, method or decision.

Example: Believing that driving across the country is safer than taking a plane because you remember seeing a horrific plane crash on the news.

Backfire Effect: When one's beliefs are challenged by contradicting evidence, the belief becomes stronger.

Example: "You can give me all the evidence you want, I know what I know! The more evidence you try to give me against my belief, the more I am convinced that I am right."

Bandwagon Effect: When one does something primarily because others are doing it.

Example: "Mom, I am going with Bobby and Jimmy to jump off the Brooklyn Bridge."

Belief Bias: The tendency to judge the strength of arguments based on how plausible their conclusions are rather than how strong the argument itself is.

Example: (To a person who already believes in God) "God exists because... look at that beautiful sunset!"

Ben Franklin Effect: If person A has done a favor for person B, person A is more likely to do another favor for person B than if person B did a favor for person A.

Example: "Can you take out my garbage on Tuesday?" "Why not, I did it last Tuesday."

Bias Blind Spot: One's inability to recognize one's own biases.

Example: "Of course you are voting that way. This is because of the confirmation bias. I, on the other hand, am voting the other way because I am reasonable."

Bizarreness Effect: That which is bizarre or strange is more likely to be remembered than that which is normal.

Example: Most memory strategies include making bizarre stories in your mind to remember objects and numbers. This is very effective.

Cheerleader Effect: The bias that causes us to find individuals more attractive when they are in a group.

Example: "Those guys are gorgeous!... Oh, wait. Now that they split up, I am looking at them individually and they really aren't that good looking."

Childhood Amnesia: The inability to remember anything before age two or three.

Example: "My first memory is of me sitting on my father's lap when he told me about his grandfather. I think I was about three years old then."

Choice-supportive Bias: The tendency to retroactively ascribe positive attributes to an option one has selected. This is also known as *post-purchase rationalization*.

Example: "That $40 bar of soap I bought at the multi-level-marketing seminar is well worth it because it is GMO-free!"

Clustering Illusion: This is the tendency to erroneously see random clusters in data as significant or meaningful.

Example: "This mutual fund did amazing in the past. Clearly, the mutual fund manager knows what they are doing!" *This is unlikely the case. If we look at all mutual funds, by mere chance and luck alone, some will do very well.*

Confirmation Bias: The tendency to interpret new evidence as confirmation of one's existing beliefs or theories.

Example: "I know my political position is right because all of the media outlets I subscribe to also agree with me."

Congruence Bias: A bias in research where one has an over-reliance on direct testing of a hypothesis while ignoring indirect testing.

Example: If a researcher wants to know if smoking pot leads to homelessness, she might just (incorrectly) look at how many homeless people smoked pot before being homeless. The indirect testing needed might be also to see how many successful people smoked pot before they were successful.

Conservatism: The tendency to revise one's belief insufficiently when presented with new evidence.

Example: Gert believes in the Loch Ness Monster. Gert is shown how every photo and story used as "proof" has been discredited. Gert is now less convinced, but still has an unreasonably strong belief.

Consistency Bias: The psychological tendency to see oneself as consistent which affects our actions.

Example: If you see yourself as the type of person who gives to charity, and someone asks you for money for their charity, even if you don't exactly support the idea of their cause, you are likely to give to them to remain consistent with your self-image.

Context Effect: A concept within cognitive psychology that has to do with how environmental factors affect our perception of stimuli.

Example: A joke might be hilarious at a comedy club, but the same joke at a funeral is not at all funny.

Continued Influence Effect: This refers to the way false information enters memory and continues to affect beliefs even after the false information has been corrected.

Example: Accusations were made about politician X being a rapist. All allegations were clearly found to be baseless, yet the mere idea destroyed any chances for politician X to win.

Contrast Effect: Adding or subtracting value to subjects or objects based on how we analyze them as compared to what we perceive as a normal case.

Example: People who are happy with their salary are later unhappy with their salary when they find out that their coworkers are getting paid more.

Courtesy Bias: The tendency to tell people what we think they want to hear.

Example: "That tattoo of your mother on your arm really suits you!"

Cross-race Effect: The tendency to more easily recognize and distinguish between faces that match one's own race (or the race with which one is more familiar).

Example: The quasi-racist remark "they all look the same to me" is based on this effect. More accurately, people of unfamiliar races look more similar to each other than people of one's own race.

Cryptomnesia: When forgotten memories return to consciousness and are mistaken for original thoughts and ideas.

Example: "I have this great idea for a book: Imagine a young girl who has this dream that she is taken to this strange land where she meets a lion, a scarecrow, a tin man..." "Wait a minute. You are describing *The Wizard of Oz*." "No, I made this up!"

Curse of Knowledge: Assuming that others with whom you are communicating have the same background knowledge about the topic(s) as you do.

Example: Many bad teachers assume that the students already know what the teacher knows, so they lose the students in the process of teaching.

Declinism: The tendency to believe that a society or institution is tending towards decline.

Example: "Things were so much better in the past. We need to make this place great again!"

Decoy Effect: Since choices are often made relative to what is being offered rather than absolute preferences, by introducing an option that is of lesser value but similar to one of the other options, one's choice can be manipulated whereas he or she would tend to choose the higher value option that is similar to the "decoy" option introduced.

Example: If you offer 100 people $10 or a pen worth $10, most of them will choose the $10. If you add in a third option, a cheap pen worth 25 cents, more people will then choose the expensive pen.

Defensive Attribution Hypothesis: Refers to a set of beliefs used as a shield for oneself against the fear that one will be the victim or cause of a serious mishap.

Example: "I will never get into a drunk driving accident. I know my limits!"

Denomination Effect: People are less likely to spend larger bills than their equivalent value in smaller bills.

Example: If an item cost $20, and person A has a $20 bill, and person B has 20 $1 bills, all other things being equal, person B will be more likely to buy the item.

Disposition Effect: The tendency of investors to sell assets whose price has increased, while keeping assets that have dropped in value.

Example: Stocks A and B were both purchased for $10 each. Stock A is now worth $20, and stock B is now worth $5. The investor is more likely to sell stock A with all other factors considered equal.

Distinction Bias: The tendency to view two options as more different from one another (distinctive) when evaluating them simultaneously than when evaluating them separately.

Example: "I can see how different the twins are when they are both in the same room. Otherwise, they really do seem identical."

Dunning–Kruger Effect: When people are too ignorant to realize the extent of their own ignorance.

Example: Politician X thinks he can easily solve the problems we have in the Middle East. This is because he knows very little about the problems.

Duration Neglect: The psychological observation that people's judgments of the unpleasantness of painful experiences depend very little on the duration of those experiences.

Example: If person A has his hand in ice-cold water for 10 seconds, and person B has his hand in ice-cold water for 30 seconds, both people are likely to rate the unpleasantness of the experience the same.

Egocentric Bias: The tendency to rely too heavily on one's own perspective and/or have a higher opinion of oneself than reality dictates.

Example: "The world is full of beautiful women everywhere one goes!" (Says the guy who has never left his Swedish village where women outnumber men 4 to 1).

Empathy Gap: The perceptive difference between attitudes, preferences, and behaviors while in a visceral state versus in a calm state.

Example: "I can't imagine why that woman fainted when seeing the decapitated head. We see these in movies all the time."

Endowment Effect: The hypothesis that people ascribe more value to things merely because they own them.

Example: John would never buy a trinket for $5, but if he were given the trinket, he probably wouldn't sell it for $5 either.

Experimenter's or Expectation Bias: This is a research-related bias. This is the tendency for researchers (experimenters) to believe, certify, and publish data that agree with their expectations for the outcome of an experiment, and to disbelieve, discard, or downgrade the corresponding weightings for data that appear to conflict with those expectations.

Example: A Christian researcher does a study on the effectiveness of prayer. She finds no effect, so she does not publish the study with the negative results.

Extrinsic Incentives Bias: The tendency to attribute extrinsic motives (e.g. money) rather than intrinsic motives (e.g. education) when weighing the motives of others rather than oneself.

Example: When a manager thinks more money will be a greater motivator to her staff rather than a recognition program.

Fading Affect Bias: The tendency to forget information associated with negative emotions more quickly than information associated with pleasant emotions.

Example: One is more likely to remember the details of their upcoming vacation and less likely to remember the details of a business trip that one is not looking forward to taking.

False Consensus Effect: The tendency to overestimate the extent to which one's own opinions, beliefs, preferences, values, and habits are normal and typical of those of others.

Example: "Nobody likes going to the movies anymore. I have not been to the movies in years."

False Memory: An apparent recollection of an event that did not actually occur.

Example: Many innocent people were sent to prison based on the false memories of children who "recalled" sexual abuse—thanks to a process known as *suggestion* by therapists who essentially implanted the memories.

Focusing Effect: The tendency to weigh attributes and factors unevenly, putting more importance on some aspects and less on others.

Example: Dating a horrible human being just because she has big boobs.

Forer effect or Barnum effect: The tendency to give high accuracy ratings to descriptions of one's personality that supposedly are tailored specifically to them but that are, in fact, vague and general enough to apply to a wide range of people.

Example: I know very much about you. Yes, you, the person who is reading this right now. You are smart, and you appreciate the value of using reason. You are the kind of person who is not afraid to read a book to expand your level of knowledge.

Framing Effect: The tendency to react to a particular choice in different ways depending on how it is presented.

Example: (in universe #1) "We can either go see that awesome movie that got rave reviews, or stay home and watch TV." "Let's go see the movie!"

(in universe #2) "We can either leave the comfort of our own home and go see that movie, or relax at home watch that amazing new show on TV." "Let's stay home!"

Frequency Illusion: The tendency to notice instances of a particular phenomenon once one starts to look for it, and to, therefore, believe erroneously that the phenomenon occurs more often than it does.

Example: You start to look for "signs" that you should take a new job, and you start to see them everywhere. *Actually, you are just interpreting common events in such a way that support your conscious or unconscious desire to take or reject the job.*

Functional Fixedness: The tendency to limit oneself to using an object only in the way it is traditionally used.

Example: Running out to the garage to get a hammer to hammer in a small nail to hang a picture frame, when you are surrounded by other objects, such as paperweights, that can do the job just fine.

Fundamental Attribution Error: The tendency to explain someone's behavior based on internal factors and to underestimate the influence that external factors have on another person's behavior.

Example: "Billy is acting out because he is an unruly kid with no discipline." *Actually, Billy is acting out because he is seven, and he has been stuck at grandma's house all day sitting down trying to be polite.*

Generation Effect (Self-generation Effect): The tendency to better remember information if it is generated from one's own mind rather than simply read.

Example: Stories that are made up are better remembered by the person making up the story than if that person read the story.

Google Effect: The tendency to forget information that can easily be found online by using Internet search engines such as Google.

Example: "What is the capital of Wyoming?" "Let me see... 'Siri, what is the capital of Wyoming?'" *"Cheyenne is the capital of Wyoming."*

Group Attribution Error: People's tendency to believe either (1) that the characteristics of an individual group member are reflective of the group as a whole, or (2) that a group's decision outcome must reflect the preferences of individual group members, even when information is available suggesting otherwise.

Example: "That white cop unjustly shot that black kid. White people are racist!"

Halo Effect: The tendency for an impression created in one area to influence opinion in another area.

Example: "My teacher really knows his stuff when it comes to math. I bet he is also a whiz at chess!"

Hard–easy Effect: The tendency to be overconfident about the correctness of answers to difficult questions and underconfident about answers to easy questions.

Example: This frequently happens with multiple choice questions where people consistently second guess their answers to easier questions and are more confident on the ones that they actually get wrong.

Hindsight Bias: The tendency to see a past event as having been predictable, despite there having been little or no objective basis for predicting it.

Example: "I knew that he was going to hit a home run!"

Humor Effect: The tendency to better remember humorous items than non-humorous ones.

Example: Memorize three mental images. Later try to recall them all and see which you remember better. 1) a man walking by a lake 2) a woman running up a mountain, and 3) Will Ferrel streaking through the quad.

Hyperbolic Discounting: The tendency for one to increasingly choose a smaller, sooner reward over a larger, later reward as the delay occurs sooner rather than later in time.

Example: People would rather have $10 now than $20 a year from now, even though that $20 represents a 100% increase over 1 year.

Identifiable Victim Effect: The tendency of individuals to offer greater aid when a specific, identifiable person (or "victim") is observed under hardship, as compared to a large, vaguely defined group with the same need.

Example: "A single death is a tragedy, a million deaths is a statistic."

IKEA Effect: The tendency to place a disproportionately high value on products one partially creates.

Example: "Do you like this table? It is my favorite piece of furniture." "It looks like an ordinary table." "Yea, but I assembled it!"

Illusion of Asymmetric Insight: The tendency to perceive one's knowledge of others to surpass other people's knowledge of them.

Example: We think we know our spouse better than he or she knows us.

Illusion of Control: The tendency for people to overestimate their ability to control events.

Example: "Don't worry. I have practiced quite a bit for my part in the play. The play is going to be great!"

Illusion of External Agency: A set of attributional biases consisting of illusions of influence, insight, and benevolence.

Example: "I just managed not to fall off that cliff! There must be a guardian angel looking out for me!"

Illusion of Transparency: The tendency for people to overestimate how well they understand others' personal mental states.

Example: "Timmy is fine. He's just upset because he didn't win." *Actually, Timmy is upset because his dad called him a "loser."*

Illusion of Truth Effect (Illusory Truth Effect): The tendency to believe information to be correct the more it is repeated.

Example: One of the ways the Russians influenced the 2016 presidential election was to flood the Internet with false information and narratives about the Democratic candidate.

The more this information was heard, the more it was believed, despite the continual debunking efforts.

Illusion of Validity: The tendency for one to overestimate his or her ability to interpret and predict accurately the outcome when analyzing a set of data that appears to show a consistent pattern.

Example: Wine connoisseurs often think they have a valid method for determining good wine from bad wine when in fact, many blind studies have shown that even of the best of them have a difficult time telling the difference between a $500 bottle of wine and a $10 bottle.

Illusory Correlation: The tendency to perceive a relationship between variables (typically people, events, or behaviors) even when no such relationship exists.

Example: Good luck is frequently associated with rituals or "good luck charms."

Illusory Superiority: The tendency for one to overestimate his or her own qualities and abilities, relative to others.

Example: In several studies, a vast majority of those interviewed believe that they are better than average when it comes to driving. Of course, only about 50% can be better than average.

Impact Bias: The tendency for people to overestimate the length or the intensity of future feeling states.

Example: Sandy thinks she would be miserable for months if she was dumped by Troy. Troy dumped Sandy. Sandy was only miserable for a couple of days and quickly got over it.

Information Bias: Believing that the more information that can be acquired to make a decision, the better, even if that extra information is irrelevant for the decision.

Example: Phil holds off on accepting the job because he is waiting to find out if he will be going to Sweden in the summer, even though he would take the job whether he was going to Sweden or not.

Ingroup Bias: The tendency to favor one's own group.

Example: Choosing to sit next to a person roughly your same age, same gender, and same race rather than someone in one of these different groups.

Insensitivity to Sample Size: The tendency to judge the probability of obtaining a sample statistic without respect to the sample size.

Example: Willie thinks that because he played roulette three times and won twice, that if he plays 30 times, he will win about 20 times.

Irrational Escalation: The tendency to make irrational decisions based upon rational decisions in the past or to justify actions already taken.

Example: It was rational to threaten violence as a last resort if country X did not comply with policy Y. Country X did not comply with policy Y, so an attack was launched. This led to a counter attack which led to more attacks until full-blown nuclear war destroyed the entire world. The end.

Just-world Hypothesis: The tendency to believe one will get what one deserves that often leads to a rationalization of an inexplicable injustice by suggesting things the victim might have done to deserve it.

Example: The idea that homeless people are homeless because they are lazy, uneducated, substance abusers who brought their situation upon themselves.

Law of the Instrument: The tendency to over rely on a familiar tool.

Example: A Freudian psychotherapist might think that most problems are a result of oppressed feelings from childhood.

Less-is-better (less-is-more) Effect: A type of preference reversal that occurs when the lesser or smaller alternative of a proposition is preferred when evaluated separately, but not evaluated together.

Example: Choosing an expensive $45 pen over a cheap $55 desk clock. However, if both options were presented together, then choosing the $55 desk clock.

Loss Aversion: The tendency to prefer avoiding losses to acquiring equivalent gains.

Example: One would theoretically do more to protect from losing $100 then he or she would for gaining $100.

Mere Exposure Effect: The tendency to develop a preference for things merely because of familiarity with them.

Example: One might prefer an old car to a much better new car, simply because one is familiar with the old car.

Misinformation Effect: When a person's recall of episodic memories becomes less accurate because of post-event information.

Example: After the riot had broken out, a group of people started the false narrative that an elderly woman was struck by a police officer. Due to this narrative spreading, many of the witnesses of the riot recalled seeing the woman being struck by the police officer (although it never happened).

Moral Luck: The tendency to ascribe moral praise or condemnation to a moral agent when they have no control of the factors that brought about the moral judgment.

Example: Carl and Jason go out for a night of drinking at the local bar. They both drive home intoxicated in their separate cars. Carl gets pulled over by a cop and arrested for DUI, while Jason did not. Carl is seen as morally inferior to Jason.

Negativity Bias or Negativity Effect: The tendency for negative things to have a greater effect on one's psychological state and processes than neutral or positive things of equal intensity.

Example: People are more affected emotionally by the death of a stranger than the birth of one.

Normalcy Bias: The tendency to believe that things will always function the way things normally function.

Example: Many people don't take proper precautions for a potential disaster because of this bias.

Observer-expectancy Effect: The tendency for a researcher's cognitive bias(es) to cause them to subconsciously influence the participants of an experiment.

Example: If a researcher is investigating ESP, and is determined to prove it exists, she might give the participants subtle facial cues as to which option in the experiment to choose, thus contaminating the results of the experiment.

Omission Bias: The tendency to judge harmful actions as worse, or less moral than equally harmful omissions (inactions).

Example: A person who passes a kid drowning and does nothing might be seen as a cold-hearted ass-clown, but not a murderer.

Optimism Bias: The tendency to believe that one is at less at risk of experiencing a negative event compared to others.

Example: "Car accidents are horrible, but I am very careful and that won't happen to me!"

Ostrich Effect: The tendency to ignore a dangerous or risky situation.

Example: Sometimes people will rationalize or make excuses for why they don't want to do something when the real reason has to do with this bias.

Outcome Bias: An error made in evaluating the quality of a decision when the outcome of that decision is already known.

Example: When our leaders take a military action, we might support the decision initially. However, if the military action is a failure or leads to bigger problems than it solved, we criticize the leaders for making the decision.

Outgroup Homogeneity Bias: The tendency to perceive out-group members as more similar to one another than in-group members.

Example: All people on the other team are essentially the same —mean and nasty, whereas all those on our team have all different personalities.

Overconfidence Effect: The tendency for one's confidence in his or her judgments is reliably greater than the objective accuracy of those judgments, especially when confidence is relatively high.

Example: "I know I'm right!"

Pareidolia: A psychological phenomenon in which the mind responds to a stimulus by perceiving a familiar pattern where none exists.

Example: Seeing Jesus in toast.

Peak-end Rule: An event makes its mark in our memories more by what happens at its end than at any prior point, then at its peak.

Example: Judging a really bad movie as good just because it had an exciting ending, then watching the movie a second time and being terribly disappointed for the first 98% of the movie.

Pessimism Bias: The tendency for people to exaggerate the likelihood that negative things will happen to them.

Example: "Society is collapsing!"

Picture Superiority Effect: The tendency for pictures and images to be more likely remembered than words.

Example: Most marketing includes images for this reason.

Planning Fallacy: The tendency for predictions about how much time will be needed to complete a future task and underestimate the time needed.

Example: "I can be ready in 10 minutes." *In fact, it takes the person 20 minutes.*

Projection Bias: The assumption that one's tastes or preferences will remain the same over time.

Example: "I can't imagine life without you!" *Earnestly says the guy who just met the girl and had a great first date. Two dates later, he can't wait to break it off.*

Pseudocertainty Effect: The tendency to perceive an outcome as certain while in fact it is uncertain.

Example: "Are you sure you can stop at the store on the way home?" "I'm positive!" *Actually, something came up at work, and he didn't make it to the store.*

Reactance Bias: The tendency to do something different from what someone wants you to do in reaction to a perceived attempt to constrain your freedom of choice.

Example: An employee is asked by his boss to file a report by noon. He doesn't like being his boss' puppet, so the employee files the report by 1:00 instead.

Reactive Devaluation: The tendency to devalue a proposal if it originates from an antagonist (i.e., some source that the person does not like).

Example: A politician makes an excellent decision that will be of great benefit to the country, but because the politician is a Republican, many liberals think it is a bad decision.

Response Bias: A category of cognitive biases that influence the responses of participants away from an accurate or truthful response.

Example: Most people (non-professionals) who conduct surveys are not well-aware of these biases. Therefore, the results of their surveys can be inaccurate.

Restraint Bias: The tendency for people to overestimate their ability to control impulsive behavior.

Example: This is a huge problem in dieting, being a faithful spouse, getting work done, and just about every other area of life. Once we realize that we have much less willpower than we think we do, we can control our environment in ways that don't tempt our restraint (e.g., don't buy candy for the house when you are on a diet).

Rosy Retrospection: The tendency to remember and recollect events more favorably than when they occurred.

Example: "Back in the '80s, people were friendly and life was grand!"

Selective Perception: The tendency to select, categorize, and analyze stimuli from our environment to create meaningful experiences while blocking out stimuli that contradict our beliefs or expectations.

Example: "Clearly the world is falling apart. Everywhere I look I see hatred and anger."

Self-selection Bias: In statistics, the self-selection bias arises in any situation in which individuals select themselves into a group, causing a biased sample with nonprobability sampling.

Example: If you are wondering how people like your new website, and have a pop-up window on your website that invites feedback, you are allowing people to comment only if they feel the need. This means, you never hear from those who are indifferent or those who became so frustrated that they didn't get to the form or don't want anything to do with it.

Self-serving Bias: The tendency for people to attribute positive events to their own character but attribute negative events to external factors, generally used to protect one's self-esteem.

Example: Tracy broke up with Tommy. While she simply said, "it's not working out," Tommy is convinced it is because Tracy is a "bitch" rather than being open to the possibility that it has something to do with him.

Semmelweis Reflex: A metaphor for the reflex-like tendency to reject new evidence or new knowledge because it contradicts established norms, beliefs or paradigms.

Example: Throughout the centuries, scientific facts have met much resistance until they could no longer be ignored, due to strong, conflicting religious beliefs. Even today, there are still those who refuse to accept that the earth is not flat.

Sexual Overperception Bias: The tendency to believe that others are more sexually interested in you than they actually are.

Example: "Dude, she wants me." *No, she doesn't.*

Sexual Underperception Bias: The tendency to believe that others are less sexually interested in you than they actually are.

Example: "He is so sweet! He is really loves listening to all my stories about my cats!" *No, he doesn't.*

Shared Information Bias: The tendency for group members to spend more time and energy discussing information that all members are already familiar with and less time and energy discussing information of which only some members are aware.

Example: Group A makes poor decisions because they ignore important information that only a few of the members have and focus instead on what every member knows.

Social Comparison Bias: The tendency to dislike and compete with someone who is seen as physically, or mentally better than yourself.

Example: Rod meets Carl for the first time. Carl is good-looking, well-built, and holds a PhD in physics. Rod can't stand Carl but can't pinpoint why.

Social Desirability Bias: The tendency of survey respondents to answer questions in a manner that will be viewed favorably by others.

Example: In the survey question that asks, "How often do you have racist thoughts?" Participants are far more likely to downplay that number than report it honestly because they don't want to be seen as "racist."

Source Confusion: The misattribution of the source of a memory.

Example: Sandy thinks she was abducted by aliens, when in fact, she is confusing actual events and scenes from *Close Encounters of the Third Kind*.

Status Quo Bias: The tendency to prefer the current state of affairs.

Example: The idea that people generally resist change, is true due to this bias. We pass up good opportunities because we prefer the status quo.

Subadditivity Effect: The tendency to judge the probability of the whole to be less than the probabilities of the parts.

Example: If we are asked to estimate the chance that we will die from natural causes, we might guess 50%. If we were provided a list of natural causes of death and asked to estimate each one, that number would likely add up to over 50%. This might have to do with our inability to consider all the components within a whole unless they are detailed for us.

Subjective Validation: The tendency for a person to consider a statement or another piece of information to be correct if it has any personal meaning or significance to them.

Example: A fortune cookie reads "You will learn something surprising today." Later that day, you learn that the B train is running late. You recall the fortune cookie, and deem that information "surprising," while "validating" the claim through your subjective interpretation.

Suggestibility: The tendency to believe that what someone says is true or may be true.

Example: Highly suggestible people require very little evidence or good reasons to accept information as true. This explains in part why so many people believe in astrology, Tarot card readings, people who claim to communicate with the dead, etc.

System Justification: The tendency to defend and bolster the status quo, that is, to see it as good, fair, legitimate, and desirable.

Example: "I know the poor appear disadvantaged, but they are not victims of the system, they are victims of themselves!"

Telescoping Effect: The tendency for one to perceive recent events as being more remote than they are and distant events as being more recent than they are.

Example: "I just went to the doctor no more than a year ago." *Actually, he last went to the doctor three years ago.*

Third-person Effect: The tendency to perceive that mass media messages have a greater effect on others than on oneself.

Example: "People are such suckers when it comes to what they believe in the media!"

Trait Ascription Bias: See *Actor–observer Bias*.

Triviality/Parkinson's Law of: The argument that members of an organization give disproportionate weight to trivial issues.

Example: When discussing how the AIDS drug will be distributed in Africa, the committee spent 80% of their time discussing the packaging of the drug.

Ultimate Attribution Error: The tendency to attribute negative outgroup and positive ingroup behavior to internal causes and to attribute positive outgroup and negative ingroup behavior to external causes.

Example: "Liberals like us have a deep compassion for our fellow humans whereas conservatives just care about themselves."

Unit Bias: The tendency to think that a unit of some entity (with certain constraints) is the appropriate and optimal amount.

Example: Americans are getting fatter partly because the portion "small" has increased significantly over the years. Next time you order a "single scoop" of ice cream, notice how many scoops they give you.

Worse-than-average Effect: The tendency to underestimate one's achievements and capabilities in relation to others.

Example: If someone is really good at tennis, they might think that others are just as good.

Zero-risk Bias: The tendency to prefer the complete elimination of a risk even when alternative options produce a greater reduction in risk (overall).

Example: Travis is offered two bets: 1) he could wager $10 for a 1 in 2 chance at winning $100 or 2) he could wager nothing and get a free $10 bill. He chooses the second option, even though he is clearly better off (statistically) choosing the first option.

Zero-sum Bias: The tendency to intuitively judge a situation to be zero-sum (i.e., resources gained by one party are matched by corresponding losses to another party) when it is actually non-zero-sum.

Example: People often object to government programs to take care of the sick because they think the money spent will be "lost," when in fact, preventative care saves countless dollars in increased productivity, future health care costs, and in other areas. In other words, government-supported health care is not zero-sum.

Bo Bennett, PhD

The Reductios: Techniques for Exposing Fallacious Reasoning

There are two techniques that are well-suited for exposing fallacious reasoning and bad arguments. These are the *reductio ad absurdum* (reduce to absurdity) and what I call the *reductio ad consequentia* (reduce to the consequences). What we are essentially doing with these techniques is testing the argument presented to see if there are either any contradictions (absurd conclusions) or undesirable conclusions.

The *reductio ad absurdum* is a mode of argumentation or a form of argument in which a proposition is disproven by following its implications logically to an absurd conclusion. Arguments that use universals such as, "always," "never," "everyone," "nobody," etc., are prone to being reduced to absurd conclusions.

The general strategy of the *reductio ad absurdum* is as follows:

Assume P is true.

From this assumption, deduce that Q is true.

Also, deduce that Q is false.

Thus, P implies both Q and not Q (a contradiction, which is necessarily false).

Therefore, P itself must be false.

Consider the following argument:

I am going into surgery tomorrow so please pray for me. If enough people pray for me, God will protect me from harm and see to it that I have a successful surgery and speedy recovery.

We first assume the premise is true: if "enough" people prayed to God for the patient's successful surgery and speedy recovery, then God would make it so. From this, we can deduce that God responds to popular opinion. However, if God simply granted prayers based on popularity contests, that would be both unjust and absurd. Since God cannot be unjust, then he cannot both respond to popularity and not respond to popularity, the claim is absurd, and thus false.

The key to the *reductio ad absurdum* is the **absurdity** to which the argument reduces. The word "absurdity" has multiple meanings. The primary meaning is synonymous with "contradiction," and a secondary meaning is synonymous with "ridiculous," or even "I don't like that conclusion." The primary use of the *reductio ad absurdum* exposes a fatal and objective logical flaw in the argument, whereas the secondary use is far less meaningful. In fact, I strongly advise against using the *reductio ad absurdum* to demonstrate that the argument reduces to unfavorable conclusions as it waters down the effectiveness of the classic use of this technique. To see if an argument reduces to unfavorable conclusions, use the *reductio ad consequentia*.

People like to make rules to justify their positions. This can be a form of rationalization, but more often it is an honest and conscious attempt to provide a good reason for one's position. The problem is, very often, the rules that one creates lead to less-than-desirable consequences. To be clear, this isn't the *appeal to the consequences* fallacy where the consequences are undesirable, therefore the claim is false; **it the use of a rule to support a position without realizing that the same rule would require that support for other positions not supported, therefore, invalidating the rule.**

Let's look at some examples.

Person #1: Abortion is not wrong because the fetus is not conscious.

Person #2: Does that mean we can terminate the lives of people who are unconscious due to dehydration or too much alcohol?

Person #1 made a "rule" as to why abortion is not wrong. Person #2 pointed out that by using the same rule we would be forced to come to an undesirable conclusion: that it is okay to terminate the lives of people who drink too much. Person #1 can clarify the rule to make it more specific, perhaps, "I meant that terminating the life is acceptable because the fetus was never conscious." What person #1 cannot do while claiming to be acting rationally, is stand by their rule and deny the consequences of applying that same rule to other situations.

Let's look at another example.

> *Person #1: God allows suffering and evil because it ultimately leads to the best possible world. In other words, the greater good. He can see the future positive consequences that we are unable to see.*
>
> *Person #2: So everything bad that happens is ultimately a good thing?*
>
> *Person #1: Yes.*
>
> *Person #2: So if a gunman breaks into an elementary school and kills 100 children, that's a good thing?*
>
> *Person #1: No, it is an evil act that leads to a greater good.*
>
> *Person #2: Then why should attempt to stop it?*

In this example, the "rule" is implied from a reason. The rule would be "allow suffering and evil in the world only when it leads to a greater good (or the best possible world)." The consequences of that rule would necessarily mean that our attempts to stop suffering or evil are futile because regardless of our action, whatever happens, will be the best possible outcome. Even if our futile attempt to stop evil will make us a better person, the fact that we don't attempt to stop it also means it is for the greater good and our indifference is required for the best possible world.

And one more example.

> *Person #1: You should vote for people of color. There are too many white people in office.*
>
> *Person #2: Should I vote for candidate X, the woman of color who is a Trump supporter and agrees that climate change is a hoax by the Chinese?*
>
> *Person #1: No, not her.*

In this example, person #2 pointed out what can be an exception to the rule. It has been said that to every rule there is an exception (even that rule?), so should we never attempt to make rules? No, rules generally make useful heuristics. The point of *reductio ad consequentia* is to demonstrate that the rule being made is problematic, and at worst, invalid. Perhaps person #1 really meant "all things being equal, you should vote for the candidate that adds more diversity to our government." This is a much more nuanced and reasonable position than the simple rule to vote for people of color. As more exceptions are added to rules, the less useful and more invalid the rule becomes.

People make rules to justify their positions, but due to the *confirmation bias*, they rarely put that rule to the test and attempt to falsify that rule. This is an effective strategy in argumentation and in testing one's own beliefs because it can expose an irrational justification for one's position. If one's accepted rule can no longer be used, they will attempt to come up with a replacement, which can lead to a different stance on one's position.

While there are many other techniques for exposing flawed reasoning, they are beyond the scope of this book. Consider these two techniques a primer.

Types of Lies

Here is a list of types of lies that are also **not** logical fallacies. All of these are involved in the reasoning process and can lead to accepting bad arguments. For a complete list of types of lies with definitions and references, see the Wikipedia page on "lies." The purpose of including this list is so that these are not mistaken for logical fallacies.

- Bad faith
- Barefaced lie
- Big lie
- Bluffing
- Bullshit
- Contextual lie
- Cover-up
- Deception
- Defamation
- Deflecting
- Disinformation
- Economical with the truth
- Exaggeration
- Fabrication
- Fib
- Fraud
- Half-truth
- Honest lie
- Jocose lie
- Lie-to-children
- Lying by omission
- Lying in trade
- Memory hole
- Minimisation
- Misleading and dissembling
- Noble lie
- Pathological lie

- Perjury
- Polite lie and butler lie
- Puffery
- Speaking with forked tongue
- Weasel word
- White lie

Top 25 Most Common Fallacies

I hesitated to include this section because I don't want my readers to focus on the top 25 and ignore the rest. However, I would be doing you, the reader, an injustice if I didn't tell you that, in my estimation, these top 25 fallacies, or some variation of them, account for *close to half* of all fallacious reasoning. Therefore, if you just learn these very well, your ability to reason will be significantly improved. So here they are in alphabetical order.

- Ad Hominem
- Appeal to Common Belief
- Appeal to Emotion
- Appeal to Faith
- Ambiguity Fallacy
- Anonymous Authority
- Argument by Emotive Language
- Argument from Ignorance
- Begging the Question
- Equivocation
- Failure to Elucidate
- False Dilemma
- Hasty Generalization
- Magical Thinking
- Moving the Goalposts
- Poisoning the Well
- Prejudicial Language
- Questionable Cause
- Red Herring
- Reductio ad Hitlerum
- Slippery Slope
- Special Pleading
- Strawman Fallacy
- Weak Analogy

- Wishful Thinking

Practice Identifying Fallacies

In this section you can practice identifying logical fallacies. My answer for each question is on the page that follows the question.

Practice Situation #1

Person 1: I am sickened by the number of killings in this country in which a gun was used!

Person 2: People have been killing each other long before guns were invented. Don't blame the gun; blame the person.

Question: Is person two committing the *strawman fallacy*? Why or why not?

Bo's Answer To Practice Situation #1: Person one makes an emotive statement, not a factual claim. Person two's response *could* be considered a *strawman* since it addresses an argument person one never made—an argument that claims nobody was murdered before guns (of course people have been killing each other before guns). If an argument could be inferred from person one's statement, then it might be that guns have led to more deaths than a time before guns—an argument which would require support and elucidation.

In this situation, I would avoid calling either party out on fallacious reasoning. All too often the argument gets derailed by chasing claims of fallacies when the focus should be on the content of the original argument. If I were person two, rather than assume an argument or claim was being made, I would ask what exactly person one is claiming before creating an argument.

Focus on good communication, not on winning an imaginary argument.

Practice Situation #2

Person 1: Poverty is a serious issue in the U.S.

Person 2: We are far better off than many other countries!

Question: Is person 2 committing a fallacy? If so, which one and why?

Bo's Answer To Practice Situation #2: I would argue that, on first glance, it *appears* that person two is committing a fallacy, and it falls under *relative privation*. The fallacy is in the comparison of an unfair worst-case scenario (third-world country poverty) to our case (poverty in the U.S.). Person one is clearly stating that poverty is a problem, and person two appears to be minimizing the importance of that problem by comparing it to something extreme. Person two's comparison does not negate person one's claim that poverty is a real issue (implied importance).

In fairness to person two, what he or she said was factually correct, but facts alone don't excuse one of fallacious reasoning. If person two's intent was **not** to dismiss person one's claim that poverty in the U.S. was a real issue, then it could be argued that his or her comment was not fallacious, but rather made to put the problem in perspective (globally) or perhaps even the intent of person two is to call attention to the larger problem of poverty in third-world countries.

The bottom line is we cannot know the intent of others unless we refrain from calling "fallacy" every chance we get and keep a dialog open. Give the other person the chance to explain what they mean. Then, if the fallacy is clear, go ahead and call "fallacy."

Practice Situation #3

> Person 1: "Well, for years science thought that the universe was only 4 billion years old. Why should we believe science when it now says that the universe is 13 billion years old?"

Question: Is this a fallacy? If so, which one and why?

Bo's Answer To Practice Situation #3: Reification fallacy. Science does not think—science is the process in which scientists draw conclusions based on the best available evidence. It might be reasonable to not trust in people, but what they are really doing is stating that they are not trusting the scientific process, that is, they are not trusting the process of **drawing conclusions based on the best available evidence**. In doing so, they are implicitly (if not explicitly) rejecting reason.

We don't *believe in science*, we *trust in the scientific process*. Conclusions drawn using the scientific method may change—that is the nature and the strength of the scientific process: to bring us closer to the truth as more and/or better information becomes available. Reification of science allows people to demonize science—like it is SATAN incarnate—since it is much more difficult to demonize a *process*.

Practice Situation #4

> *Richard Branson was quoted as saying, "There is no way I would ask others to go on a Virgin Galactic flight if I didn't feel it was safe enough for myself."*

Question: Is this a fallacy? If so, which one and why?

Bo's Answer To Practice Situation #4: Quotes are generally a goldmine of fallacies simply based on the fact that they have to be short and are incomplete as far as being an argument, and are often taken out of context. In this particular example, we don't exactly know what Branson's intent was, and this would give us some indication of fallaciousness on his part. For example, if he had said, *"There is no way I would ask others go on a Virgin Galactic flight if I didn't feel it was safe enough for myself.* **Therefore, you should go on a Virgin Galactic flight,"** then this could be seen as a form of the *blind authority fallacy*. If you, the reader, accepted this as a valid reason to go on the plane, you would be guilty of fallacious reasoning, as well.

Based on the quote and the situation, I would have to argue for Branson in that the quote was a more of a reflection of his confidence in his product than a plea for others to accept his authority blindly.

Practice Situation #5

Person 1: X happened to me, and I turned out okay.
Therefore, X is not harmful.

Question: Is this a fallacy? If so, which one and why?

Bo's Answer To Practice Situation #5: In short, it can be considered the *anecdotal fallacy*. This is accepting one example in place of statistically relevant information.

This example represents seriously flawed thinking where people cannot accept, or refuse to accept, that an issue extends beyond their perception. Scientifically speaking, these kinds of claims are analogous to conducting a flawed study with a sample size of one, then generalizing the conclusions to the population—an extreme form of the *hasty generalization fallacy*. This is like the rich having the attitude that **they** don't need universal healthcare therefore, it is a bad thing; the scientifically inept claiming that **they** don't see any signs of climate change therefore, it's not happening; and the rest of the American public who, through lack of knowledge rather than malicious intent, deny the existence of real problems because they don't personally experience any of these problems.

I don't mean to be too hard on anecdotes. They do have their place in rhetoric: like pumping people up at Amway conventions.

Practice Situation #6

Person 1: So you are a utilitarian?

Person 2: Yes.

Person 1: Imagine you are on a bridge with someone else with a track under the bridge. On the track is five workers, also on the track is a runaway trolley that is heading straight for the workers.

Person 2: What's the point of your thought experiment?

Person 1: To refute your system of morality. Anyway, the trolley will kill all five workers if it reaches the workers and the only way to stop the trolley is to push the person next to you onto the tracks and use the corpse as a trolley stopper. What will you do?

Person 2: I push, of course, since I produce more happiness saving five people than saving one person.

Person 1: But killing people is always immoral, and since utilitarianism requires you to push, it must be immoral.

Question: Is there a fallacy in here somewhere? If so, where, which one, and why?

Bo's Answer To Practice Situation #6: The only clear fallacy in this scenario is that person one is *begging the question* by saying that killing people is always immoral. Even if person two agreed to the premise that killing was always immoral, person two could state that any system being used in the same moral dilemma would necessitate some immoral action—either the immoral killing of one person or the more (arguably) immoral neglect of saving five lives. Based on one's values, one can certainly argue that doing nothing and allowing five people to die is far more immoral.

This could be a self-defeating argument if a) person two agreed to the premise that killing was always immoral, and b) agreed with the premise that any moral system that requires an immoral action must itself be immoral. I am not sure if anyone would agree with those premises, however.

Practice Situation #7

I read a study where 9 out of 10 people who go to the gym regularly have Facebook accounts. I didn't realize lifting weights caused narcissism.

Question: Is this a fallacy? If so, which one and why?

Bo's Answer To Practice Situation #7: The big fallacy I see is the *questionable cause fallacy* (three counts). The person is unjustly a) attributing having a Facebook account to narcissism, b) attributing lifting weights to going to the gym regularly (people can go to the gym for many other reasons) and c) being fit with going to the gym regularly (not everyone who goes the gym regularly is "fit," especially due to poor eating habits).

Practice Situation #8

We are all caught up and twisted by our rejection of Allah as king. It undermines both our ability to discern and our ability to interpret truth. Sin is self-deceptive. This means that you can fill a room with the most intelligent and brilliant minds in the universe for as long as you like. And they will not come to the truth.

Question: Spot the fallacies.

Bo's Answer To Practice Situation #8: This argument is ripe with fallacies. Let's break this down:

> *We are all caught up and twisted by our rejection of Allah as king.*

This demonstrates classic *question begging*. This assumes the conclusion: that Allah is king. It is also an *unfalsifiable hypothesis* (or just *unfalsifiable*) by stating that "we are all caught up and twisted by our rejection," since there is no possible way to test this claim. Further, *emotive language* is being used by saying we "reject" Allah as king rather than simply don't believe.

> *It undermines both our ability to discern and our ability to interpret truth.*

Question begging again. The conclusion that there is ultimate "truth" out there is assumed rather than argued. And it is an *unfalsifiable hypothesis* that this "undermines both our ability to discern and our ability to interpret truth."

> *Sin is self-deceptive.*

Begs the question that "sin" exists (sin, defined as breaking a divine law). This is an *unfalsifiable hypothesis* that it is self-deceptive. Also, this entire argument is a major *self-defeating argument*:

> *P1: We are all sinners (including the authors of all holy texts)*

> *P2: Sin is self-deceptive and undermines both our ability to discern and our ability to interpret truth*

> *C: Therefore, I can't possibly claim that this argument I am trying to make is true.*

Practice Situation #9

If you don't have a uterus, your opinion on abortion is irrelevant.

Question: Is there a fallacy here?

Bo's Answer To Practice Situation #9: First, with any politically, religiously, or ideologically-charged idea, we need to do our best to leave our biases and personal opinions at the door; otherwise, emotion will likely trump reason. Now to the question.

Sounds like a *non-sequitur*, where the conclusion does not follow from the premises. In more informal reasoning, it can be when what is presented as evidence or reason is irrelevant or adds very little support to the conclusion. Let's break it down:

> *Premise: If you don't have a uterus,*
>
> *Conclusion: then your opinion on abortion is irrelevant*

The claim is made, but with no support. *Why* is a uterus required to have a relevant opinion on abortion?

Another technique for determining if a position is reasonable or not is to see if the argument can be reduced to absurdity by considering situations that fit the argument. For example,

> *Are you actually suggesting that a father's opinion on whether or not to keep his child is irrelevant, that is, not closely connected or appropriate to the matter at hand?*

I would assume this person making this argument is referring to male legislators but extended the "rule" to the point of fallaciousness by including "all people without uterus'."

Practice Situation #10

> *Person 1: Felons should not be allowed to vote. If we can't trust them to be on the streets, then we can't trust them to choose our leaders.*
>
> *Person 2: I disagree. An article by the New York Times suggests that not only would felons probably not sway any elections in the long run, but most of them probably would opt out of voting anyway.*
>
> *Person 1: The New York Times is biased. Therefore, your argument is invalid.*

Question: Is there a fallacy here? If so, which one and where?

Bo's Answer To Practice Situation #10: The response "*The New York Times* is biased, therefore your argument is invalid" commits the *genetic fallacy*.

Let's rework this into an argument where we can see the *genetic fallacy* more clearly:

> P1: The New York Times suggests that felons being allowed to vote would have very little effect on any election outcome.
>
> P2: The New York Times is biased.
>
> C: Therefore, felons should not be allowed to vote.

And here is an example that is *not* fallacious based on simply not trusting the source:

> P1: The New York Times suggests that felons being allowed to vote would have very little effect on any election outcome.
>
> P2: The New York Times is biased.
>
> C: Therefore, I am not convinced that felons should be allowed to vote.

So to recap, there are three elements that we need to consider for this type of argument to decide if it is fallacious or not:

1) The quality of the source

2) The claim being made (opinion or fact)

3) The objection to the argument (claiming it is false/not accepting it as true)

Practice Situation #11

> You could give me 1,000 studies by Ph.D. holding scientists telling me something is true, and I wouldn't believe you because I'll find you 1,000 more telling you the opposite.

Question: Is there a fallacy here? If so, which one and where?

Bo's Answer To Practice Situation #11: I would first call this statement a general misunderstanding of the scientific process and an *exaggeration*. There is an element of truth to the statement—academics (even of science) often come to different conclusions given the same data. But such a split (50/50) on an issue where 1000's of studies have been done is extremely rare, and just usually when the conclusions are highly generalized such as "sugar is bad for you" rather than a specific conclusion such as "sugar is a main contributor to diabetes."

I would also agree that the statement contains a fallacy: the *argument from authority*. "Ph.D. holding scientists" means very little in this context unless the PhD is in the field of the research having to do with the claim being made. I am a "PhD holding scientist," but my PhD in social psychology does not make my opinion on nuclear physics any more valid.

Practice Situation #12

P1. Company A has done bad thing X and Y

P2. Person Z has consumed products from company A

C1. Therefore, person Z tolerates or supports bad thing X and Y by consuming company A's products.

C2. This means person Z is morally guilty/complicit.

Question: Is there a fallacy here? If so, which one and where? Is this a good argument? Why or why not?

Bo's Answer To Practice Situation #12: What we have here is an opinion in argument form. The conclusions do not necessarily follow (*non sequitur*). I see this as more of a philosophical discussion than a problem of logic. For example, if one follows a well-being based moral system, then they may follow the rule, "If company A has an overall positive effect on well-being, I will support it." So bad thing X and Y is forgiven by good thing A and B. Or perhaps one is a virtue ethicist who will not tolerate what they perceive to be a moral failing despite the "greater good." Other factors need to be considered as well, such as the practicality of alternatives (e.g., "Ford is racist, but BWM is not, but there's no way I can afford a BMW!"), if the person really thinks bad thing A and B are bad things, if they knew about it, etc.

The biggest problem I have against this "complicit" argument is that people are acting as self-appointed moral police, who are judging others by their specific moral code and values.

I do think boycotts have their place and certainly can be effective in seeing immediate, positive social change. I think boycotters need to be well-informed and have their facts straight before taking action. I think the boycotters should then make a well-reasoned argument and let people join their cause rather than casting accusations of moral bankruptcy if they don't.

Questions and Answers

Over the years, readers of *Logically Fallacious* and students of fallacious reasoning have asked some fantastic questions. Here are some of my favorites.

What is the best way to defend against an ad hominem?

The best way to deal with them is to prevent them! Of course, you don't have full control over how people respond, but you can *influence* the way they respond by the way you state your argument. Be as diplomatic as possible and try not to appear as if you are coming across as judgmental. Rather than

> *I believe that going out late at nights to go to pubs to get drunk is a waste of time, money, energy, and health, and that you're much better off never doing that and going to sleep early.*

Try stating it more as an invitation to a discussion, softening some of the language:

> *While I can understand the appeal of intoxication, staying out late and drinking to intoxication comes with the cost of time, money, energy, and health, that I believe is too heavy a price to pay. A social life is very important, but a good social life doesn't have to require so much personal sacrifice.*

This kind of statement is less likely to enrage those who disagree with your position. Of course, people will still attack you. When they do, humor can be an effective way to both diffuse the anger and point out that they are not addressing the point.

> *While the nursing home does want me in bed by 8 o'clock, I choose to connect with people socially in different environments that are far more conducive to my schedule, pocketbook, vitality, and health.*

Is not the belief in the existence of a supernatural being (God) a logical fallacy?

The belief itself is not a fallacy, but the reason for the belief often is. For example:

I believe in God because how else could everything have got here? (argument from ignorance)

I believe in God because he gave his only son for my sins. (emotional appeal)

I believe in God because the Bible clearly says he exists. (circular reasoning)

Rather than a blanket fallacy of belief, one would really need to explore the reasons.

How can we stop an infinite regression by constantly asking "why" or "how do you know that"?

The regression you mention can be very useful in questioning one's assumptions, but it can also be fallacious. Each "how do you know" question is essentially questioning the truthfulness of the previous statement. At some point, the burden of proof shifts to the person asking "how do you know" to demonstrate that what you have claimed is false. For example:

Person A: *People who regularly eat donuts for breakfast are almost all obese.*

Person B: *How do you know? (reasonable - burden is on person A to provide evidence for the claim)*

Person A: *I research this area, and conducted a meta-analysis comprising 12 studies that have been done in the last decade. The results were clear.*

Person B: *How do you know you didn't make a serious mistake? (reasonable, but less so - burden of proof can be argued either way)*

Person A: *I have been doing this for years and I am good at it. Besides, my work was peer reviewed and no serious mistakes were found.*

Person B: *How do you know that this time you didn't make a mistake and that those who reviewed your work didn't all make errors as well?* (unreasonable - we leave *rational skepticism* and enter *denialism*)

Person A: *What makes you think that I might have and that all those who reviewed my work made errors as well?*

Person B: *Err... because, I..., just seems that way...*

Person A: *How do you know?*

A deeper philosophical issue here is epistemology and foundational knowledge. There are many schools of thought here, and not worth getting into in casual argumentation. The technique above should prove very useful.

How do I know if I am simply rehearsing my prejudices?

Prejudice is an unjustified or incorrect attitude (usually negative) towards an individual based solely on the individual's membership of a social group. Simply acknowledging that you might be prejudice is a very good start—asking the question begins the critical thinking process. Prejudice includes the three components of attitude: *affective*, *cognitive*, and *behavioral*, so you need to think about each area in terms of the possible prejudice. To illustrate this point, let's use an example from the headlines: the riots in Baltimore.

Affective. How do I feel about each "side" of this situation? Do I have negative feelings for the police or authority? Do I have negative feelings for those low on the socioeconomic scale? Usually, feelings cannot be fully understood using reason (if we try, we often just *confabulate*—or make up reasons). Strong negative feelings for one of these groups is an indicator of prejudice.

Cognitive. If I were to describe each group as honestly as possible, would either description be overwhelmingly negative? If so, this is an indicator of prejudice.

Behavioral. How do I act towards a group? Do I discriminate in any way? Do my behaviors reflect the way I feel or what I believe about this group? If so, this is an indicator of prejudice.

Prejudice exists on a spectrum, so it is certainly possible for some people to be more prejudice than others, and a low level of prejudice does not have to be problematic, especially if it is mostly in the affective and cognitive domains. For example, if a White guy finds himself having uncontrollable negative feelings around a Black guy, but the White guy reasons that this feeling is an irrational response (perhaps conditioned from his youth) and behaves in such a way that the prejudice is undetectable, then not only is this not necessarily problematic, but it is commendable. Changing the way we feel is often a long process facilitated by deliberate reasoning. The more we reason that feelings we have are irrational, the more likely those feelings are to change.

Is there such thing as a sexist fallacy?

A teacher tells the classroom before a test that boys are better at math than girls are. The girls will most likely second-guess themselves and do poorly on the test.

I don't think this would qualify as a fallacy, but it certainly is problematic. The phenomenon described in your scenario is what is referred to in social psychology as *stereotype threat*, which is like a self-fulfilling prophecy based on stereotypes. There has been much research exploring the possible reasons why girls tend to score lower on math, and all the research points to social and cultural issues—the strongest evidence pointing specifically to stereotype threat[15].

As for the comments of the teacher, she would be perpetuating this harmful myth and activating the stereotype threat, being a causal factor in the girls' reduced performance. This might be better classified as ignorance or bad teaching, rather than fallacious reasoning. As for the girls, they have every reason to

---

[15] Tomasetto, C., Alparone, F. R., & Cadinu, M. (2011). Girls' math performance under stereotype threat: The moderating role of mothers' gender stereotypes. Developmental Psychology, 47(4), 943–949. doi:10.1037/a0024047

trust their teacher and cannot be expected to know about stereotype threat. The effects of stereotype threat are unconscious, that is, there is no or little "reasoning" on the part of the girls who are given this information. It is the background processes at work that lead to the girls doing worse on the test.

Can "fallacious detecting mode" hamper creativity?

Yes, it can. I cannot recall the exact research, but I have come across much research over the years that suggest analytical thinking does hamper creative thinking. From a neuroscientific point of view, this makes sense given that our frontal lobes (where analytical thinking takes place) are shut down when we dream, and that moments of insight often hit us in altered states of consciousness, like waking up or falling asleep.

If fallacious reasoning were to spark an idea, leading to another idea or part of the solution to the big picture, would it be wrong?

The "wrongness" of the conclusion needs to be judged based on the conclusion itself, not the process in which the conclusion was reached. The reasoning could be fallacious, but the conclusion still correct. This would be like saying that we should not smoke if we want to avoid lung cancer because a leprechaun told me so. If we call "talking with leprechauns" our "creative process," we are incorrectly relying on a flawed method for determining empirical facts. Other creative processes can be very effective in problem-solving where there is an objective answer, but this gets into a new area that extends outside the scope of your question.

Can it be absolutely true that there are no absolute truths?

The short answer is no.

The longer answer: This borders on a "Yogibearra-ism" (e.g., "Always go to other people's funerals, otherwise they won't come to yours.") but known in logic as a *self-defeating statement.* These are good ways to make people laugh, but not good uses of reason. It is fallacious to make a self-defeating statement (again, unless as a statement of irony).

Here is a non-fallacious dialog related to absolute truth:

> Sally: "There is no absolute truth."
>
> Bob: "So is THAT absolutely true??" (asked rhetorically)
>
> Sally: "I don't know. In my worldview, my statements are probability based; they're not based on a false sense of certainty."

Is including the line "just food for thought" a legitimate way of making a bad argument? For example, "Just food for thought, if foods were meant to be genetically modified, they'd appear that way in nature."

This is similar to the "just playing devil's advocate here" line. An important part of critical thinking is to consider as many possibilities as possible, so "food for thought" should be welcomed. However, it could be used as a way of just simply making a bad argument and prefacing it with "just food for thought" to get out of having to defend it. This is like saying, "No offense, but you are a jackass." The "no offense" does not excuse you for calling the person a jackass.

> Just food for thought, if foods were meant to be genetically modified, they'd appear that way in nature.

The best response to this would be an analogy that clearly shows the error.

> Just food for thought, if people were meant to take medicine, there would be penicillin trees.

We save lives through "unnatural" means such as surgery, medicines, and technology because nature doesn't care about us any more than it cares about the survival of the virus' and bacteria that kill us. The example given is a clear *appeal to nature*.

There are some famous people who have mocked God and resulted in their untimely death. To give just one example, the designer of the Titanic said, "Not even God can sink this ship." Of course, we all know what happened to the Titanic. My question is, would this be considered a coincidence or is the fact that the ship sank proof that God exists?

There are some famous people who have mocked God and resulted in their untimely death.

This statement is clearly problematic in many ways. To begin with, it is an *unfalsifiable* assertion. By the phrase "and resulted in" we are claiming causality (second problem) where no such causality as been established (we only have correlation). This is a clear *questionable cause* fallacy.

Now to your question. You ask, *"would this be considered a coincidence or is the fact that the ship sank proof that God exists?"* This question is a *false dichotomy*; there are other options here. First, it is certainly *not* "proof" of God's existence, and I say this as a logician and not an atheist. At most, one can claim that it *evidence for* God's existence. But in my opinion it is extremely poor evidence, and here is why:

First, what about the billions of people who mock God who live healthy, happy, and long lives? This is an example of the *confirmation bias*, only looking at examples that support a conclusion, and ignoring all those that falsify it.

Second, weak predictions and "prophecies" are those that are open-ended. So if I generically predict that you are going to die, and you do... eight years later, that doesn't make me psychic. If people died the moment they mocked God, then there would be something worth investigating.

Third, I would not even call these coincidences as a coincidence is defined as "a remarkable concurrence of events or circumstances without apparent causal connection." Again, these might be "remarkable" if the people died within moments of "mocking God," but they didn't. These aren't coincidences; they are **statistical probabilities** based on the number of people who mock God (billions) and the number of people who eventually die (everyone) or the number of tragedies that occur in the world (too many).

Is it fallacious reasoning to reject a source as evidence for an argument because of a dislike or distrust of the source, without looking at the validity of the source?

This can be the *genetic fallacy*—basing the truth claim of an argument on the origin of its claims or premises. I say "can be" because considering the source is not only reasonable but important.

For example, if someone tells you that they heard from *The Weekly World News* that President Obama was actually and illegal alien... from Mars, you would be out of your mind to even consider investigating the claim based on the source. But the *New York Times*, while perhaps biased, is a reasonable news source and should not be dismissed based on the source.

I know that using the phrase "experts say that," is the *anonymous authority* fallacy. I was wondering, when using someone's statement as evidence for a claim, is there any standard to determine who is a legitimate expert?

There is no standard, per se. When you cite expert authority (which is not in itself, fallacious) then one must take into consideration:

1) the level of expertise of the source

2) if the source is really an expert on the given topic

3) the way the response is phrased

For example, the following go from most fallacious to legit.

> *My grandmother says that chicken soup is great for colds.*
> *Therefore, it must be.*

> *My doctor tells me that exercise keeps the immune system*
> *strong. Therefore, it does.*

> *My doctor tells me that exercise keeps the immune system*
> *strong. I trust his advice.*

What is the main difference between the *appeal to popularity* and the *appeal to common belief?*"

Not much of a difference when both refer to a belief. But the *appeal to popularity* is more generic that can be applied to ideas, products, and other non-beliefs. For example,

> *The new Tickle-Me-Buzz-Lightyear toy cannot stay on the*
> *shelves. Therefore, it is a great toy!*

This more accurately is about us reasoning that because a toy sells well (is popular), that it must be good; therefore, *appeal to popularity* is a better fit. However, if we said,

> *Parents everywhere believe that the Tickle-Me-Buzz-*
> *Lightyear toy is the best toy ever; therefore, it is a great toy!*

This is would be common belief.

Not much of a difference, and it really does not matter that much. Informal fallacy names are just a way to help us identify the problematic reasoning. You can call it "fallacy of stupidity" and it wouldn't really matter, as long as you realized that just because something is popular or common, does not make it good/right/true.

What do you think about this argument against the riots? The riots are causing many buildings to be destroyed. Destruction is bad. Therefore, the riots are bad.

I think it makes as much sense as:

> *These life-saving antibiotics cause diarrhea.*
>
> *Diarrhea is bad.*
>
> *Therefore, life-saving antibiotics are bad.*

Let's look at the form of the argument:

> *A (diarrhea) is part of group B (life-saving antibiotics).*
>
> *A has the property X (bad).*
>
> *Therefore, B has the property X.*

This is a classic *fallacy of composition*.

Remember that with fallacies of form like this one, the form is fallacious, not necessarily the conclusion. Consider the following:

> *Murder causes suffering.*
>
> *Suffering is bad.*
>
> *Therefore, murder is bad.*

Technically, this is fallacious in form no matter how right it sounds. Without going into foundations of moral reasoning, let's just say that murder is bad because of the overall reduction to well-being. We can think of times we suffer for the greater good (like surgery).

In summary, the argument against the riots you present is fallacious, but that doesn't mean that riots aren't bad.

If one claims that something shouldn't be debated because of the negative consequences of debating the issue, is this the "appeal to consequences" fallacy?

At its foundation, this is an opinion. If we do X, the results will be Y, and Y is too steep of a price to pay for X. While this is technically appealing to the consequences, it wouldn't be a fallacious appeal, as a truth claim is not involved. In other words, the appeal is not an attempt to convince someone that the issue *can't* be debated; it is to convince someone that the act of debating the issue comes with too high of an emotional cost; therefore, it *shouldn't* be debated. I think most people can sympathize with this argument who try to stay away from ideologically-charged social media posts, knowing the consequences would be too great (e.g., spending the better part of their day defending their position).

What if the word "shouldn't" was replaced with "can't?" This is a great example of exercising the principle of charity. It is still clear that they are expressing an opinion rather than stating a fact, and they are not claiming that it is impossible to debate the issue. This would still not be fallacious.

If you do not trust doctors' advice regarding the Coronavirus, then you should not trust them on any other medical issue as you need to be consistent. Is this a fallacious argument?

I would say yes, because "doctors" are not necessarily experts on virology (*appeal to false authority*). Further, advice on the Coronavirus generally incorporates other issues of personal/economic well being, which could be an issue depending on what is meant by "trust."

Researchers specializing in the Coronavirus and virologists are generally the experts here; doctors (as in generic practitioners) generally follow the advice of the specialists if they are good; otherwise, they may be giving their personal opinion. No matter who the experts are, we should put our trust in the science. Doctors can ignore or be unaware of the current science.

When doctors give advice, they should do so with the understanding that there are choices, and make those choices clear. For example, "If you do decide to go out to eat, realize that you are increasing your risk of exposure to the virus." If by "trust" we mean "I acknowledge this, and I accept the risk," then I see no problem. However, if by "trust" we mean "This guy doesn't know what the hell he is talking about," but when the same doctor says "take two aspirin and call me in the morning," and the patient does so acknowledging the sound advice, then there is clearly an inconsistency in reasoning.

True or fallacious? When you single out one race and say 'that' race matters, you ARE implicitly saying other races don't matter as much.

That is only one option. For example, if parents are witnessing their two children drowning and the wife turns to the husband and says, "Save Billy. Billy's life matters," the implication is clear (poor Timmy!) Another option is that the common perception of the race is that it doesn't matter or matters less than other races, so explicitly stating that it matters is putting it on equal ground with the other races. This is clearly what is meant by "Black lives matter."

Why isn't there a "Fake News" fallacy for calling news you don't like, "fake?"

Calling news "fake" because you don't like it is clearly a real problem these days, but it is not really a fallacy. There is no argument being made; it is simply a dismissal of claims or even facts without offering a reason. Just substitute "nonsense" or "poppycock" for "fake news," and we can see this phenomenon has been around for a long time.

The main fallacy behind the "Fake News," claim is the *Genetic Fallacy*, where certain networks are "very bad;" therefore, facts from them are "Fake News." The error in reasoning is a cognitive bias (the *confirmation bias*) where we reject/dismiss information we don't like and tend to accept information we do like.

Does "What is the greatest contributor of carbon dioxide affecting climate change?" beg the question?

This poses an interesting question: when does a fact become a fact? If I wanted to know if the earth bulges more at the poles, I wouldn't preface the question with "assuming the earth is not flat..." or feel obligated to cite research supporting a spherical earth. Yes, it technically *begs the question* that the earth is spherical, but in non-fallacious way (i.e., it is not unreasonable to work with accepted facts, even though not everyone accepts certain facts). According to NASA Carbon Dioxide affects climate[16]. This is good enough for me to be accepted as fact. There is a point where the burden of proof shifts to those denying accepted facts, like in the case that we shouldn't be expected to provide proof that the earth is not flat to flat-earthers. This shifted burden of proof means that the question begging fallacy does not apply. People can disagree, and that is the fun part about informal fallacies—they are arguments in themselves.

Many people think if you're old enough to fight for your country you should be old enough to drink. Is this a weak analogy?

I would ask why. **Why** do you (does the person) think that if one is old enough to fight in a war, then one should be old enough to drink? Once we have a reason, we can evaluate the argument. Until then, we just have a claim.

Let's look at some possible answers:

1. Fighting in a war requires a certain level of responsibility, and that level is more than enough to drink alcohol.

2. Fighting in a war requires a certain level of maturity, and that level is more than enough to drink alcohol.

---

[16] https://climate.nasa.gov/causes/

3. Fighting in a war requires a certain level of self-control, and that level is more than enough to drink alcohol.

The assumption here, of course, is that 18 year olds are responsible, mature, have enough self-control, etc. to fight in a war. Another possibility is that they are not these things, but we need people to fight, so we make do at the risk of harming those enlisted. But let's go with the former assumption. The level of responsibility, maturity, and self-control is adequate for X (fighting in a war), so does that make it adequate for Y (drinking)?

I see this as an argument where the situation matters. For example, in wartime where there is a dire need for soldiers, the level of required personal characteristics (responsibility, maturity, etc.) can be far lower than during times of general peace. If allowing 18-20-year-olds to drink has a massive downside and little upside for the community, the level of required personal characteristics could be significantly high. If one can show that the level of required personal characteristics for fighting is greater or the same as drinking, it would be a strong analogy.

Is it a fallacy when pro-life/pro-choice advocates say that if you are pro-life, then you clearly don't care about women's rights or if you are pro-choice, then you clearly don't care about the unborn?

Yes. This would be a *strawman fallacy*. Jumping from one of these positions to "not caring about" women's rights or the unborn is an unwarranted conclusion. This mirrors typical black and white thinking common in political rhetoric. Of course, reality is much more complicated, as is common with moral dilemmas. We can care about two things but care about one slightly more.

Is saying "You are either with us or against us" a fallacy?

In most cases of the generic and common, "you are either with us or against us," we are talking about a *false dilemma* (dichotomy) and *equivocation*. The equivocation is in regards to what it means to be "with" someone. There are situations where being with X necessarily means being against Y, as is supporting one of the playing teams in the Superbowl. But in most situations being "with" X doesn't mean one must be "against" Y. Consider the most common example of a social cause. Support for a social cause is on a continuum. People use the "with or against" trope to manipulate one into blind loyalty, or at least a level of support that is unwarranted.

One could also refrain from supporting X or Y, remaining neutral. Perhaps one doesn't have enough information to give their support to X or Y or just supports the idea but doesn't do anything actively. But what if it is claimed that not actively supporting X is supporting Y by default? Does this mean if you are not with X you are with Y? Not necessarily. Consider a situation where a kid is being bullied. You witness it, but say or do nothing. Can we conclude that you support bullying (i.e., you are with bullying and against anti-bullying)? No. There could be many reasons you don't interfere (some good, some not good) that have nothing to do with you supporting bullying. Here is where equivocation comes in again. Perhaps the anti-bullying folks will say that in that situation, you were "against" them because of your inaction, given that you could have done something but chose not to. This line of reason leads to absurdity because we can say that they are then "against" (name any cause here—say preventing child rape) because they can easily donate to child rape prevention charities but choose not to.

The "with or against us" trope is a fallacy and often just manipulative rhetoric.

Is there a fallacy in the statement: "I don't trust any 3rd party fact checker and simply by saying the 'least biased' you prove they are biased."

Perhaps the *nirvana fallacy*. In an ideal world, there would be zero bias. We don't live in an ideal world, so we have to use the best solution.

I know this is hard for extremists to comprehend, but facts can't be biased. They are either true or false. Very often, when people claim fact check sites are "biased" what they mean is that these sites spin a narrative along with the facts, just list the facts that go with their narrative, and ignore facts that counter their narrative. This is a fair criticism. What isn't fair, is rejecting a fact because it is from a biased fact check site. This would be the *genetic fallacy*. It is important to isolate the facts from the narrative.

Example:

> *Trump signed bill X into law on Dec 12, 2020. (fact - true or false)*

> *Trump, the orange buffoon, signed the most racist and idiotic bill into law on Dec 12, 2020. (fact mixed with biased narrative)*

This is an exaggeration for demonstration only. I know of no fact check site that would write something this biased, but you get the point.

Any fallacies in the argument, "Any science that doesn't agree with our narrative ain't science?"

That's not an argument, but a *claim* or *opinion*. It is tempting to say that they are factually incorrect as well, but we cannot know that unless we know their "narrative." Narratives are not the same as science, and there can be quite a bit of ambiguity in what exactly it means for a narrative to agree with science.

A good example is with COVID. Two competing narratives might be to "open up schools" and "keep schools closed." Advocates of both can claim that "science" is on their side, but they would both be wrong. Science *informs* policy; it doesn't *support* it (science *can* support an *argument*, given that one of the premises requires a scientific fact). This is a common misconception that stems from the is/ought problem. Science tells us what is, not what ought to be—**which is what most narratives attempt to do.** Even if science can tell us that if schools are open, there is a 95% chance that 1/2 of the children will die, "science" doesn't support or "agree" with the narrative that schools should be closed. **We need to add in the goals.** In this case, the goal of the child's well-being (and what that means, exactly). These goals are usually controversial.

Consider the following inductive argument:

> *P1. An allowable ratio of child deaths by COVID due to schools being open is 1 out of 1 million students or fewer.*
>
> *P2. Through scientific methodology, we have found with 95% confidence that 50% of students will die if schools are reopened.*
>
> *C. Therefore, science supports the narrative that schools should remain closed.*

Without the "ought" or value judgment in premise one, the science only supports claims of what *is*. Policy contains "oughts" by definition, as do most narratives (but not definitionally).

In conclusion, the claim "Any science that doesn't agree with our narrative ain't science," is vague and not helpful.

Would it be *hasty generalization* to call the protests in 2020 "riots?" Especially, when statistics came out that the majority of protests were peaceful?

No. The problem isn't drawing the conclusion; it's defining "riot." Riots can break out of protests, which they did, but that doesn't make the entire event itself a "riot." This is an area ripe with political bias and spin. One can legitimately refer to the event in 2020 as "riots" as well as "protests." We just need to keep in mind that they are referring to different events. The riots were subsets of the protests.

Implying that the protests, as a whole, were "riots," might be best characterized by the *ambiguity fallacy*.

About the Author

Bo Bennett, PhD. Bo's personal motto is "Expose an irrational belief, keep a person rational for a day. Expose irrational thinking, keep a person rational for a lifetime." Much of his work is in the area of education—not teaching people *what* to think, but *how* to think. He is the founder and president of Archieboy Holdings, LLC., a holding company for many web properties as well as a publishing company for his books.

Bo holds a PhD in social psychology, with a master's degree in general psychology and bachelor's degree in marketing.

For a complete bio and updates on Bo's latest projects, visit BoBennett.com.

Made in United States
North Haven, CT
30 December 2021

13878649R00276